CONCEPT FORMATION AND KNOWLEDGE REVISION

Concept Formation and Knowledge Revision

by

Stefan Wrobel

GMD,
Sankt Augustin, Germany

KLUWER ACADEMIC PUBLISHERS
DORDRECHT / BOSTON / LONDON

A C.I.P. Catalogue record for this book is available from the Library of Congress.

ISBN 978-1-4419-5146-5

Published by Kluwer Academic Publishers,
P.O. Box 17, 3300 AA Dordrecht, The Netherlands.

Kluwer Academic Publishers incorporates
the publishing programmes of
D. Reidel, Martinus Nijhoff, Dr W. Junk and MTP Press.

Sold and distributed in the U.S.A. and Canada
by Kluwer Academic Publishers,
101 Philip Drive, Norwell, MA 02061, U.S.A.

In all other countries, sold and distributed
by Kluwer Academic Publishers Group,
P.O. Box 322, 3300 AH Dordrecht, The Netherlands.

Printed on acid-free paper

Printed in the Netherlands

CONTENTS

FOREWORD

by Katharina Morik, Universität Dortmund

Machine learning Ð as artificial intelligence in general Ð grows from three different roots:

cognition: cognitive processes are investigated by formalising parts of them partially;

theory: theoretical computer science offers formal means to describe the properties of implemented systems;

applications: practical needs demand new systems to be developed.

Let me shortly describe each point so that I can indicate the contributions of this book and justify why this book is worth any minute of reading it for readers from all three orientations of artificial intelligence.

Cognition

Modeling cognitive behavior means to select the features that are to be formalised and those that are considered irrelevant for the investigation at hand. Using computational techniques, the formalised model of behavior is operational, i.e. it itself behaves according to the formalisation. In contrast to a model in the form of written text, the impact of modeling decisions can be seen easily. In this way, operational models offer vivid descriptions and ease the communication about cognitive processes. Particularly, operational models are well suited for the description of interactions between cognitive capabilities. The detailed description of a single capability such as, e.g., the clustering of different items into a category, or the recognition of an instance as a member of a class, is already quite complex. The description of the interaction of several capabilities, however, is much more demanding. Here, textual descriptions are either too general but understandable, or they are detailed but the resulting outcome is hard to determine. An implemented system allows for observing the input-output behavior which is the result of a detailed model.

Mathematical psychologists (e.g., Anderson, 1991) and cognitively oriented researchers in machine learning (e.g., Michalski, 1993, Fisher, 1987) have modeled processes of concept acquisition and categorisation. However, these studies were only concerned with one learning process, namely to acquire a concept hierarchy from examples or observations. It is clear, however, that learning processes are embedded into other cognitive and even emotional processes. In this book, *concept formation* is operationally modeled *as an embedded process*. Knowledge-base maintenance is chosen as the context for learning. Other contexts are possible. The principled point is that this book presents concept formation together with the demand that triggers learning. The interaction of concept learning and theory revision is modeled. The revision of a knowledge base because of new and contradictive information is modeled as a demand for learning. The model does no longer abstract away that learning is directed towards a goal. Learning is modeled as a demand-driven activity.

The issue of an adequate representation for concepts has been discussed in psychology since the work of Rosch (1975). The most challenging view has been presented by Murphy and Medin (1985): they argue that a concept is related with other concepts not only hierarchically but in a relational structure that enables inferences. In essence, a concept structure is a theory. In order to model such a notion of concepts the representation in terms of attribute-values is no longer sufficient, but relations have to be represented, too. The classical approaches to machine learning that use an attribute-value representation and learn just one concept or a hierarchy of concepts are no longer adequate. In this book, a restricted first-order logic is used for representing concepts. Relations between concepts are made explicit and are exploited for reasoning. Hence, the learned concepts are in fact a theory that can be used for problem solving.

Theory

Systems are descriptions of (cognitive) processes – but they also need to be described themselves. The formal description of computer programs has been called *knowledge level description*. Only such a description makes it possible to relate psychological theory and computational models in a sound way. Only the formal semantics of a computer program makes it comparable to other implementations and allows for stating precisely its properties. The formal description informs users about the behavior they can expect from the system. The theoretical properties help system developers in assessing their software products. They tell whether the computer program is already within the range of the best possible implementation, or not. If a problem is very hard, its solution cannot be computed fast – no matter, how good the programmers are. Therefore, the hardness of problems is an important property that is investigated in theoretical computer science. Currently, the application of results from theoretical computer science to artificial intelligence is a hot research topic.

In this book, the formal semantics of the representation formalism is presented and its properties are proven. The representation formalism for learning is a (restricted) first-order logic with higher-order concepts. Restricted first-order logics are in the focus of the new, rapidly growing field of *inductive logic programming*. It is aimed at overcoming the limitations of classical learning approaches. Instead of an attribute-value representation that is incapable of expressing relations, restrictions of first-order logic are investigated that are more expressive but still computationally tractable. Showing the formal properties of a restricted higher-order logic is, hence, an important contribution to the state of the art.

The book substantially contributes also to another field that gained attention recently, namely *knowledge revision*. As knowledge bases have to be changed over their life time, modules for integrating new knowledge and handling conflicts between new and given knowledge are necessary. The theoretical descriptions of such modules turned out to be very hard and has become an active research area. Gärdenfors (1988) has defined properties for revision operators. For several representation systems, these properties have been investigated (e.g. for the KL-ONE type of formalisms by Nebel, 1989). In this book, an operator for knowledge revision in the framework of restricted first-order logic is presented and its properties are shown.

One major problem of knowledge revision was that the operators and their properties concerned all consequences of a knowledge base. It was impossible to adequately handle the difference between explicit knowledge (stated by entries in the knowledge base) and implicit knowledge (obtained from the knowledge base by inference). Moreover, the intuitive notion of *minimal change* could not be captured appropriately. Stefan Wrobel now succeeded in formalising minimal base revision, stating a property of syntactic minimality, and showing the enhanced Gärdenfors properties for his new revision operator.

Applications

Research on machine learning has been motivated by the problems to build up a knowledge base. Since quite a while I have been advocating a view of knowledge engineering that considers it a never ending process where the use of the knowledge base and its construction and maintenance is closely interrelated. The field of case-based reasoning (Kolodner, 1993) and the framework of assisting computers (Hoschka, 1991) share this view. Recently, the problems of maintaining a knowledge base and the need for system tools that support a knowledge engineer in inspecting, revising, and updating a knowledge base has become widely acknowledged.

This book presents tools that support a knowledge engineer. The concept formation tool learns from examples a concept definition in terms of rules.If invoked by the knowledge revision tool it gathers its examples automatically. The knowledge revision tool allows to handle contradictions in the knowledge base either automatically or interactively. A comfortable user interface has been developed that displays all knowledge items involved in a contradiction and offers choices to the user which item is to be deleted or refined and which must be kept as it is. The tools are fully integrated into the system MOBAL (Morik *et.al.*, 1993).

Conclusion

The ideal to combine the three sources of artificial intelligence research has almost never been reached. Such a combined and integrated research requires the researcher to master different ways of thinking, different working styles, different sets of literature, and different research procedures. It requires capabilities in software engineering for the application part, in theoretical computer science for the theory part, and in psychology for the cognitive part. The most important capability for artificial intelligence is to keep the integrative view and to create a true original work that goes beyond the collection of pieces from different fields.

In presenting the long way

- from psychological investigations that indicate that concepts are theories and point at the important role of a demand for learning

- to an implemented system which supports users in their tasks when working with a knowledge base

- and its theoretical foundation,

this book achieves such an integrative view of concept formation and knowledge revision.

Katharina Morik, June 1994

References

D. H. Fisher. Knowledge acquisition via incremental conceptual clustering. *Machine Learning*, pages 139 – 172, 1987.

P. Gärdenfors. *Knowledge in Flux › Modeling the Dynamics of Epistemic States.* MIT Press, Cambridge, MA, 1988.

G.L.Murphy and D.L.Medin. The role of theories in conceptual coherence. *Psychological Review*, pages 289 – 316, 1985.

P. Hoschka. Assisting-computer – a new generation of support systems. In W. Brauer and D. Hernandez, eds., *Verteilte K nstliche Intelligenz und kooperatives Arbeiten,* pages 219 – 230. Springer, Berlin, New York, 1991.

J.R.Anderson. The adaptive nature of human categorization. *Psychological Review*, pages 409 – 429, 1991.

J. Kolodner. *Case-Based Reasoning.* Morgan Kaufmann, San Mateo, CA, 1993.

R. S. Michalski. Beyond prototypes and frames – two-tiered concept representation. In VanMechelen, Hampton, Michalski, and Theuns, editors, *Categories and Concepts › Theoretical Views and Inductive Data Analysis*, pages 145 – 172. Academic Press, London, 1993.

K. Morik, S. Wrobel, J.-U. Kietz, and W. Emde. *Knowledge Acquisition and Machine Learning › Theory, Methods, and Applications.* Academic Press, London, 1993.

B. Nebel. *Reasoning and Representation in Hybrid Representation Systems.* Springer, Berlin, New York, 1989.

E. Rosch. Cognitive representations of semantic categories. *Journal of experimental psychology: General*, pages 192 – 232, 1975.

ACKNOWLEDGEMENTS

One of the biggest pleasures in completing a book is writing the section that acknowledges the important roles others have played in the course of the work, so here it is.

Since this book has grown out of my thesis work, my first and foremost thanks goes to Prof. Dr. *Katharina Morik* of the University of Dortmund, my advisor and leader of the machine learning projects I have worked in at the Technical University of Berlin and at GMD. From the original suggestion of the topic to the completion of this book, her advice, guidance, comments and encouragement have been invaluable, and have especially helped me in the difficult moments of this thesis. As project leader, she created a collaborative team-oriented research environment from which this work has greatly benefited. Her research on sloppy modeling and balanced cooperative modeling has provided the much-needed paradigmatic foundation for all of our work. Another important acknowledgment goes to Prof. Dr. *Wolfgang Wahlster*, the second reviewer. He provided important questions and comments and a very thorough and detailed review which has also helped to improve this book.

I also appreciate very much the important roles that my colleagues in the machine learning projects in Berlin ("Lerner") and at GMD ("MLT") have played. Without them, this work would have been impossible. Dr. *Werner Emde* was one of the machine learning pioneers in Berlin, and originated, together with Prof. Dr. C. Habel and Prof. Dr. C.-R. Rollinger (at that time project leaders in Berlin), the idea of integrating knowledge revision and concept formation [Emde *et al.*, 1983]. Werner developed the inference engine that is the heart of MOBAL, and after which the formal semantics developed in this work was patterned. *Jörg-Uwe Kietz* has been a particularly careful critic of the things I have written, and has helped me spot and fix a number of inconsistencies and bugs in my concepts; the reader will find several footnotes in the text where such contributions are acknowledged. Jörg-Uwe, among many other things, developed the new rule discovery tool RDT and its interface to CLT without which concept formation would still be impractically slow, and saved my life a number of times with Macintosh advice. *Edgar Sommer* did a great job in developing the prototype application of MOBAL to telecommunications access control with Alcatel Alsthom Recherche, which is still a major showcase application for knowledge revision. In the old days in Berlin, finally, *Sabine Thieme* and the author developed the user interface for BLIP, MOBAL's predecessor; many ideas from this interface were kept for the current version in MOBAL.

I further wish to thank all colleagues and students in the immediate environments of our projects at TU Berlin and in the AI research division of the Institute for Applied Information Technology at GMD for stimulating discussions and interesting answers to my questions, be they about arcane philosophical issues or about some tricky UNIX or TeX commands. In particular, I am thankful to the machine learning seminar group from University of Dortmund and GMD for discussing and helping to improve chapters 3 and 4.

Of the various other readers of my work who have provided important criticism and suggestions for improvement, I want to acknowledge in particular Prof. Dr. *Ingo Wegener* at the University of Dortmund and Dr. *Joachim Hertzberg* and Dr. *Gerd Brewka* of GMD who provided valuable comments on previous drafts. Prof. *Tom Dietterich* and the anonymous reviewers of the ML Journal forced me to substantially improve an article, and thus chapter 5, and discussions with Prof. *Stevan Harnad* during a visit to GMD provoked me to write chapter 6.

I gratefully acknowledge Academic Press who have allowed me to reuse here some of my contributions to our book about MOBAL [Morik *et al.*, 1993].

I have placed the people from my real life outside of computer science last, but they certainly are not least! It is much more difficult to acknowledge what they have done for me here, so I will be brief and just mention who they are: namely my family, my parents and brother, my friends, and most important of all, *Lucie Hamelbeck*, the very special woman in my life whom I thank for much much more than I could ever hope to express in these lines. Thanks to all of you for being there.   — SW

1

INTRODUCTION

Ever since the advent of computers, people have been intrigued by the possibility of making computers exhibit behavior similar to the general intelligent capabilities of humans. Since the early fifties of this century, this goal is being addressed in the subdiscipline of computer science that has come to be known under the name of Artificial Intelligence (AI) [Charniak and McDermott, 1985; Winston, 1992]. We can define the goal of this discipline in a general fashion as the construction of computer models of behavior that is regarded as intelligent in humans. Over the course of AI's history, the kinds of behavior that have been studied have varied, and there is no universally accepted position on what form the computer model is to take, and whether it is to be regarded as an embodiment of intelligence or, as the author believes, merely an operational description of intelligence (see [Morik, 1992, ch. 1]).

Despite this considerable diversity in approach, however, one central assumption is almost universally accepted in AI, and this is the importance of *representation*, i.e., the choice of how to express in the computer the "knowledge" that the operational model is supposed to manipulate and reason about. AI was quick to realize that the right choice of representation is a difficult problem, and is a crucial element for both theoretical and practical success. Depending on the chosen representation, things can be easy or difficult to express, and using them for producing the desired behavior may need a shorter or longer computation time, or may not be possible at all.

While in the early years of AI, the task of selecting representations was regarded as a manual process to be left to the designer of an AI model or system, recent years have seen more and more interest in the question of whether it could be possible to automatically have an AI system select a representation, or at least automatically change the representation supplied by the system designer based on experience with this representation. This is

1

the task of *representation adjustment* as it is being studied in the Machine Learning (ML) subfield of AI, and constitutes the general problem that gave rise to the work reported in this book.

As the title indicates, this work has taken a specific perspective on the general problem of representation adjustment by treating representation change as a *concept formation* task. Since concepts, i.e., the generalized descriptions of sets of objects or events that stand behind the words of our language, provide our "vocabulary" for speaking about the world, our working hypothesis is that they are one of the most important representational tools available to humans and computers, and that forming new concepts is a central part of the representation adjustment problem. Since concept formation is a well-studied problem in cognitive psychology, this also means that our concept formation oriented approach can draw upon a large body of work in this field, and indeed uses psychological insights about the *goal-oriented* and *context-based* nature of human concept formation as guidance to develop a computational model of demand-driven representation change. As such, our work also links into the developing topic of *goal-driven learning* [Ram and Leake, to appearb].

Since, as we will see below, our approach uses a logical representation, our work can also be seen as part of a new and rapidly developing subfield of Machine Learning known as *Inductive Logic Programming* (ILP) [Muggleton and De Raedt, 1994], a name that emphasizes the intersection of inductive learning research with results from logic programming. Besides presenting a method for concept formation in first-order representations, this work includes further contributions to ILP as necessary prerequisites for the concept formation approach proper. First and foremost, as indicated by the title, these are in the area of *knowledge revision*. Knowledge revision refers to the problem of revising a system's knowledge whenever this knowledge produces incorrect inferences[1]. We develop a general knowledge revision approach based on minimal base revisions with exception sets, and then use these exception sets as a context for triggering concept formation. As a further prerequisite, we will also have the occasion to examine the formal properties of a logical representation language with higher-order logical constructs.

Situated at the intersection of both psychological and AI work on representation change, concept formation, and knowledge revision, our work will trace a path from psychological results via theoretical examination to a computer implementation, and back to a discussion of some fundamental philosophical criticisms concerning the connection of symbolic AI models to the world around them (the issue of *groundedness*).

---

[1]If, as in our case, the system's knowledge is represented by a logical theory, this problem is also called *theory revision*.

First, however, we will use the rest of this introductory chapter to more precisely define the setting and structure of this work. We begin by making explicit our assumptions about the goals and methodology of AI research, because they have implications for the kinds of representation we want to consider, and for the general organization of the rest of the work (section 1.1). We then define precisely what we will regard as a representation, and identify which part of the representation adjustment problem we want to address (section 1.2). After a brief illustration of the importance of representation change (section 1.3), we identify the particular point of view from which we address the representation adjustment problem, namely regarding representation adjustment as a demand-driven *concept formation* problem (section 1.4). We illustrate this perspective with an introductory example in section 1.5. After a brief description of the context of this research in the knowledge acquisition and machine learning system MOBAL (section 1.6), we conclude the introduction with an overview of the book as a "reader's guide" (section 1.7). A detailed summary of the contributions of this work can be found in the concluding chapter (chapter 7).

1.1 METHODOLOGICAL ASSUMPTIONS

Even though widely used by now, the name of the discipline Artificial Intelligence is not uncontroversial, as it conjures up a view of researchers primarily interested in building artificial intelligent creatures. While it is true that this perspective has always been held by a certain research community that now branches out from AI under the name of Artificial Life, it does not properly represent the field at large.

1.1.1 The descriptive approach to AI

Following Morik [1992, ch. 1], we can define the central goal of AI as modeling with the help of computers the kind of behavior that is regarded as intelligent in humans, in order to

- understand human behavior,

- make computers better adapted to humans,

- or make human capabilities available on computers.

As pointed out in [Morik, 1992, ch. 1], different interpretations of the kind of models that are to be constructed, and of the role of the computer in the modeling process, correspond to the three basic approaches to AI research:

Engineering approach. The engineering approach is primarily interested in enlarging the scope of tasks that can automatically be performed by computers in order to make industrial or administrative processes more effective or economical.

Descriptive approach. In this approach, the computer systems being constructed are interpreted as operational models of an intelligent process that differ from written, textual models primarily because of their operationality which makes it considerably easier to define the predictions of such models, and perhaps validate them in comparison to the process that is being modeled.

Constructive approach. This approach regards the model that is built as an embodiment of intelligence, not a description, and the resulting computer system as an artificial creature. Structures in the model are postulated to correspond to structures in the process that is being modeled.

Depending on which of the above approaches is being followed in a piece of AI research, very different criteria apply to judge the adequacy of a constructed model. In the engineering approach, one is only interested in obtaining the desired behavior, so any model that will produce this behavior within the given limits of time and computational resources will do. In the descriptive approach, we must also require that the structures in the resulting model be easily interpretable by humans, because otherwise, the explanatory capability of the description will be low, even if the required behavior is produced. In the constructive approach, finally, the emphasis is on model structures that can plausibly be interpreted as corresponding to the structures in the modeled process.

For the work to be presented in this book, we have adopted Morik's position that AI research is best situated at the intersection of the engineering and descriptive approaches, i.e., that the relevant dimensions for a computational model are whether it produces the required behavior in a technical sense, and whether it can also be interpreted as a useful description with explanatory value to humans.

1.1.2   Implications for representation

In the context of an operational model of an intelligent phenomenon, there are two things that must be "represented" in some form: we must represent the computational process that constitutes the model, and we must represent in the computer the "knowledge" about the world that is to be manipulated by this operational process. If we want our model to have good explanatory value to humans, we want both of these to be expressed in a form that is as explicit and easily understandable as possible. In the scientific perspective, this enables the understanding, communication, and evaluation of our results; in the engineering perspective, this allows the user to better understand the behavior of the system that he or she is using for a particular purpose.

While the goal of explicitness is thus the same for both the representation of the modeled process and the representation of the knowledge that is manipulated by this process, different means to reach these goals are appropriate. For the modeled process, we have chosen the material contained in this book as the most appropriate "representation", i.e., the natural language descriptions that are given, and their formal counterparts that precisely define the behavior of the modeled process. These can be used both by researchers and system users to understand the behavior of the operational model. For the knowledge to be operated upon by the model, however, we must go one step further, since this knowledge is the subject of communication not only between humans, but also between humans and the computer. Users must enter knowledge to be used by the operational model, and they must be able to easily understand the results produced by the model. We thus need a precisely defined language in which knowledge is to be represented in the computer, and communicated back to the user. As stated in the introduction, this language for representing knowledge is the sense in which the term representation is used in AI, and we will limit ourselves to this meaning of the term in the following.

So what is an appropriate type of representation in our context? Clearly, an answer to this question is dependent on our research goals, and on the kind of intelligent phenomenon we want to model. The chosen type of representation should be able to easily represent the knowledge that is involved, and should enable the construction of operational methods for dealing with this knowledge.

As we will see in chapter 2, our goal in this book is to examine the formation of a particular kind of concepts, namely *object* or *event* concepts. For these kinds of concepts, as contrasted to sensor or motor concepts, a particular class of representations has turned out especially adequate, namely the class of *symbolic* representations. A symbolic representation relies on syntactic tokens (symbols, "words") with individually assignable meaning which are then rulefully composed to make up a formal language in analogy to the syntactical rules that make up our natural languages. If a formal semantics is given for such a representation (see chapter 3), the meaning of an individual statement in the representation is clearly defined. Such representations, which have been the main tool of work on (object or event) concept formation in AI and cognitive psychology, thus provide one way of meeting the requirement of explicitness in our context. We have therefore chosen to use a symbolic representation as the basis for our concept formation model; section 1.2 more precisely defines what we mean by such a representation.

1.1.3   Implications for interdisciplinarity

In our view, the adoption of a descriptive approach to AI also has implications for the position of AI work in relationship to its neighboring disciplines, in particular psychology. If we want our models to have a descriptive and explanatory capability with respect to intelligent phenomena as they occur in humans, as stated in the general definition of AI above, we cannot define our phenomena solely with respect to technical requirements as in the engineering approach. We must also consider the available psychological data about human phenomena, and can build upon psychological models to identify structures to incorporate into computational models. The role of psychological work is thus a threefold one. First of all, it helps to define the phenomena to be described by the model, and operationalized by the computer implementation. Second, it may provide useful hints towards structural or functional components of computer models. Third and last, it can be used to test the predictions of a computer model against empirical observations.

In this work, we will use psychological results in the first and in the second sense, i.e., we will look at psychological research to define a range of phenomena in concept use for classification which we can then use as a yardstick for our model. In particular, they will help us identify the required level of expressiveness for our representation. Second, we will look at results about concept formation to see which constraints psychologists have found humans to use. This will point us towards one particular class of constraints, goal-oriented constraints, that have been used very little in previous research, and will form the basis for our model. Even though the final model might offer insights into psychological phenomena, we have only evaluated it empirically in technical terms, and have to leave a comparison of its predictions to human performance to future research (see chapter 7).

1.2   KNOWLEDGE REPRESENTATION

We are now ready to define what we mean by a representation in this book. We will adopt the standard definition of symbolic representations in AI as follows. A *knowledge representation system* consists of the following[2]:

---

[2]Many authors use the term *logic* for a knowledge representation system defined in this fashion.

■ a set of (atomic, indivisible) symbols which form the basic *vocabulary* of the representation system;

■ a set of rules for defining the *syntax* of the representation, i.e., specifying how the atomic symbols may be combined together into larger expressions;

■ a specification of the *semantics* (meaning) of expressions in the representation, i.e., a mapping of the atomic symbols to objects or relations in the world (an *interpretation*), and rules for deciding whether an expression is true in a given interpretation;

■ and finally, a proof procedure for deciding whether a given statement follows from a given set of expressions according to the semantics of the representation.

By a *representation formalism*, we usually refer to the specification of syntax, semantics, and proof procedure of a representation; a *representation language* consists of a representation formalism plus a specific set of atomic symbols as the vocabulary.

The above definition of a representation also serves to identify the scope of the problem of automatic representation adjustment, since many of the above components of a representation cannot be specified or modified without access to the real world and knowledge about the range of phenomena that the representation is intended to capture. We will therefore follow standard practice in Machine Learning work on representation adjustment (indeed, standard practice in all of AI and computer science), and assume that the representation *formalism*, which includes syntax, semantics, and proof procedure, is chosen by the system designer.

This leaves the level of representation language, i.e., the set of atomic symbols available within a formalism, as the domain of automatic representation adjustment procedures. Even here, however, we need to recognize that some part of the work has to come from the human system designer, namely the selection of which parts of the world are to be represented in a system's knowledge representation, and which ones are to be abstracted from. Subramanian [1990] has called this the task of developing a *conceptualization* for an application domain. Without at least an initial vocabulary, automated representation adjustment cannot proceed. In this view, the task of representation adjustment is to introduce additional new defined symbols into a pre-specified set of already existing symbols.

To be even more precise about the task of representation adjustment, note that the basic vocabulary of a representation formalism can be subdivided into two groups. The first group can be thought of as names for *objects* in the world.

In a first-order logical representation, these are the (atomic) *constants* of the vocabulary from which additional terms to denote objects can be constructed using function symbols. The second group of symbols is used to denote *properties* of objects. In a first-order logical representation, these are the predicates in the vocabulary which can be used to construct statements about objects. Since we do not have access to the objects in the real world, we will assume that our vocabulary of "names" is sufficient, or if needed, is extended by the user. The precise task of representation adjustment is thus to introduce new names for properties of objects, and define their meaning with respect to the properties previously available in the representation.

In machine learning, this particular type of representation adjustment has acquired the name *new term* problem, even though, as we outlined above, we do not introduce names for objects (terms), but really new property descriptors. Better names would thus be *new feature* problem or *new predicate* problem. Whenever we speak about introducing new terms in the following, the reader should thus be aware that in the logical sense, we are not referring to new terms, but rather to new predicates.

1.3   THE IMPORTANCE OF REPRESENTATION
ADJUSTMENT

Given that we have to leave aside the level of representation formalism, and restrict ourselves to changes of the representational vocabulary, it may seem that such changes could have only a negligible effect on the representation problem at large. Indeed it is true that the global properties of a representation, i.e., its *expressiveness* and its *computational properties* for reasoning and learning, are largely determined by the choice of representational formalism. Nonetheless, in many problems, the introduction of the right new vocabulary into the representation can make the difference between success and failure.

This is especially obvious in Machine Learning applications, where the simplicity of an inductive hypothesis, e.g., a rule or a decision tree, has a crucial influence on whether this hypothesis can actually be found by the learning system. Here, the introduction of the right new term may mean that a rule that was previously too complex to learn all of a sudden falls within the range of hypotheses learnable by the system. A classical example of this is given by Quinlan's work on learning chess endgame concepts [Quinlan, 1983]. Quinlan had originally chosen a positional description of the pieces on the board as a conceptualization for the domain, i.e., it included descriptive elements only for the different kinds of pieces, and for the rank and file of their position. While in principle, this representation was sufficient to learn the required concept, the representation of this concept would have required so many different rules for all the different positions that in practice, Quinlan was not successful with the ID3 learning program. Only after he introduced additional derived descriptors describing e.g. whether one piece threatened another, the learning program was able to actually find the required concept.

Similar experiences have been reported for work on problem-solving systems [Amarel, 1968; Korf, 1980]. We can thus see that even when restricted to the introduction of new terms that are defined based on previously existing vocabulary, approaches to automatic representation adjustment can make a significant contribution in an AI system. Nonetheless, the fundamental criticism of the kind of model presented in this book, namely that such models seem unable to account for the creation of truly new terms "from scratch", merits further discussion, and we will return to this problem at the end of this book (chapter 6).

1.4 REPRESENTATION ADJUSTMENT AS CONCEPT FORMATION

We will now describe the particular perspective on representation change and the new term problem that separates this work from previous research. Previous research on the new term problem has mostly taken place within a paradigm that is often referred to as *constructive induction* [Michalski, 1983]. Constructive induction approaches take the direct approach to the introduction of new defined terms by specifying a set of construction operators that take elements from the existing vocabulary, and combine them into new descriptors according to fixed rules. This approach has been most successful when domain-specific information is used in the specification of these operators, because this ensures that the newly constructed term will actually be useful in the domain.

A well-known example of such an operator is Michalski's *maximum* operator [Michalski, 1983]. It is applied to a binary descriptor that describes an ordering relation, and produces a descriptor that designates the maximum element of the ordering. For the "above" relation, this construction operator would thus add the descriptor "top". Other systems have similarly exploited domain-specific knowledge to ensure that their constructive induction operators add "good" descriptors. BACON [Langley *et al.*, 1986], for example, is a learning system designed to discover physical laws of a certain form. To perform this search, BACON constructs new (numerical) terms from the ones initially given, and exploits its knowledge of the likely form of physical laws (they tend to have small exponents) to restrict its operators. The mathematical discovery system AM [Lenat, 1982] had mathematics-specific heuristics that suggested interesting concepts to form.

Whenever domain-specific knowledge is not available, constructive induction approaches must rely on general operators that combine two or more existing terms by forming their conjunction, disjunction, or some more complex expression. Various forms of such general operators have been proposed, e.g. the intraconstruction operator in inverse-resolution learners [Muggleton and Buntine, 1988; Wirth, 1989; Rouveirol and Puget, 1990], Rendell and Seshu's *FC* operator [Rendell and Seshu, 1990], or the operators used for adding conjunctions or disjunctions of existing descriptors in STAGGER [Schlimmer, 1987] or the FRINGE systems [Pagallo, 1989] (see also section 5.5.3).

The problem with such general operators, however, is that their application is very difficult to control. If applied to the existing vocabulary without any restrictions, they can produce an exponential number of new terms: any subset of the original set of features can be combined to form a new feature. In first-order languages, or if we can recombine new features repeatedly, such operators can even produce an infinite number of syntactically different new features. Various methods have been devised to cope with this problem in the different approaches. Most of them rely on techniques similar to cross-validation: the performance of newly introduced features is measured empirically by determining the classification accuracy of the rules that were learned with the new features. While some of these techniques have been demonstrated to improve accuracy in selected applications, a complete solution to the general problem will require additional constraints, especially when first-order representations are considered.

In this book, we therefore propose to turn the constructive induction approach to representation adjustment "upside down". Instead of considering the set of *terms* in the initial vocabulary, and deciding which ones of them to combine into a new one, we want to begin by considering the set of *domain objects* (instances, individuals, cases, events) in the representation, decide which ones of these objects should belong to one group, and then introduce a new term defined so that it exactly describes this group. This point of view is strongly suggested by results from psychology about the importance of the conceptual system for the problem-solving performance of humans. Chi, Glaser, and Rees [1982] have examined the shift in conceptual structure that takes place in the transition from novice to expert in a domain, and found that the key reason for the better performance of experts was their ability to group together relevant experiences under a common concept, a common name so they could treat them together in problem solving.

Where a constructive induction approach starts out by introducing a new descriptor definition (intension), thus defining a new set of objects (extension), the approach we want to follow in this book first identifies a set of objects to be aggregated (extension), and then induces a definition (intension). With these steps, our approach corresponds directly to the problem of *concept formation* as it has been studied in psychology and Machine Learning. More precisely, by concept formation we refer to the following task (borrowing terminology from [Easterlin and Langley, 1985]):

■   *Given* a set of object (instance, event, case) descriptions (usually presented incrementally)

■   *find* sets of objects that can usefully be grouped together (*aggregation*), and

■   *find* intensional definitions for these sets of objects (*characterization*)[3].

The non-incremental variant of this task is usually referred to as *conceptual clustering*. In the context of representation change, an additional requirement is:

■   *Define* a new name (predicate) for the new concept, and introduce it into the representation, so that it can be used e.g. in the definition of further concepts, or for the description of future input objects.

In hierarchical concept formation systems [Michalski and Stepp, 1983; Lebowitz, 1987; Fisher, 1987a; Gennari *et al.*, 1989], this latter step is usually not included, i.e., these systems aggregate objects and characterize them, but do not give them names that are available elsewhere.

It is obvious that just by turning constructive induction upside down, the problem of controlling the introduction of new terms does not automatically go away. Corresponding to the problem of search control in constructive induction approaches, the central problem in a concept formation approach is how to find useful sets of objects to be grouped together. Since the search space to be considered is the powerset of the set of known objects, we again have an exponential number of candidates. The key advantage of the concept

---

[3]Our use of the term concept formation is thus more general than the definition used by Gennari *et. al.* [Gennari *et al.*, 1989] who included the additional requirement of forming a hierarchical organization, and also restricted the term to divisive, hill-climbing methods.

formation perspective on constructive induction, however, is that it allows us to bring the large body of psychological work on concept formation to bear on the problem of introducing new terms: As we will see in chapter 2, human concepts arise not from the combination of a set of existing properties, but from a set of objects that need to be referred to for some purpose, and only then acquire a characterization in terms of common properties. Existing work in Machine Learning has only explored a small subset of the constraints that psychologists have identified for human concept formation; in particular, we will see that one particularly powerful source of constraints, namely the goals and problem-solving context of concept formation, has received very little attention up to now, and will actually use this constraint as the basis for our own model.

1.5   AN INTRODUCTORY EXAMPLE

A small example may help to clarify the distinction between constructive induction and concept formation approaches to representation change. It is taken from a prototype domain that we have developed as a testbed for our approach, and which we will use throughout this book. The domain is concerned with the basics of German traffic law, i.e., knowledge about where and where not to park, about the fines one might have to pay, points that one might get on the traffic violation record, etc. Knowledge is represented in an extended function-free Horn-clause representation that is more precisely defined in chapter 3 — here we hope that the reader will find it sufficiently familiar for understanding the example, based on our experience which shows that this representation is explicit enough to be readily employed by most users even without formal training.

The problem solving goal in our sample domain is to derive a classification of traffic violation cases with respect to who is responsible for the violation, whether a fine will be paid, how many points will be received on the violation record, and whether a person will go to court. The basis of the domain consists of 15 violation cases plus a number of background knowledge rules; table 1.1 shows an example of a case.

The facts in event1 state that the vehicle with the license number b_au_6773 was involved in the traffic violation, that a person with the initials sw is the owner of this vehicle, and that the vehicle is a sedan. The traffic violation consisted of the fact that the vehicle was parked in a bus lane and consequently towed away. The fine was DM 20, which was paid by the person responsible for the violation (sw). The person did not appeal against the decision, he/she

```
involved_vehicle(event1,b_au_6773)
owner(sw,b_au_6773)
sedan(b_au_6773)
car_parked(event1,place1)
bus_lane(place1)
car_towed(event1,b_au_6773)
responsible(sw,event1)
fine(event1,20)
pays_fine(event1,sw)
not(appeals(sw,event1))
not(court_citation(sw,event1))
not(tvr_points_p(event1))
```

Table 1.1   A Case of Traffic Violation (event1)

did not receive any points on his/her traffic violation record, and did not have to go to court.

The basic representational vocabulary available in such a representation are the *predicates* that have been used. In this domain, the initial vocabulary provided by the user consisted of the predicates shown in table 1.2, along with the names of the argument sorts (types), and a descriptive comment.

As it turns out, the initial vocabulary shown in table 1.2 lacks one crucial concept that is necessary to properly represent the domain, and to learn the proper rules e.g. about who is responsible for a violation. In German traffic law, there is a set of minor violations that are treated differently from all other violations. In particular, for minor violations, the owner, and not the driver, is responsible. Without this concept, information about minor violations cannot be made explicit and remains hidden in a large number of different rules; with the concept, a small set of rules can be used for defining the concept, and a single rule is then sufficient to express who is responsible for a violation. Table 1.3 shows the minor violation concept that was introduced by the goal-driven concept formation approach to be described in this book[4].

In the course of this book, we will see how such a complex new concept can be introduced into a representation by exploiting the problem-solving context of the knowledge revision module of a learning system. Such a complex concept can be found only because the system first uses the constraints from problem-solving to decide which cases to put into a common group, and then

---

[4] The new name, of course, was provided by the user, the system had just used concept1.

involved_vehicle/2: <event>, <vehicle>:
    <Vehicle> was involved in <event>.
owner/2: <person>, <vehicle>:
    <person> is the owner of <vehicle>
car_parked/2: <event>, <place>:
    The vehicle involved in <event> was parked in <place>.
bus_lane/1: <place>:
    <place> is in a bus lane.
responsible/2: <person>, <event>:
    <person> is responsible for <event>.
fine/2: <event>, <amount>:
    <event> results in a fine of <fine>.
pays_fine/2: <event>, <person>:
    <person> paid the fine resulting from <event>.
appeals/2: <person>, <event>:
    <person> appeals against the decision made in <event>.
court_citation/2: <person>, <event>:
    <person> has to go to court for <event>.
tvr_points_p/1: <event>:
    <event> costs points on the traffic violation record (tvr).
eco_expired/1: <vehicle>:
    The emission control certification of <vehicle> has expired.

Table 1.2   Initial vocabulary of predicates provided in the traffic law domain (subset)

parking_violation(X) → minor_violation(X)
involved_vehicle(X,Y) & eco_expired(Y) → minor_violation(X)
involved_vehicle(X,Y) & lights_necessary(X)
                    & not(headlights_on(X,Y)) → minor_violation(X)
unsafe_vehicle_violation(X) → minor_violation(X)

minor_violation(X) → not(tvr_points_p(X))
minor_violation(X) & appeals(Y,X) → court_citation(Y)

Table 1.3   The newly added minor violation concept

invokes an inductive learning method to find the above description for these cases. For a constructive induction approach, the above description would have to have been constructed from the initial vocabulary of predicates that were given in table 1.2 — without any indication as to why exactly this complicated combination of these predicates was interesting to consider.

1.6 THE CONTEXT OF THIS WORK IN MOBAL

The work described in this book was implemented as part of the knowledge acquisition and machine learning system MOBAL [Morik *et al.*, 1993]. MOBAL is a knowledge acquisition system that integrates machine learning techniques according to the *balanced cooperative modeling* paradigm of K. Morik [Morik, 1987; Morik, 1989b; Morik, 1989a; Morik, 1990; Morik, 1991; Morik, 1993]. This paradigm regards knowledge acquisition as a cyclic interactive process of building a model of a domain in which both user and (learning) system contribute to the development of the model in a balanced fashion. Central requirements of the paradigm are system support for the inspection of a knowledge base, for its inductive extension, and for both monotonic and non-monotonic interactive revisions of the evolving model.

MOBAL consists of a number of interacting modules that address the above requirements, namely a powerful graphical interface, an inference engine [Emde, 1989], tools for sort taxonomy construction [Kietz, 1988] and predicate structuring [Klingspor, 1991], and the first-order learning algorithm RDT [Kietz and Wrobel, 1992]. MOBAL also contains an interface to the common knowledge representation language CKRL of the MLT (machine learning toolbox) system developed in the ESPRIT project of the same name (P2154) [Morik *et al.*, 1991]. In order to implement the methods for knowledge revision and concept formation developed in this book, the knowledge revision tool KRT, and the tools for concept formation and rule set restructuring, CLT and RRT, were designed and implemented by the author within MOBAL. Furthermore, a formal description of the core of MOBAL's knowledge representation, including syntax, semantics, and computational properties, was performed. Since the latest release of the system (3.0), MOBAL features an external tool concept that allows third-party learning algorithms to be used from within the system (see appendix); a predecessor of this facility was used to perform the empirical experiments in chapter 5.

The work described in this book could not have taken place without this embedding into the MOBAL system, and neither without the context provided by the work of all the colleagues who have worked on MOBAL; they are fully acknowledged at the beginning of this book.

1.7   OVERVIEW OF THE BOOK

Following the research methodology suggested by section 1.1.3, the chapter following this one (**chapter 2**) is concerned with the psychological results that are available about the nature of human concepts and concept formation processes. Besides giving an overview of these results, the goals of the chapter are twofold. First of all, if we want to develop a model of concept formation, we should do it in a representation formalism that is powerful enough to capture the range of phenomena empirically known about human concepts. We will make a catalogue of the recorded properties of human concepts, compare them to the capabilities of knowledge representation formalisms, and conclude that only a first-order representation is a sufficient formalism for our purposes. Second, from work on human concept formation, we will identify four types of possible constraints on concept formation, and examine what types of constraints have been used in previous concept formation research in Machine Learning. We conclude that a particularly important type of constraint, goal-oriented constraints derived from a problem solving context, has not received much attention, and will select this type of constraint as the basis for our model.

The next two chapters on the one hand provide the necessary basis for our concept formation approach, but on the other hand offer a contribution in their own right. **Chapter 3** links up the representational requirements from psychology with the knowledge representation that is offered by the MOBAL system. In order to have a sound formal basis for our approach, we precisely define a subset called $\Re$ of this representation, and develop formal characterizations of its syntax, semantics, and computational properties. Our main result in this chapter is interesting in particular from an inductive logic programming perspective, as we show that our representation, which is an extended clausal formalism with selected higher-order logic statements, can be given both a standard two-valued semantics, as well as a multi-valued semantics taken from generally Horn programs. We show that for the two-valued semantics, the positive-literal (true Horn clause) subset of our representation has a fact-correct (sound and complete) proof theory which answers queries in polynomial time if the maximal arity of predicates and the maximal branching factor of rules is fixed. For the multi-valued semantics, we show that our proof theory is actually sound and complete. In the context of our main topic, concept formation, the results of this chapter mean that we have a sound and well-understood representational basis for our approach.

Given a representation formalism, we need to make more precise just how we want to exploit a goal-derived context to focus our concept formation activities. To this end, in **chapter 4**, we briefly describe the problem solving that underlies processing in MOBAL, and then identify the knowledge revision activities of the system as a particularly suitable context for concept formation. We formally define the knowledge (or theory) revision problem, and develop a set of requirements that any revision operation should satisfy based on results from work on theory contraction. We then show how the support set construct of MOBAL's knowledge representation can be used to define a minimal base revision operation $\dot{-}$ that meets these postulates. Along the way, we also demonstrate that performing truly minimal specializations of theories, as has been advocated by some researchers in Machine Learning, is an undesirable strategy. We then supply an operationalization of the revision operator $\dot{-}$ based on a two-tiered confidence model which can be used to specify which are the more and which are the less important member statements of a theory. We further argue that in many cases, additional specialization beyond our minimal base revision operation is needed, and introduce the concept of a *plausibility criterion* to decide which rules need to be further reformulated. We conclude with a set of operators and a search strategy for performing such reformulations in MOBAL's knowledge revision tool KRT.

With representation and knowledge revision context in place, **chapter 5** describes the concept formation process proper as it is implemented in the CLT and RRT modules of MOBAL. We begin by defining exactly how the instance and exception sets formed during knowledge revision operations can be used as aggregates for concept formation, and define the necessary additional operators for KRT's reformulation step so that concept formation can be triggered. Given an aggregate from KRT, the remaining task is to induce an intensional characterization for this aggregate, and to evaluate the new concept to see if it should be introduced into the representation. We show how MOBAL's learning module RDT can be used for characterization by partially instantiating its syntactic hypothesis model, and define a structural criterion for evaluation. Given a new concept, an important question is whether it can be used to improve the structure of the rule base. We show how operations known from work on inverse resolution can be adapted for this purpose. The chapter concludes with an evaluation of the effect of new concepts on the structure of the knowledge base. We define a quality measure $\geq_q$ on knowledge bases, and show that new concepts are guaranteed to be an improvement along this measure, and report the results of an empirical experiment in which new concepts were shown to improve the accuracy of the knowledge base.

Thus having defined our concept formation approach, **chapter 6** as promised takes a step back and returns to an issue that we briefly touched upon above, namely whether concept formation methods of the type we have developed here can ever introduce "truly new" concepts or features into a representation.

This is a fundamental criticism of symbolic approaches in general, and its originators claim that without a true sensorial grounding in the world, this can never be possible. We take a closer look at the issue of grounding, and argue that it is not the physical sensorial grounding that is crucial, but the embedding into *some* environment where problems are solved and feedback is received. Since Brook's notion of situatedness is also found to relate too much to the robotics paradigm, we propose the term *embeddedness* to denote this type of connection to the surroundings.

In the concluding **chapter 7** finally, we summarize our results, and discuss some directions for future work. Among others, we give a first sketch of a model in which the goal-driven approach to representation change is applied to the task of incrementally processing real-valued sensorial input from an environment, and automatically change the segmentation rules to arrive at a higher-level symbolic vocabulary.

As a final note to the reader, even though we have presented the chapters of the book in a sequential ordering here, it should be obvious that given the interrelations we have described here, different reading strategies are possible. We have tried to support a selective style of reading by giving each chapter its own introductory paragraph where pointers to necessary material from other chapters are given. Given the introduction, chapter 2 about the psychological aspects, chapter 3 about representation, and chapter 4 about knowledge revision can be read selectively; chapter 5 relies on results established in preceding chapters, and probably should not be read without having looked at chapter 2 and chapter 4 first. Chapter 6 is a general discussion and only presupposes some knowledge about symbolic AI approaches. Have fun!

2

THE PSYCHOLOGY OF CONCEPTS AND CONCEPT FORMATION

> Without concepts, mental life would be chaotic. If we perceived each entity as unique, we would be overwhelmed by the sheer diversity of what we experience and unable to remember more than a minute fraction of what we encounter. And if each individual entity needed a distinct name, our language would be staggeringly complex and communication virtually impossible. [...] In short, concepts are critical for perceiving, remembering, talking, and thinking about objects and events in the world. — E. Smith and D. Medin, *Categories and Concepts*, p. 1 [Smith and Medin, 1981].

In the preceding chapter, we saw that the design of a representation system requires choices on two different levels. First, there is the level of representation *formalism*, i.e., the choice of syntax and semantics for the representation. Then, there is the equally important choice of a representation *language*, i.e., the vocabulary to be made available in the chosen formalism. We also saw that this vocabulary is to be looked at not as a set of syntactical terms, but as a system of *concepts*.

In this chapter, we want to take an in-depth look at the psychological evidence that is available about human concepts and their formation. This will allow us to develop requirements that representations should meet on both the formalism and the language level. On the formalism level, these requirements result from the fact that any representation formalism we choose must be powerful enough to express the kinds of concept definitions psychologists have found necessary to explain human concepts. On the language level, the issue is which concepts should be included in the representation, and which ones should not. If seen from a dynamic (representation change) perspective, this is equivalent to the question of which concepts should be newly formed, and which ones are better left aside. There, the psychological evidence about the constraints that are exploited by human concept formation processes are relevant.

The rest of the chapter follows the course suggested by the preceding paragraph, starting out with a brief introduction to recent psychological research on concepts (section 2.1). We will then look at the properties that human concepts were experimentally found to possess (section 2.2.1), and describe some psychological models that were designed to explain these properties (section 2.2.2). From the discussion of these models, we will propose a set of minimal requirements for a representation formalism. In particular, we will show why attribute-based formalisms are insufficient, and why restricted first-order formalisms are needed (section 2.2.3).

The next part of the chapter (section 2.3) is then devoted to the issue of representation language, i.e., the question of forming new concepts. We will show that the "correlated feature" hypothesis is a likely candidate to serve as the basis of concept formation, even though it is insufficient alone (section 2.3.1). We therefore discuss possible other constraints that psychologists have identified as influential in human concept formation, and describe how they could be or have been exploited in machine learning models (section 2.3.2). In particular, we will focus on constraints that arise from goal-oriented problem solving activity (section 2.3.3). The next section contains a review of previous work in Machine Learning, and the kinds of concept representation and concept formation constraints it has used (section 2.4). We conclude with a summary of our argument for a demand-driven approach (section 2.5).

2.1 PSYCHOLOGICAL RESEARCH ON CONCEPTS

In this section, we want to give a brief overview of recent trends in the psychological study of concepts to provide a context for the rest of the chapter. Instead of trying to cover all subdisciplines of psychology, we concentrate on those that we will draw upon most strongly in the rest of this chapter: *cognitive psychology* and *developmental psychology*.

2.1.1 Cognitive psychology

Within most cognitive psychology research, concepts are examined in the cognition of adult, mature individuals. Concept formation, consequently, is usually being studied in the short time frame of experimental laboratory tasks. There is no emphasis on individual concepts, which serve only as data points to support the general models. Even though mostly not computationally operational, the models are often expressed in nearly operational terms. In this, cognitive psychology is relatively close to artificial intelligence.

It is useful to distinguish two (overlapping) phases of recent concept research in cognitive psychology. In the first phase (strongly influenced by the work of Rosch [1978]), there was a focus on the tasks of concept learning from examples and categorization, mostly studied for object categories (both natural and artificial). The methods used had a strongly quantitative, "empirical" flavor, and included categorization time and accuracy measurements, feature listings, and similarity and typicality ratings. The main result of this phase was the insight that contrary to the classical-logical (Aristotelian) view, human concepts had a rich internal structure. Some instances of a concept were found to be more typical than others, and concept membership was found to be graded, not all or none. Sections 2.2.1 and 2.2.2 describe those findings and the resulting concept models in more detail.

In the second phase of cognitive psychology research on concepts (beginning in the 80ies), there was a stronger emphasis on category formation from observation (as opposed to forming a concept for a category that is already defined extensionally by positive and negative examples). More abstract concepts were included, the tasks became more complex and were embedded in a realistic context (as opposed to using e.g. nonsense syllables). In addition to the methods used in the first phase, more qualitative and "content-oriented" analyses were performed. Important observed phenomena were the context and transformation effects in categorization, and the goal- and task-oriented nature of concept formation that we will discuss in more detail below (section 2.3.3).

2.1.2 Developmental Psychology

In contrast to cognitive psychology with its emphasis on adult cognition, the field of developmental psychology studies concepts and the process of concept formation from an *ontogenetic* perspective, i.e., in the context of the development of an individual from birth to adulthood. The concepts that are examined include the most complex and abstract ones (like "time" or "living thing"). Often there is a strong emphasis on detailed analyses of the development of individual concepts in an exemplary fashion (see [Carey, 1985]), rather than on general models of the concept formation process.

The models that are developed in this branch of psychology often do not share the methodological focus on operationality that cognitive psychology or cognitive science have imported from AI. Rather, one finds accounts of concept formation that consist first and foremost of a descriptive part, i.e., it is recorded when which stages in a child's development occur, as was done e.g. by Piaget. The explanations of observed behavior are usually expressed in terms that are not directly interpretable in an operational fashion, so that these models cannot always be transferred easily into the realm of AI and machine learning.

The major early results of developmental psychology (e.g. by Piaget [Piaget, 1977; Sigel, 1983] or Wygotski [Wygotski, 1964]) are the description of possible levels of concept representation (see section 2.2.2), of different stages of conceptual development in children, and of various strategies for concept formation (see section 2.3.2). More recent research, however, has concentrated less on the dependency of conceptual capabilities on age, and more on the interdependencies of various conceptual processes with each other. The resulting reexamination of children's capabilities led to much lower age limits than previously believed (see the reviews in [Gibson and Spelke, 1983; Mandler, 1983]) and to more process oriented models (e.g. by Nelson [Nelson, 1983], section 2.3.3).

2.2 CONCEPT REPRESENTATION

After the brief overview of psychological research above, our goal in this section is to develop a set of requirements for the expressiveness of a representation formalism that is to be used for the study of concept formation. It must at least be able to represent the concept structures that psychologists have used to describe human concepts. So what are the key properties of human concepts?

2.2.1 Properties of human concepts

The term *concept* is being applied to a wide range of phenomena in human behavior. The most widely used view of concepts is based on their function of collecting a set of individuals into a group with certain common properties. In this view, one distinguishes between the *intension* and the *extension* of a concept. The intension is the "meaning", the "essence" of the concept, and determines its extension, i.e., which entities will be accepted as members of the concept[1]. We will refer to this view as the *classificatory concept* view[2].

---

[1] Often, the term *category* is used to refer to the extension, whereas the term *concept* is used to refer to the intension.

[2] Stegmüller [Stegmüller, 1970, p. 19] introduces classificatory concepts as the simplest form of scientific concepts that are superseded by *comparative* and *quantitative* concepts.

Most research in cognitive psychology and AI is tacitly based on this view of concepts, and the object and event concepts ("car", "accident") examined there fit perfectly well into the classificatory view.

For other concepts, such as those examined in developmental psychology ("time") and the philosophy of science ("gravitation"), the basic distinction between intension and extension is not so easily applicable. Which entities would we identify as members of the concepts "time" or "gravitation"? Those concepts are best characterized as explanatory schemata [Nersessian, 1984] without a classificatory function; this is the *explanatory concept* position. The classificatory and the explanatory views of course do not exclude each other; they simply cover different parts of our mental repertoire.

Yet another class of phenomena to which the term *concept* is often applied are motor action and perception or sensor "concepts". There, one may even debate whether it is correct to speak of concepts, e.g. for actions such as "grasping", visual or auditory patterns. In developmental psychology, such concepts are often seen as the basis of the representational system. Bruner, for example, describes the conceptual system as rooted in an *enactive*, sensorimotor level, upon which are built an *iconic*, perceptual level, and finally a *symbolic* level that houses the kind of classificatory concepts discussed above [Bruner, 1973; Sigel, 1983]. Piaget and Wygotski have made similar assertions.

In this chapter, we are concerned with the properties of classificatory concepts on the symbolic level, for now ignoring their rootedness in perceptual and sensorimotor levels[3]. The key observations that psychologists have made about such concepts are summarized in the following paragraphs.

The first group of observations is based on the results of experimental *feature listing* tasks, where subjects are asked to list as exhaustively as possible the features or components they think belong to a specified concept. From these results, it is apparent that people include relatively complex information in their features:

I.1 Nonnecessary features The simplest possible view of concepts is the classical one where a "concept" consists of a set of features that are singly necessary and jointly sufficient (see 2.2.2). People, however, also include in answers features that are nonnecessary, i.e., only true of some or most of the members of the concept. In studies cited by Smith and Medin [1981], it was even shown that nonnecessary features are actually used in categorization [Hampton, 1979], and that similarity correlates with nonnecessary features in certain cases [Rips *et al.*, 1973].

---

[3] We will, however, return to this issue in a later chapter (chapter 6).

I.2 Disjunctive concepts A further point is made by the empirical observation of disjunctive concepts, where there may not be any features that are shared by all members of a concept. Contrary to what might be argued, disjunctive concepts are not limited to technical or mathematical domains. Rosch *et.al.* [1976] found that for many abstract categories (such as "furniture" or "vehicle"), people list very few if any features, indicating the strongly disjunctive nature of the underlying concepts.

I.3 Relational information Shifting our attention to the kind of features that people list in feature listing tasks, we find that a feature can describe elementary perceptual attributes of an object ("round", "red"), but just as often information about the object's function (a vehicle is "used for transportation") or its relation to other objects (an apple "has a core") [Murphy and Medin, 1985].

I.4 Features as concepts As a final observation, it has been noted that features themselves are not atomic units of description. Instead, people tend to have a lot of knowledge about features [Murphy and Medin, 1985]. "Red", for example, is usually thought of as a feature, but people can list a lot of features of the color "red" in turn.

The second set of observations is based on experiments where people are asked to *categorize* a presented stimulus, i.e., name a concept to which the stimulus belongs, or simply decide whether or not the stimulus belongs to a specified concept. Here, it turned out that concepts and conceptual systems have internal structure:

II.1 Typicality For most categories, people find it a simple and natural task to rate individual members with respect to how typical or representative they are of the concept [Smith and Medin, 1981]. More importantly, in several experiments [Rips *et al.*, 1973; Rosch *et al.*, 1976], the typicality rating of an object was found to correlate with the time and error rate of categorizing this object into the category. The more typical the object, the faster and more reliably the categorization was performed, which indicates that the mental concept representations themselves may incorporate some sort of typicality structure.

II.2 Basic levels Another interesting observation can be made if people are asked to categorize a stimulus without identifying with respect to which concept it is to be categorized. In this task, people tend to produce concepts of an intermediate level as answers, e.g. naming an object a "chair" rather than an "office chair" or a "piece of furniture". On this *basic level*, categorization is faster and more reliable [Rosch *et al.*, 1976].

II.3 Superordinate Distance The last observation in this group again refers to the structure of the conceptual hierarchy. Interestingly, a concept is not always rated most similar to its immediate superordinates. Sometimes, more distant (higher) superordinates are found the most similar. This is the case e.g. for "chicken", which is rated more similar to "animal" than to "bird" [Smith and Medin, 1981].

The final set of observations is about the nature of the categorization process itself and indicates some of the factors that influence categorization:

III.1 Unclear cases The first indicator for the complexity of categorization is the fact that membership in a category is not all or none. Objects can be partial members of a category, or members in certain respects. In those unclear cases, people have trouble deciding, and categorizations vary [McCloskey and Glucksberg, 1978]. This is the case e.g. when deciding whether a radio is furniture, or whether a tomato is a fruit.

III.2 Context effects Another well documented phenomenon is the dependence of categorization (and similarity) judgments on context [Tversky, 1977], where context refers to the information available at the time of categorization. Using an example from Murphy and Medin [Murphy and Medin, 1985], if you see someone jumping into a swimming pool, you may categorize this into the concept "drunk" during a party, but also as "heroic" if you knew someone was drowning.

III.3 Multiple categorizations The final observation is closely related to the context effect phenomenon. It can be empirically observed that people usually have a set of categories that they could apply to an object in a given situation. Here, it is not the available information that determines which category will be picked, but the goals of the observer [Barsalou, 1982]: the observer chooses from the multiple possible categories the one that is most related to his current goals.

This concludes our discussion of empirical observations about human concepts. Table 2.1 presents a summarizing overview of the three groups that we have presented. As we will see below, they present quite a challenge for many psychological models of concept structure, and have direct implications for the necessary expressiveness of representation formalisms for concept formation.

2.2.2 Models of concept structure from psychology

The models with which people have tried to explain the above phenomena fall into five general classes [Smith and Medin, 1981], which we describe in the

I. Features	*II. Internal Structure*	*III. Categorization*
Nonnecessary features	Typicality	Unclear cases
Disjunctive concepts	Basic levels	Context effects
Relational information	Superordin. distance	Multiple categoriz.
Features as concepts		

Table 2.1   Important empirical observations about human concepts

following sections: *classical* models, *probabilistic* models, *exemplar* models, *hybrid* models, and *theory-oriented* models.

Classical Models

The classical model of concept structure dates back to Aristotle, and should be familiar from all mathematics textbooks: A concept is defined by a set of defining features, which are individually necessary and jointly sufficient. One can recognize an object as a member of the concept by checking all the features, and can infer all the features with certainty from knowing that an object is a member of the concept. The concept hierarchy is created by the subset relation between the features, e.g. a polygon is a closed object made out of lines, a triangle is a polygon made of three lines.

Classical concept models in this pure form are merely a historical reference point nowadays, since they cannot explain any of the psychological phenomena mentioned above: all features must be defining, so nonnecessary features (I.1) or disjunctive concepts (I.2) cannot be represented; the approach treats features as atomic (I.4), and needs to hide relational information in them (a polygon "made out of lines", I.3). Except in formal domains, finding the defining features of a concept has turned out impossible.

The approach treats all concept members equally, so no typicality effect can be modeled (II.1). It correctly predicts that objects with less features are categorized faster, but does not identify any distinguished basic level (II.2) and predicts uniform superordinate distance (II.3). Multiple categorizations can be represented, but the approach cannot explain how the right one is selected (III.3), nor how context effects (III.2) or unclear cases could arise (III.1).

As a result of these problems, the classical view in psychology today appears only in modified forms, e.g. in hybrid models, or with additional assumptions as in the theory-oriented models (see below).

Probabilistic models

In probabilistic models, a concept is still defined by a set features, but those features need not be defining. Instead, the features of a concept are *salient* ones that have a substantial probability of occurring in instances of the concept, i.e., properties need only be *characteristic*, not defining. Each feature[4] has a weight attached to it that specifies its importance. Categorization is performed by checking the features, and requiring that the weighted sum of those that match be above a certain threshold[5]. Inferences from concept membership are no longer certain, but only probabilistic. The concept hierarchy is no longer based on the subset relation of features, since concepts do not necessarily have to have the features of their superordinates.

By abandoning the requirement that all features be defining, many of the phenomena discussed in section 2.2.1 can be explained. Since category membership is now expressed by a percentage value, it is easy to explain typicality by assuming that the higher the match value of an instance, the more typical it is of the concept (II.1). Since the feature set of a concept is not required to be nested within the feature set of its superconcept, it is no problem to account for cases where distant superordinates are rated more similar than the immediate parent (II.3). The basic level effect can be explained by introducing a *category utility* measure that combines ease of categorization with amount of possible inferences [Gluck and Corter, 1985] (II.2).

Nonnecessary features and disjunctive concepts can be represented by selecting appropriate feature weights (I.1, I.2). Unclear cases arise if a match does not quite reach the membership threshold (III.1). Just as the classical approach, the probabilistic models discussed above treat features as atomic (I.4), and thus have to hide relational information in them (I.3). Likewise, context effects and multiple categorizations cannot be explained by these models without further assumptions (III.2, III.3).

Exemplar models

The exemplar view is even less constraining than the probabilistic view: it drops the requirement that a concept be a summary description of a category as a set of features. Instead, the general assumption is that a concept

---

[4] Or set of features, as in the Hayes-Roth' model [Hayes-Roth and Hayes-Roth, 1977].
[5] The concrete implementation of the weighted sum computation varies between the different models.

consists of a collection of representations of some or all of its "exemplars". Exemplars are interpreted as immediate representations of actual category members, or as "prototypical instances", i.e., allowing for some amount of abstraction/generalization so that each exemplar represents a subset of the category [Rosch, 1975; Rosch, 1978]. This allows the exemplar view to represent any concept, even the non-linearly separable ones that cannot be expressed probabilistically[6]. An entity is categorized as a member of a concept if it retrieves a criterial number of the concept's exemplars before retrieving a criterial number of exemplars of any other contrasting concept[7] [Medin and Schaffer, 1978].

The exemplar view, if properly instantiated, can explain the same phenomena as the probabilistic approach, and also fails to account for context effects or multiple categorizations unless additional assumptions are made. Even though there is evidence that people actually use exemplars [Holyoak and Glass, 1975; Collins and Loftus, 1975], the exemplar view is a problematic model of concept structure due to its lack of constraints and a much too strong reliance on processing assumptions.

Hybrid Models

Given the difficulties with some "core-only" models, an interesting possibility is to look at models that allow for an independent identification procedure, i.e., one that may contain different information from the core. This approach goes back to Miller and Johnson-Laird [Miller and Johnson-Laird, 1976], and was briefly reconsidered by Medin and Smith in [Smith and Medin, 1981] and [Medin and Smith, 1984]. It allows for another degree of freedom in developing concept models, since the representations of core and identification procedure may now be chosen independently. For this reason, we will call those models *hybrid models*.

Clearly, by adding a probabilistic recognition procedure to a classical core, the problems of the classical approach with typicality, basic levels, and superordinate distance can be fixed. There is also some empirical evidence for a hybrid model of concepts consisting of a classical core and a probabilistic/prototypical identification procedure (see [Murphy and Medin, 1985]): People insist on concepts having defining features even if they cannot provide them. Classical mathematical concepts were found to show typicality effects: 22 was rated a more typical even number than 18 [Armstrong *et al.*, 1983]. In an exper-

---

[6] As pointed out by Fisher [Fisher, 1987b], probabilistic models acquire the same power if probabilities are associated with *sets* of features as well.

[7] The probability of retrieving an exemplar is taken to be proportional to the similarity between the entity to be categorized and the exemplar.

iment involving the concept of "grandmother", subjects used characteristic features of the concept for identification ("age"), but defining features from the presumed core ("has grandchildren") for justifying their categorizations [Landau, 1982].

Theory-oriented models

Despite considerable differences, the four views of concept structure presented above agree on one central point: all four assume that concepts are represented as sets of features, and thus have problems explaining phenomena (I.3) and (I.4), because they ignore people's knowledge about features. The same is true for context effects and multiple categorization (III.2, III.3), which cannot be explained in the above models because they provide no possibility to link the set of concepts with the rest of an observer's world model. Together, those observations have led Murphy and Medin [Murphy and Medin, 1985] to look at categorization as an *inference* process that may utilize both information about the features of a concept, as well as any other information the agent may possess. In other words, categorization means constructing an *explanation* of why an object belongs to a concept under the given circumstances.

To make possible such a view of categorization, Murphy and Medin argue for concepts to be tied in much more closely with the mental theory and goals of the categorizer. They discuss a model where this theoretical knowledge is stored locally in the core of each concept, extending Miller and Johnson-Laird's [Miller and Johnson-Laird, 1976] proposal of theory-based core plus perceptual identification procedure for lexical concepts. They "use *theory* to mean any of a host of mental 'explanations,' rather than a complete, organized scientific account." [p. 290] According to this proposal, then, a concept's core is a "micro-theory" defining and explaining the concept's meaning. Those micro-theory concepts are then linked to each other by causal and explanatory links, forming the macro-theory of the agent. Murphy and Medin do not specify exactly what form their concepts and theories should take, so their proposal must be seen as a blueprint for a set of possible theory-oriented models.

If properly instantiated, such a model could explain the observations that were so troublesome for the other four classes of models, since now information about features is representable, as is relational information. If categorization is an inference process, it is also possible that current context and goals of the observer are taken into account.

2.2.3 Minimal requirements for representation formalisms

Now that we have discussed empirical observations about the properties of human concepts, and the models of concept structure that psychologists have come up with to explain those observations, we are ready to answer the question we posed in the introduction to this chapter: what is the necessary expressive power of a representation formalism to represent the kinds of models we have just presented? Is a propositional formalism sufficient, or must we resort to first order logic?

On first sight, it may seem that most of the observations in table 2.1 can be explained by models that make reference only to "features", e.g. the probabilistic or a hybrid model. Using the standard AI meaning of "feature", this suggests that an attribute-based, propositional formalism might suffice. As we pointed out above, however, psychological models take considerably more liberty in what is to count as a feature. In section 2.2.1, we saw that almost all concepts need relational information for their definition (observation I.3). This information is simply hidden inside of "features" such as "has 4 wheels" or "used to open a can", thus making it impossible to represent the relationship between those features and the concepts "wheel" and "can" that are implicitly referenced. Thus, even the seemingly feature-based models discussed above do include relational information by using relational features, so one needs a formalism that can represent relational information even for those models.

Secondly, people have a great deal of knowledge *about* features (I.4 above). As Medin *et al.* [1987, p. 277] state, "the constituent components of concepts are not irreducible primitives but rather participate in a variety of interproperty relationships." If we want to represent this knowledge, and explain the context and multiple categorization effects (III.2, III.3), we definitely cannot make do with a propositional formalism. As Murphy and Medin have pointed out, all of those observations require an embedding of concepts into theories for their explanation, i.e., we must be able to speak about features as full-fledged objects about which we can make statements.

The least expressive formalism within which relational information of the above type can be represented are function-free Horn clauses (DATALOG formalisms in the terminology of [Ceri *et al.*, 1990]), or other formalisms of similar expressive power[8]. While thus being necessary for the representation of certain psychological phenomena and models, we should emphasize that the

---

[8] As an important example, the class of *description logics* or *term-subsumption languages* (KL-ONE [Brachman and Schmolze, 1985] is a well-known instance) was shown to have members whose expressive power is comparable to function-free Horn-clauses while still being tractable [Donini *et al.*, 1991].

above formalisms are most likely not sufficient to explain all the phenomena we have listed in section 2.2.1; indeed it is likely that the treatment of internal concept structure will require some probabilistic additions to such formalisms.

In summary, there is a psychologically well-founded argument for the use of at least function-free Horn logic in the computational study of concept formation. In our work on concept formation to be reported below, we have consequently chosen such a formalism, instead of the attribute-based formalisms that are still more common in machine learning. In chapter 3, we will present the chosen formalism in more detail, and we will also have the opportunity to discuss which psychological phenomena can and which ones cannot be addressed in such a formalism. First, however, we need to turn our attention to the second part of the psychology of concepts: to the issue of concept formation.

2.3 CONCEPT FORMATION

To examine the nature of concept formation processes is to take a dynamic view on the problem of selecting the right representation *language* within a representation formalism. Assuming the results of concept formation processes are concepts that are actually needed in the conceptual system, an answer to the question of which concepts are formed, and in what way, also constitutes an answer to the language selection problem, since we can then use concept formation processes to extend an initially insufficient language.

The goal of this section is to discuss the available psychological observations about human concept formation in order to identify where they can be exploited in the construction of computer models of concept formation. What are the constraintsconcepts formation,constraints on that determine which concepts are formed?

2.3.1 Correlated features: the basis of concept formation

At first sight, the models of concept structure that were discussed in section 2.2.2 seem to be a possible source of constraints on concept formation. Unfortunately, these models per se do not specify which concepts are formed, they only specify the form of those concepts that *are* formed. They do not pick out any category as better than another. The bias inherent in the various representation forms is a constraint only with fixed feature sets; it disappears if arbitrary other features can be introduced. The probabilistic models discussed above, for example, cannot represent categories that are not linearly separable, i.e., that cannot be expressed as a linear combination of features. With different features, however, the same category may become linearly separable. Furthermore, empirical data cast doubt on whether linear separability is important for actual concepts [Medin and Schwanenflugel, 1981]. The classical view fares a little better, since it excludes all concepts for which no defining features can be found, but as we saw above it is implausible as a concept model. The other classes of models (exemplar, hybrid, theory-oriented) can represent any concept, so there must be other sources of constraints.

Murphy and Medin [1985] have discussed two possible general constraints on which objects can be aggregated into a concept: the similarity hypothesis and the correlated feature hypothesis.

The similarity hypothesis. Simply stated, the similarity hypothesis claims that the most important constraint in forming a category is that its members be *similar* to one another, and dissimilar to objects from other categories. Similarity could for example be determined by some kind of a matching process between the features of the objects.

Unfortunately, the similarity explanation presupposes what it is trying to explain: it is well-defined only if we can rely on a concept (e.g. set of features and weights) to specify how to run the matching procedure. Otherwise, anything can be made similar by changing the things attended to by the matching procedure. Indeed it can empirically be shown that the similarity between two objects is not a universal constant, it rather depends heavily on the context and the task for which the similarity is to be judged [Tversky, 1977].

The correlated attribute hypothesis The correlated attribute hypothesis, developed by Rosch [Rosch *et al.*, 1976; Rosch, 1978], postulates "that natural categories divide the world up according to clusters of features, that they 'cut the world at its joints.' That is, attributes of the world are not randomly spread across objects, but rather appear in clusters" [Murphy and Medin, 1985, p. 293]. The most useful and efficient categories are taken to be those that reflect the cluster structure of correlations. As an explanation for concept formation, this means that categories develop to group objects with a cluster of features and to exclude objects with different features.

There is a significant amount of empirical evidence that people detect and use feature correlations [Medin *et al.*, 1982; Cohen and Younger, 1983; Younger and Cohen, 1984]. Thus, the correlated attribute hypothesis at least seems to account for part of the concept formation process. It also does not suffer from the circular ill-definedness of the similarity hypothesis, since it only requires the detection of feature correlations, and not knowledge of feature weights.

Nonetheless, several problems remain. The most severe is certainly that it still is not clear what is to count as a feature, and how people manage to perceive an essentially unstructured world in terms of features. Assuming that the world is structured a priori, i.e., that it contains information that an observer would only have to absorb, is a common assumption in the information-processing paradigm of Cognitive Science and AI, but nonetheless a controversial one. We will return to this point in chapter 6. But even if we assume that correlations are "objectively" present, and that elementary observations are already expressed as features, it is not clear how the correct correlations would get picked out; additional constraints are necessary. Thus, even though there is a good amount of evidence for correlated features as the basis of concept formation, they alone are insufficient.

2.3.2   Structural and theory-based constraints on concept formation

In this section, we will briefly survey two possible sources of constraints on concept formation, namely structural and theory-oriented constraints. A third source of constraints, goal-derived constraints, is discussed in a separate section (2.3.3).

Structural constraints One possible source of constraints is the structure of individual concepts and of the entire conceptual system. Above, we have pointed out that for individual concepts, structural constraints are hard to come by, since none of the models of concept structure discussed in section 2.2.2 provide any real constraints on the concepts they can represent. Also, we saw that similarity did not work since it cannot be determined without having a concept first.

Another possible constraint on individual concepts could be to require them to be as "simple" as possible. Naturally, this brings up the question of how simplicity could be measured. In machine learning programs that employed this measure (e.g. CLUSTER [Stepp and Michalski, 1986]), simplicity was assumed to be proportional to the length of the concept's representation in terms of a fixed descriptor set. Even though this seemed to work well there, simplicity is as questionable a constraint as similarity, since it makes sense only with respect to a fixed representation language. In a changing representation, what was complex may become simple after a while.

For entire conceptual systems, it seems more feasible to specify sensible constraints. One very basic such constraint could be the one that was suggested for scientific theories by Stegmuller [Stegmuller, 1970] who required that good classification systems be *exhaustive* and *disjoint*, i.e., that they cover each object of the domain in question, and that each object is covered by exactly one leaf concept. A similar constraint was proposed in psychology by Keil [Keil, 1979], as reported by Carey [Carey, 1985]: Keil hypothesized that ontologically basic categories would form a strict hierarchy, and that there would be no concepts across different branches of this hierarchy. Unfortunately, human conceptual hierarchies do not exhibit these claimed characteristics. In particular, they are not disjoint (see point III.3 in section 2.2.1).

A final constraint that we should mention here is based on a structural measure, but with an orientation towards the classification and prediction goals of a conceptual system. Based on the category utility measure that Gluck and Corter [Gluck and Corter, 1985] had introduced to identify the basic level in conceptual hierarchies, Fisher [Fisher, 1987b] has developed a measure of the expected number of attributes correctly predicted over an entire partitioning of objects, and uses this constraint to decide how to aggregate. This constraint was empirically shown to correctly predict the basic-level effect for category systems.

Despite these successful proposals of structural constraints, several authors have plausibly argued that structural constraints can only go so far. We only want to briefly remind the reader of Goodman's [1955] famous argument that there could not be any structural criteria that make an inductive process prefer the predicate *green* (with the usual meaning) over the predicate *grue* (meaning "green before the year 2000, and blue after") in an inductive hypothesis (see [Carey, 1985, p. 196]). In our own work on concept formation, structural constraints have not been a major focus, even though we use structural constraints to decide whether to keep or discard a newly formed concept (see section 5.3.2).

Theory-based constraints As Murphy and Medin [Murphy and Medin, 1985] persuasively argue, there is strong evidence that people's existing theories of the world provide strong constraints on which concepts are formed and which ones are not. Specifically, Murphy and Medin present evidence that prior theories are important in filtering out from the space of possible correlations those that are deemed to be plausible, and that people actually use those correlations for concept formation. In one study, Medin *et al.* [1987] asked people to sort entities into categories, and offered them two sets of correlated attributes for doing this. The two sets differed with respect to how easy it was to come up with a causal explanation for the correlation. Indeed, subjects were found to strongly prefer the causally linked correlated attributes for aggregating categories, and they also offered the causal link as an explanation of why they categorized the way they did.

In other studies, the strong influence of prior theories on the perception of correlations has been shown to result in *illusory correlations*, i.e., correlations that were suggested by people's theories, but were not actually present in the data. Murphy and Medin cite a number of studies where this phenomenon was observed [Chapman and Chapman, 1969; Crocker, 1981; Wright and Murphy, 1984].

2.3.3 Evidence for the goal orientation of concept formation

In our work on a computational model of concept formation to be presented in chapter 5, we have been particularly interested in another important constraint on concept formation: the interrelation of concept formation with goal-oriented problem solving activities. The importance of goal-directed action for the formation of concepts has been recognized very early in developmental psychology. As early as 1934, the Russian psychologist Wygotski introduced his own work on concept formation by referring to previous research of N. Ach and F. Rimat in Germany as follows [Wygotski, 1964, p. 112][9]:

> "This is one of the main results of Ach and Rimat's research. They have shown that the associational view of concept formation is wrong, pointed out the productive and creative nature of concepts and the role of the functional momentum in their formation, and emphasized that a concept can arise and develop only if there is a *specific need*, the need for a concept, within a specific, conscious, *purposeful activity* that is directed towards reaching a *specific goal* or towards the solution of a specific task."

In this pointed form, Wygotski's position can be understood only with reference to the psychological discussion at his time, where a lot of research on concepts rested on the "definition method" as experimental task. This definition method is basically the feature listing task of modern cognitive psychology (see section 2.2.1): subjects are asked to verbally define a specified concept. With this methodology, all dynamic aspects of concept formation can only be speculated about, and one is limited to a study of the static structure of concepts.

---

[9] Translated from the German edition by the author; italics added by the author.

By contrast, Wygotski's experimental method of "double presentations" was the following. The subjects are presented with a number of small objects of different shapes and colors all labeled with an artificial word as their class name. Initially, the subjects may look at the label for only one object, and are asked to group with it all other objects that they think are likely to be labeled by the same word. After each trial, the experimenter checks the solution (without giving the correct solution to the subject) and then presents to the subject the label of another object, which can be of the same or a different class as the first.

By this, Wygotski could vary the vocabulary available to the subject, which he believed to be the key means of concept formation, in a controlled fashion while maintaining the same experimental task (object grouping) over the entire process. Thus, in this experimental setup, concept formation was indeed studied in the context of purposeful activity, even if this activity was of an artificial nature. Despite his initial emphasis on goals and problem solving activity, Wygotski's main interest in "Thought and Language" is not in the influence of goals and problem solving, but in the role of language in learning and concept formation processes, and in particular, the properties of the shift from internal to external language. He thus does not identify where and how the problem solving context given by his experimental setup influences the concepts that are formed.

Concept formation from event contexts

Fortunately, there is more recent research that can at least partially identify how these factors influence concept formation. A case in point is Nelson's [Nelson, 1983] model of how concepts and categories could be derived from event representations. According to Nelson, *events* are the relevant context for the formation of concepts even in very young children. This hypothesis is supported by empirical evidence showing that for children aged 8 to 12 months, one may not switch events (e.g., games played) without eliciting a reaction, while the objects involved in the events seem to be substitutable (e.g. in object hiding tasks [Le Compte and Gratch, 1972; Nelson, 1979]).

The representation of event knowledge is supposed to consist of social *scripts* [Schank and Abelson, 1977], which includes action schemata in the sense of Piaget, plus "representation of objects, persons and person roles, and *sequences* of actions appropriate to a specific scene." Several studies are cited that show that children possess a number of scripts at the age of one year already. The granularity of such scripts may vary from small "scenes" such as "rolling a ball" to larger events such as "eating a meal".

Based on scripts, concept formation can be understood as the process of separating out parts of the script (objects, actions, properties) so they can be treated as independent mental objects. In the script, parts are connected by their linear sequential relation. In the developing concept, on the other hand, they are connected by their occurring in a common context. In the linguistic terminology adopted by Nelson, concept formation from scripts means shifting from *syntagmatic* relations in the event to *paradigmatic* relations in the concept. This view parallels data on free word associations cited by Nelson [Entwistle, 1966; Ervin, 1961; Nelson, 1977], which show that younger children tend to produce syntagmatic associations, whereas older ones, just like adults, increasingly use paradigmatic associations. Nelson's proposal is further supported by findings that during the use of concepts, properties relevant to how people typically interact with instances of the concept — this is exactly what the script context specifies — are indeed more likely to be active [Barsalou, 1982].

Nelson proposes three distinct mechanisms of increasing difficulty that produce three different kinds of concepts from event representations. Those mechanisms correspond to overlapping phases of a child's conceptual development, covering the time from 1 year of age (where the existence of scripts has experimentally been shown) to the first school years:

1. Reoccurrence of the same object in different actions of one event: This leads to *single object concepts* which are essentially defined by their role in the script actions. According to Nelson, the reoccurrence of an object as a focal point of interest to the child in some activity determines what objects will be conceptualized; those selected will be analyzed for their characteristics. The reoccurrence of the object is used to separate it from its syntagmatic context, so that it can be recognized in other contexts than the original context. This of course requires from the child to be able to perceptually recognize the reoccurrence of the object[10].

2. Occurrence of different objects in the same position of different instances of an event: This leads to *categories of objects* that are defined by the common position they fill in a certain script. Children seem to possess such categories ("food") from very early on, but sometimes use a specific slot filler ("apple") to name the category of all fillers of that slot ("fruit"), which Nelson counts as further evidence for the use of across-event substitutability in category formation.

3. Reoccurrence of the same object or category of objects in different events, in the same or different positions: this leads to context-free concepts and categories, and is the most difficult process of the three, since it requires

---

[10] We again refer the reader to chapter 6 for a discussion of the issue of perceptual grounding.

established object concepts or categories, and an ability to recognize that they serve the same or (even more difficult) different functions in other scripts.

For all three of those concept formation strategies, the key point is the shift from syntagmatic to paradigmatic organization, i.e., from a set of objects that play a certain role in an activity, to a concept that is primarily characterized without reference to the initial temporal event context. Furthermore, Nelson's assertion that only "focal point[s] of interest" are subject to this syntagmatic--paradigmatic shift is very interesting, in that it pinpoints the importance of goals *external* to the concept formation process to select where to form a concept.

Ad-hoc categories

A similar point is made in an independent study reported by Barsalou [Barsalou, 1983] who examines the nature of what he calls *ad-hoc categories*. An ad-hoc category is a category that is created for and during the solution of one particular task. As an example, a person wanting to sell unwanted possessions at a garage sale may form the category "things to sell at a garage sale". Stated generally, the ad-hoc categories examined by Barsalou have the form "things instrumental to achieving goal X", and therefore exhibit as direct a goal orientation as possible.

Such a unidimensional criterion obviously can define a set of objects, and hence a category, but is there a concept behind such categories, i.e., are there mental representations of them that go beyond a mere list of category members? The evidence provided by Barsalou is mixed. On the one hand, ad-hoc categories were found to possess the same graded structure that is typical of natural kind concepts. On the other hand, Barsalou found that lists organized by ad-hoc categories were recalled hardly better than random lists, indicating that there may be no concept behind such categories.

Barsalou's explanation for those findings parallels Nelson's model in a surprising way: he assumes that the appearance of a set of objects is the initial principle of aggregation for the category, but that an additional process of characterization must occur before this category is present in memory as a concept. In this way, frequently used ad-hoc categories (like "things to sell at a garage sale", which may be useful every Saturday) may become fully accessible concepts.

Summary

There is a good amount of evidence for the use of contextual constraints as a triggering principle for concept formation. In two models by Nelson and Barsalou, Wygotski's suggestion that concepts arise out of purposeful activity is taken up in basically the same manner by assuming that entities are grouped together because they play the same role in a particular context, and that this grouping is then transformed into a concept by a separate process of abstraction or characterization. What is left open by the models discussed above is whether concepts are formed *only* when there is a specific need for this concept to solve a specific task, as Wygotski has claimed. Barsalou's evidence can really only show that *some* categories (and subsequently concepts) are formed in this fashion. Similarly, Nelson's point that only objects of "focal ...interest" are conceptualized does indicate the need for context-based selection of where to form a concept, but does not prove that all or even most concept formation processes work this way.

2.4   PREVIOUS WORK IN MACHINE LEARNING

In the preceding sections of this chapter, we have already mentioned some of the systems in Machine Learning that have addressed the problems of concept representation and concept formation. Here, we want to give a more complete overview of how concepts have been treated in existing work.

2.4.1   Concept representation models used in ML

As for concept representation, most representations in use in Machine Learning belong to the domain of attribute-value, or propositional, formalisms. The most important representations that have been used there are *rules* and *decision trees*. Propositional rules have been used e.g. in the AQ family of learning systems [Michalski, 1983] and in many successors. They take the form of a set of conjunctively combined preconditions which together are sufficient for concept membership. Decision trees, which have become popular with the ID3 [Quinlan, 1983] and CART [Breiman *et al.*, 1984] systems, classify a new object by sorting it down the branches of a tree labeled with individual decisions, i.e., they can be transformed into an equivalent rule representation by creating a rule for each root-to-leaf path in the tree.

Such propositional representations essentially belong to the classical approach discussed above, as concept boundaries are sharp, and concepts have no internal structure. Since multiple rules may be used to conclude membership, however, all of these formalisms allow the representation of disjunctive concepts and nonnecessary features. Context effects can be modeled if additional rules are allowed as background knowledge; this is often not the case, however. As propositional formalisms, these approaches also cannot easily represent and reason about the internal structure of features, or about relations between objects.

The latter problem is alleviated in systems that use first-order representations. While first-order representations have been in use in Machine Learning for a long time (e.g. RLLG [Plotkin, 1970], ARCH [Winston, 1975], INDUCE [Michalski, 1983], MIS [Shapiro, 1983]), they have only recently attracted more interest at the intersection of logic programming and inductive learning research known as Inductive Logic Programming (ILP) [Muggleton and De Raedt, 1994]. Here, many learners are now using various subsets of first-order Horn clauses as their representation (e.g. CIGOL [Muggleton and Buntine, 1988], CLINT [DeRaedt and Bruynooghe, 1989], FOIL [Quinlan, 1990b], GOLEM [Muggleton and Feng, 1992], our own learner RDT [Kietz and Wrobel, 1992], and many others).

As pointed out in section 2.2.3, just as propositional formalisms, first-order formalisms cannot deal with concepts that have internal typicality structure; they can, however, represent context and multiple categorization effects, as classification can be an arbitrarily complex first-order inference process. In a certain sense, these representations can thus be seen as operationalizations of the "micro-theory" view that embeds concepts into the whole of an agent's theory. Consequently, the problem here is not with expressive power, but with computational tractability, so we will spend some time to examine this question for our representation in chapter 3.

To address the issues of internal concept structure, the probabilistic models from psychology have been taken up in a number of learning systems. In the symbolic domain, an early example is the rule learning model by Barbara and Frederic Hayes-Roth [1977], where probabilities are even recorded for feature sets. A later model that can even account for basic-level effects is the conceptual clustering program COBWEB by Fisher [1987a] that was already mentioned; in this program, concepts are represented precisely as defined in the probabilistic model above. Probabilistic notions have also been incorporated into some of the classical decision tree learning algorithms (e.g. the probabilistic decision trees of [Quinlan, 1990a]). In addition, non-symbolic techniques in the domain of Artificial Neural Networks   have been developed that also learn graded concepts, albeit represented in non-symbolic form as networks of nodes connected by weighted links [Hinton, 1990].

Similarly, the exemplar-based view has attracted a lot of attentionexemplar models recently under the headings of Case-Based Reasoning (CBR)

[Kolodner, 1992] and Instance-Based Learning (IBL) [Aha, 1989]. In both approaches, concepts are represented by individual or slightly generalized examples or cases, which are then used to derive a solution to a new problem (in CBR) or to classify a new object using techniques similar to nearest neighbor match. An early IBL system was PROTOS [Bareiss and Porter, 1987], more recent developments are described e.g. in [Aha *et al.*, 1991]. Just as the exemplar approach described above, these systems are capable of learning graded concepts with typicality structure; they are not as powerful in their use of background knowledge and the embedding of concepts in theories, however.

The least-used concept representation model from psychology, finally, are the hybrid models. Here, only R. Michalski [1987] has made a proposal to use *two-tiered* concepts, i.e., concepts with a propositional rule core as described above, plus a flexible matching procedure. This original proposal has since then been elaborated e.g. in the AQTT-15 system [Michalski, 1990] and later in POSEIDON [Bergadano *et al.*, 1992].

2.4.2 Concept formation constraints used in ML

From the above classification of concept formation constraints, existing concept formation systems have mainly used three types: similarity-based, correlation-based, and structure-based.

The implementation of *similarity-based constraints* relies on a context-free numerical similarity function that is given two objects and computes a real number, often scaled to be in the interval [0, 1], that measures their similarity. The simplest such similarity measure is the Euclidean distance between two numerical feature vectors. Such measures are most heavily used in numerical taxonomy [Everitt, 1980], but have also been used e.g. in UNIMEM [Lebowitz, 1987] to decide when to combine two instances into a more general concept. Experience with the implemented versions of similarity-based constraints parallels the psychological findings: these constraints are simple, but the quality of the concepts that are formed depends very much on a proper definition of the similarity measure. For example, it has been noted that the effect of UNIMEM's parameters on its results remains unclear [Gennari *et al.*, 1989].

Most existing concept formation systems have therefore used constraints that are based, in differing degrees, on *correlation-based* measures. The full set of correlation coefficients, i.e., the conditional probabilities of one feature given another one, are not always used in the algorithms; instead, various simplifications have been made. The CLUSTER system [Michalski and

Stepp, 1983], for example, uses measures called "inter-cluster difference", "discrimination index", and "dimensionality reduction" in its lexicographic evaluation function (LEF), all of which indirectly express feature correlations. Inter-cluster difference is measured by counting the number of features not shared by two proposed clusters; the more non-shared features, the less the inter-cluster correlation. The discrimination index counts the number of variables that singly discriminate all clusters, i.e., that are perfectly correlated to their classes. Dimensionality reduction also relates to feature correlation, since it measures the number of variables required to distinguish all classes; the lower this number, the better features are correlated within a class.

UNIMEM [Lebowitz, 1987] uses a more direct approximation of class and feature correlation by keeping integer counters of predictability (given a class, how often did the feature appear?) and predictiveness (given a feature, how often did the class appear?) to decide when to fix a feature as part of a concept definition. Since counters are used that do not reflect the ratio of observed examples to total number of events, this measure was somewhat ad-hoc. More recent systems have therefore approximated predictability and predictiveness by relative frequency counts; this has been done e.g. in COBWEB [Fisher, 1987a] and its successor CLASSIT [Gennari *et al.*, 1989]. In these systems, the two measures are then combined into a single quality measure ("category utility") that balances predictability and predictiveness in a class (originally developed by Gluck and Corter [1985]). WITT [Hanson and Bauer, 1989] uses another correlation-based measure ("cohesion") for bottom-up clustering.

Structural constraints are also used in various systems and refer to the syntactical structure of individual concept descriptions, or to the structure of the entire conceptual system. To name a few examples, in CLUSTER [Michalski and Stepp, 1983], only aggregates that could be characterized by conjunctive expressions were considered, and those with shorter definitions (total number of "selector" conjuncts used in entire clustering) were preferred. In CLUSTER/G [Stepp and Michalski, 1986], the available descriptors had associated weights derived from a goal dependency network, and the system preferred clusterings that used descriptors with high weights. In KLUSTER [Kietz and Morik, 1994], aggregation is restricted to subsets of the set of instances of a common superconcept, and also respect findings about contrast sets [Tversky, 1977] in requiring that this set of objects be aggregated into mutually disjoint subsets (without requiring the entire hierarchy to be strict).

The other types of constraints listed in the preceding sections, namely theory-based and goal-derived constraints, have been used comparatively little so far. While there have been proposals to use existing theories to check perceived correlations (e.g. [Pazzani *et al.*, August 1986]), these have not been used for concept formation yet. Similarly, despite the strong psychological evidence for the use of constraints derived from a goal-oriented problem-solving context, such constraints have been used very little prior to our own work. Emde, Habel, and Rollinger [1983] originally proposed the basic idea of using rule exception sets to introduce new concepts which now forms the core of our method, albeit without interpreting it as a constraint based on problem-solving activities. Above, we mentioned the CLUSTER/G system, which through its use of a goal-dependency network at least acknowledged the importance of goals for concept formation, but used this information for no more than giving weights to descriptors. The general idea behind our method, namely to introduce a new concept whenever the existing vocabulary is insufficient to reach a given problem solving goal, has previously been used only in a propositional-logic constructive induction context in the STABB system [Utgoff, 1986]; recently, it has also been applied in the KLUSTER system [Morik and Kietz, 1989; Kietz and Morik, 1994]. The two systems are discussed in section 5.5 along with further related work.

2.5   TOWARDS A DEMAND-DRIVEN APPROACH

In sum then, the goal of our work is pick up the suggestions from psychology, and focus on problem-solving derived constraints that had not previously received attention. In chapter 5, we will present our model in detail; here, we simply want to identify where the model takes up the points raised by the above discussion of psychological research.

- Following Barsalou, the major premise of the model is that some concepts are formed in response to a specific need, or *demand* for the concept arising out of a specific goal-oriented activity. We will sometimes refer to this way of forming a concept as a *demand-driven* approach.

- Second, our demand-driven approach takes up Nelson's point that many concepts are formed by a syntagmatic–paradigmatic shift for objects that play a common role in some context. As we will see, this is operationalized in the model by basing concept formation on objects that play a similar role in *inference rules* of the system's theory.

- Third, we use a problem-solving context external to the concept formation process itself to select which of those object sets actually get characterized and become concepts. This problem solving context consists of the *knowledge revision* activities of the system.

- Finally, our approach bases the characterization of so-chosen concepts on correlations of their member's features. As advocated above (section 2.2.3), the concepts that are formed are embedded into the system's theory, which is expressed in a restricted Horn clause formalism.

The next chapter is devoted to a presentation of this formalism and the environment in which the concept formation process was realized.

CONCEPT REPRESENTATION IN A PARACONSISTENT LOGIC WITH HIGHER-ORDER ELEMENTS

The discussion of psychological data on human concept formation in the preceding chapter (chapter 2) has enabled us to arrive at a number of minimal requirements that a knowledge representation should meet if it is to serve as the basis of a computational model of concepts and concept formation. As a central conclusion, we observed that a propositional formalism is insufficient to represent people's knowledge about concepts, their features, and their relationships to other concepts.

In this chapter, we return to the technical aspects of representation change and concept formation, and discuss the knowledge representation language that forms the basis of the computational concept formation technique to be presented in chapters 4 and 5. As our work on concept formation has taken place in the context of the MOBAL system (see chapter 1), we use a subset of the knowledge representation provided by MOBAL's inference engine, IM-2 [Emde, 1989; Emde, 1991], to represent knowledge about concepts. In the rest of the chapter, we first informally describe this relevant subset of the representation (section 3.1). We then discuss how concepts are represented in this language, and how it compares with the requirements set up in the preceding chapter (section 3.2). To ensure that the chosen representation is a tractable basis for a computational method, we conclude with a discussion of its formal and computational properties (section 3.3), followed by related work (section 3.4 and a summary (section 3.5).

3.1 DESCRIPTION OF THE REPRESENTATION

Before we define the knowledge representation used in this book, we should clarify in a few words the relation of the formalism defined here to the knowledge representation used in MOBAL. Since MOBAL is a knowledge acquisition toolbox consisting of several modules for different tasks, a domain model in MOBAL consists of a variety of different knowledge sources which together define the set of representational constructs available in the system. The representation defined below is a proper subset of MOBAL's representation, and comprises exactly the elements that are used by KRT, CLT, and RRT, i.e., the knowledge revision, concept formation, and rule set restructuring modules described in chapters 4 and 5.

In order to facilitate the description and formal analysis, and to make things easier to follow, the definition of the representation is given here in a notation that is close to the logical notation of Prolog. In MOBAL, we use a syntactically slightly different format that maps one-to-one to the syntax presented here. The representational elements defined below are stored (in a different syntax) in MOBAL's inference engine, IM-2 [Emde, 1989; Emde, 1991], which performs forward and backward inferences, maintains a trace of all derivations, and guarantees truth maintenance. Beyond the facilities that are used in MOBAL and in this book, IM-2 has additional capabilities that are described in [Emde, 1989; Emde, 1991]. In the following, when we speak about "the representation", a "knowledge base", or a "theory", we refer to the subset of MOBAL's domain model that is defined below.

It is the purpose of this section to give an informal, exemplary description of the representation which we will refer to as $\Re$; for the formal details, we refer the reader to section 3.3, where a formal theory is defined for $\Re$.

The basic representational unit in MOBAL is a *fact*, which is simply a *predicate* with one or more arguments that are *constants*, written in lowercase as in Prolog, e.g.

>   color(object1,red).

Facts may also be negated, as in

>   not(color(object1,green)).

The negation, however, is not interpreted as negation by failure, i.e., a negated statement is only true if it is in the knowledge base or can be derived from it.

Inferential relationships between facts are expressed as *rules*, which take the form of function-free clauses, such as

>   large(Object) & dense(Object) → heavy(Object)

which states that all dense, large objects are heavy. All variables (written in uppercase) are assumed to be universally quantified. Rules need not be Horn clauses, i.e., both premises and conclusion of a rule may be negated, as in the following examples:

light(Object) → not(heavy(Object))
not(heavy(Object)) → light(Object)

Again, it is important to emphasize that the negation is *not* negation by failure, i.e., a negated premise requires an explicitly negated fact to match. A negated conclusion similarly derives an explicitly negated fact. Rules may also contain constants which are written in lowercase:

color(Object,red) → is_red(Object).

Finally, certain predicates, the so-called *computed predicates*, are predefined by the inference engine, and may also be used in rules. These include the basic arithmetic predicates of Prolog, i.e., gt, lt, ge, le, add, sub, mult, div[1]. An example rule with a computed predicate is:

weight(Object,Weight) & gt(Weight,10) → heavy(Object).

In addition to rules and facts as described above, MOBAL offers a set of higher-order representation constructs that allow quantification over predicates. A *metapredicate* is a construct that defines a correspondence between a *metafact* and a (domain level) rule, e.g. such as

opposite_1(P,Q): P(X) → not(Q(X)),

where P and Q are predicate variables, i.e., variables that must be instantiated with predicate symbols. Using this metapredicate, a metafact such as

opposite_1(light,heavy)

is translated into the domain level rule

light(Object) → not(heavy(Object)).

Metapredicates may also use arguments of the domain level rule. As an example, consider the metapredicate

---

[1]The inference engine offers additional "autoepistemic" predicates that are described in detail in [Emde, 1989]

factoring(P,V,Q): P(X,V) → Q(X),

which would translate the metafact

factoring(color,red,is_red)

into the rule

color(Object,red) → is_red(Object).

Similarly, it is possible to use *metametapredicates* and *metametafacts* to describe inferential relationships between metapredicates, e.g. their symmetry:

m_symmetrical(M): M(P,Q) → M(Q,P).

which is used to translate

m_symmetrical(opposite_1)

into the *meta-rule*

opposite_1(P,Q) → opposite_1(Q,P).

These higher-order constructs first originated in the context of the natural language system BACON [Habel and Rollinger, 1981], and were then adapted and modified in METAXA [Emde, August 1987; Emde, 1991], BLIP [Emde *et al.*, 1989], and MOBAL. Metapredicates were first introduced in BACON to represent a universal set of higher-order cognitive concepts like "transitivity" as they had been postulated by [Johnson-Laird, 1980]. In MOBAL, they have become a powerful tool for representing knowledge about the properties of predicates, and for performing inferences with rules (represented as metafacts). In MOBAL, the system can be told to ensure that any rule that is in the knowledge base is also represented by a metafact; if necessary, new metapredicates are abstracted and defined for this purpose automatically. In our formal definition below, this is not required. Below (section 3.2), we will use metapredicates to represent conceptual hierarchies.

3.2   CONCEPTS IN THIS REPRESENTATION

Given the description of our representation formalism $\Re$, we are now ready to discuss the representation of concepts in this formalism.

3.2.1 Description

Keeping in line with the arguments of sections 2.2.2 and 2.2.3, we are defining a concept not in isolation, but in a relation to a theory of which it is a part. This theory, of course, is a knowledge base of MOBAL (or rather, its $\Re$ subset). More precisely, we define a concept as follows.

Definition 3.1 (Concept) *A concept C is defined as a pair*

$$C = (c, \Gamma)$$

that consists of the concept's name c, and the ($\Re$-)theory Γ of which it is a part. Names of concepts are simply predicates of $\Re$, i.e., elements of $\mathcal{P}$.

Concepts can be unary or n-ary, in the latter case, they are also referred to as relations. Wherever Γ is clear from the context, a concept is simply referred to by its name c. Based on c and Γ, we can formally define the *intension* and *extension* of a concept as follows.

Definition 3.2 (Intension, Extension) *The intension of a concept $C = (c, \Gamma)$ is defined as*

$Int(c, \Gamma) := \{R | R$ *is a rule in Γ, and c occurs in R, either as a premise or as a conclusion*$\}$

The extension of C is defined as

$Ext(c, \Gamma) := \{F | F$ *is a fact in Γ^*, and has c as its predicate*$\}$

In this definition, Γ^* refers to the inferential closure of Γ, i.e., to the set of all statements that can be derived from Γ; a precise definition is given in section 3.3.3. For both Int and Ext, we will occasionally omit the Γ argument when it is clear from the context.

Note that these definitions of intension and extension are purely syntactic, i.e., defined only with reference to elements of $\Re$. An alternative that might better fit our intuitions would be to define the extension of a concept as the set of objects or tuples of objects that are in the interpretation $I(c)$ for a (minimal) model I of Γ. $Ext(c, \Gamma)$ as defined above easily induces such an interpreted extension by defining

$$Ext_I(c, \Gamma) := \{(I(T_1), \ldots, I(T_a)) | c(T_1, \ldots, T_a) \in Ext(C)\}.$$

---

bus_lane(Place) → no_parking(Place)
fire_hydrant(Place) → no_parking(Place)
car_parked(Event,Place) & metered(Place) & unpaid(Event)
                           → parking_violation(Event)
car_parked(Event,Place) & no_parking(Place)
                           → parking_violation(Event)
parking_violation(Event) → fine(Event,20)
parking_violation(Event) → minor_violation(Event)
parking_violation(Event) & appeals(Person,Event)
                           → court_citation(Event)

$\Big\}$ *

parking_violation(event2)
bus_lane(place1)
fire_hydrant(place2) $*Int(parking\_violation, \Gamma)$
metered(place3)
involved_vehicle(event1,b_au_6773)
owner(b_au_6773,sw)
car_parked(event1,place1)
responsible(sw,event1)

Table 3.1   A theory with the concept parking_violation

Table 3.1 shows a theory Γ from the traffic-law domain which contains the unary concept $C = (parking\_violation, \Gamma)$. As marked in the figure, the intension of this concept consists of five rules. As for the extension, note that our representation permits the extension to be defined both based on the rules that are part of the intension as well as by simply adding facts about it into the knowledge base, as was done in the example with parking_violation(event2). The extension of parking_violation is thus

     {parking_violation(event1). parking_violation(event2)}.

where the former follows from Γ via two rule applications.

For later use in concept evaluation, we will define three subsets of a concept's intension.

Definition 3.3 (Sufficient, necessary, used) *For a concept $C = (c, \Gamma)$ with intension $Int(c, \Gamma)$ the* sufficient conditions *of C are defined as:*

    $SC(c, \Gamma) := \{R | R \in Int(c, \Gamma),$ *and c occurs in R as the conclusion predicate*$\},$

the necessary conditions *of C as:*

$NC(c, \Gamma) := \{R | R \in Int(c, \Gamma), \text{ and } R \text{ has a single premise with predicate } c\}$,

and finally the uses *of C as:*

$U(c, \Gamma) := Int(c, \Gamma) \backslash (SC(c, \Gamma) \cup NC(c, \Gamma))$,

i.e., comprising all rules with premise c plus other premises that do not have c as their conclusion.

Again, we will occasionally omit the Γ argument when it is clear from context. In our example, the first two rules of the intension are in $SC(\text{parking\_violation}, \Gamma)$, the third and fourth are in $NC(\text{parking\_violation}, \Gamma)$, and the last is in $U(\text{parking\_violation}, \Gamma)$.

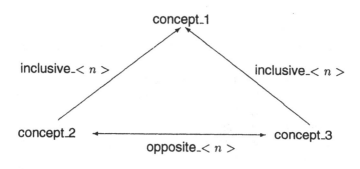

Figure 3.1   Concept hierarchy represented on the metalevel

Further knowledge about relations between concepts can be made explicit by employing MOBAL's metaknowledge. If we predefine a set of metapredicates that represent inclusion and opposition relationships between concepts, we can represent a concept hierarchy conveniently on the metalevel. For this purpose, the standard metapredicates

inclusive_1(P,Q): P(X) → Q(X)
opposite_1(P,Q): P(X) → not(Q(X))

are used, which are defined accordingly for other arities of concepts. A concept hierarchy represented with these metapredicates is shown in figure 3.1.

I. Features	II. Internal Structure	III. Categorization
Nonnecessary features	Typicality	Unclear cases
Disjunctive concepts	Basic levels	Context effects
Relational information	Superordin. distance	Multiple categoriz.
Features as concepts		

Table 3.2   Important empirical observations about human concepts (again)

3.2.2   Psychological evaluation

Let us now briefly evaluate this representation against the set of phenomena that we had identified in chapter 2, and summarized in table 2.1. This table is repeated here for convenience (as table 3.2), and contains three groups of phenomena that we will look at individually.

Group I: Features Our representation contains elements from both the classical and the exemplar model, since a concept is represented both by a summary description that lists its features, and by descriptions of its individual members, even though there is no distance measure that could be used to categorize new instances based on extensionally defined parts of a concept. By using rules to represent features, both sufficient features (rules that use the concept in their conclusion) and necessary features (rules that use the concept in their premises) can be expressed. Since multiple sufficient and necessary feature rules are allowed (see the example in table 3.1 above), concepts in this representation can contain nonnecessary features, and can be defined disjunctively (polymorphic concepts [Hanson and Bauer, 1989]). Since "features" are Horn-clause rules, they can employ relational information. Lastly, components of features, such as no_parking in the example, are in turn treated as full-blown concepts. Our representation thus accounts for all of the observations in group I of the table.

Group II: Internal Structure Our representation is less adequate to reflect psychological observations about the internal structure of concepts. Since categorization is an inference process that arrives at a yes or no answer, membership in concepts of $\Re$ is not graded, and all members are equally typical. Neither is there a distinguished basic level in our representation, both in contrast to data about human concepts. Only the observations about superordinate distance can partially be explained by observing that the representation does not require the concept hierarchy to be represented minimally: If we explicitly include a metafact/a rule expressing the relationship between a concept and a distant superordinate, we can assume that the "distance" between the two is shortened, and access facilitated.

We should point out that IM-2 offers an additional feature that is not used in MOBAL, but which could be used to model typicality effects. IM-2 can associate with each fact an *evidence point*, which is a pair of numbers each in the interval [0,1000] indicating the amount of positive and negative evidence for the fact. If such attributed facts are used in rules, the evidence contributed by each derivation is combined and results in an evidence point for the conclusion. In this fashion, it would be possible to sum the evidence from several sufficient condition rules, and produce graded membership.

Group III: Categorization Since categorization is an inference process as called for by theory-oriented models, categorization is very flexible and powerful, and can accordingly capture the context and multiple categorization phenomena mentioned in group 3 of the table: Since rules for different concepts may overlap, an object or case may be classified into several concepts; similarly, depending on the the the rest of the knowledge in the theory that contains the concept, inferences about concept membership will be different, which corresponds to the context effects cited by psychologists. This leaves unclear cases, which cannot arise in the representation $\Re$ as defined above; they would require an extension with evidence points as suggested in the preceding paragraph.

In sum then, this representation addresses many, but not all of the concerns that have been put forth by psychologists about "classical" models of concepts. This leaves us with the open question of whether the representation is also a good basis for a computational method, i.e., whether it can be given a well-defined semantics, and whether it is computationally tractable.

3.3 FORMAL PROPERTIES

In the preceding sections, we have looked at our knowledge representation language from a particular perspective, namely the static perspective of expressive power. In other words, we have informally defined a syntax for possible statements in our representation, and were then primarily interested in whether the information we found necessary for conceptual systems could be expressed with those statements. The complementary dynamic perspective on knowledge representation was assumed implicitly, but never made explicit: what does it mean to enter a certain statement into the knowledge base, i.e., which inferences will be supported by the knowledge base? Which mechanism uses the intensional definition of a concept to deduce whether a certain individual is really a member of the concept?

These questions focus our attention on the fact that a knowledge representation is not simply a language, but is really part of a knowledge representation system that is to store statements of the language, perform inferences with those statements, and answer questions about what is in the knowledge base or implied by it. This perspective is also called the *functional* view of knowledge representation [Levesque and Brachman, 1985]. As a user of a knowledge representation system, we need to know:

- What does a particular concept definition, or what do other statements in the representation mean? What is their *semantics*?

- Which inferences does the knowledge representation system provide? Are these correct and complete with respect to the semantics of the representation? In other words, will the inference system correctly categorize objects according to a given intensional concept definition?

- Are the inferences provided in reasonable time? Would it be possible to employ new concepts for categorization in a time-limited context?

From a pragmatic point of view, these questions can be answered simply by referring to the implemented system. In our case, the representation is stored and manipulated by IM-2, MOBAL's inference engine, and a detailed technical description of IM-2's inference mechanism is available [Emde, 1991]. Using the description, or its operational incarnation as a program, it can be determined which inferences will be provided, and which ones not. Through empirical tests, we can estimate how long it takes to answer queries on average knowledge bases.

Such a system-oriented characterization of a representation has some disadvantages however, which indicate the need for a formal characterization. First, the operational description does not provide a succinct characterization of the inferences delivered by the representation system, and does not provide a definition of the meaning of a statement independent of the implementation. Second, if we want to guarantee certain properties of the representation, we need to prove them, which cannot be done without first having a precise formal definition of the representation. Third, by providing a description that is independent of the program, we have a much better basis for scientific communication about the system and our concept formation method.

In the following, we will therefore develop a formal definition of the semantics of a knowledge base as a reference point against which we can measure the completeness and correctness of the inferences that are provided by the system. To this end, we will now develop a formal theory $\Re$ (consisting of syntax, semantics, and proof theory) whose well-formed formulae correspond exactly to the statements possible in the above representation. After a specification of the syntax of $\Re$ in section 3.3.1, we will first define a classical two-valued semantics (section 3.3.2). After describing a proof theory for our representation (section 3.3.3), we use the semantics definition as a reference point against which we measure the completeness and correctness of the inferences that are provided by the system (section 3.3.4). After an examination of the computational complexity of inference in $\Re$ (section 3.3.5), we change our focus to the treatment of inconsistencies in our representation (section 3.3.6), and provide an alternative, multi-valued semantics for $\Re$ (section 3.3.7).

3.3.1 Syntax

Let $\Omega = \mathcal{M} \cup \mathcal{C} \cup \mathcal{V} \cup \mathcal{P}$ be the *alphabet* of $\Re$, where $\mathcal{M} := \{$ "(", ")", ",", ":", "& ", "$\rightarrow$ "$\}$ is a set of punctuation and connective symbols, $\mathcal{C}$ is a set of constant symbols (c_1, c_2, or other lowercase letters), $\mathcal{V}$ is a set of variable symbols (X, Y, or other uppercase letters), and $\mathcal{P}$ is a set of predicate symbols (p, q, r, or other lowercase letters), where $a : \mathcal{P} \rightarrow I\!N^+$ denotes the arity of a predicate symbol. Define the set of *terms*

$$T := \mathcal{C} \cup \mathcal{V} \cup \mathcal{P}.$$

We let τ denote a type function

$$\tau : T \rightarrow I\!N$$

that assigns a type to each term such that

$$\tau(t) \begin{cases} = 0 & \text{if } t \in \mathcal{C} \\ \geq 0 & \text{if } t \in \mathcal{V} \\ \geq 1 & \text{if } t \in \mathcal{P} \end{cases}$$

We write v^t to denote $v \in \mathcal{V}$ with $\tau(v) = t$, and $p^{t,a}$ to denote $p \in \mathcal{P}$ with $\tau(p) = t$ and $arity(p) = a$. Note that instead of type, we will often say *level*, and that type is not identical to order (variables of type t are instantiated to terms of type t, and not of type $t - 1$, see sections 3.3.2 and 3.3.3).

We can now define the atomic formulae of $\Re$. If $p^{t,a} \in \mathcal{P}$ is a predicate symbol of type t and arity a, and $T_1, \ldots, T_a \in T$ are terms, then

$$L = p^{t,a}(T_1, \ldots, T_a)$$

is a *positive literal* iff (if and only if) for all $k \in \{1, \ldots, a\}$, $\tau(T_k) < t^2$. We define $functor(L) := p^{t,a}$, and $args(L) := \{T_1, \ldots, T_a\}$. If L is a positive literal, $L^- = not(L)$ is a *negative literal*, and $functor(L^-) := functor(L)$, $args(L^-) := args(L)$. For a literal L, we define $vars(L) := args(L) \cap \mathcal{V}$; if $vars(L) = \emptyset$, we say that L is *ground*, otherwise *nonground*; we further define $\tau(L) := \tau(functor(L))$. All ground positive and negative literals together make up the set $\mathcal{A}$ of atomic formulae of $\Re$. In MOBAL, these are called *facts* $(\tau = 1)$, *metafacts* $(\tau = 2)$, and *metametafacts* $(\tau = 3)$.

If $L_1, \ldots, L_n, L_{n+1}$ are literals of type t, then

$$R = L_1 \& \ldots \& L_n \rightarrow L_{n+1}$$

is a *rule* iff $vars(L_{n+1}) \subseteq vars(R)$, where $vars(R)$, the variables of a rule, are defined as $vars(R) := \bigcup_{i \in \{1, \ldots, n\}} vars(L_i)$. This restriction ensures that conclusion variables are always bound in the premises. We will assume that there is a canonical, fixed ordering on the variables of a rule, i.e., $vars(R)$ is assumed to be an *ordered* set. We define $\tau(R) := t$. As stated above and defined below (section 3.3.2), the semantics for $\Re$ treats all variables as implicitly universally quantified. We use *clause* to denote a fact or a rule of $\Re$. A clause has the form of a rule as defined above; if $n > 0$, the clause is a rule, if $n = 0$ and the clause is ground, it is a fact.

We can now complete the syntax definition of $\Re$ with a definition of metapredicates as follows. If R is a rule of type t, and RS is obtained by replacing in at least one literal of R the functor predicate with a variable of type t, then RS is a *rule schema* or rule model, and $\tau(RS) := t$. If $\{v_1, \ldots, v_m\}$ are the variables introduced into R to produce RS, and L is a positive literal of type $t + 1$, then

$$MP = L : RS$$

is a *metapredicate* definition iff $\{v_1, \ldots, v_m\} \subseteq vars(L)$, and $vars(L) \subseteq vars(R) \cup \{v_1, \ldots, v_m\}$, i.e., all predicate variables in RS must be bound in L, and L may not use variables that are not in RS. We define $\tau(MP) := t + 1$.

The set of well-formed formulae of $\Re$ consists of the atomic formulae, rules, and metapredicates as defined above. In MOBAL, only formulae of types 1, 2, and 3 are used; formulae of type 1 are said to be on the object or domain level, formulae of type 2 are said to be on the metalevel, and formulae of type 3 are

---

[2]Note that we do not require the existence of a literal argument of type $t - 1$. This is done to allow, for example, a metafact of the form size_class(10,20,small) which, given the metapredicate

size_class(V1,V2,C): size(X,S) & S $\geq$ V1 & S $\leq$ V2 $\rightarrow$ class(X,C),

corresponds to the rule size(X,10) & S $\geq$ 10 & S $\leq$ 20 $\rightarrow$ class(X,small).

said to be on the metametalevel. Metametarules are not used. This completes the definition of $\Re$.

Note that if negated premises are disallowed, the subset of $\Re$ of type 1 (the base level) corresponds to the language of function-free Horn clauses (DATALOG programs [Ceri *et al.*, 1990]) which are generative.

3.3.2 Semantics

What is the meaning of a statement of $\Re$? When can we say a fact, rule, or metapredicate is true in a domain? What is the semantics of $\Re$?

The standard way of answering this question is by specifying an *interpretation*, i.e., a mapping from the constants and predicates of $\Re$ to the objects and relations of the domain that the knowledge base is supposed to describe. The meaning of a knowledge base is then given by defining under which circumstances its statements are true in the domain of interpretation, i.e., which worlds or domains are logical *models* of a given knowledge base. For $\Re$, such a Tarskian semantics [Mendelson, 1987] can be defined as follows[3].

We will first define what we mean by an interpretation for $\Re$. Let D be a non-empty set, the set of individual domain objects. Then define D^t and D^* recursively as follows:

$$D^0 := D, \ D^t := \left(\bigcup_{a \in I\!N^+} pset(\underbrace{D^{t-1} \times \ldots \times D^{t-1}}_{a \ times}) \right) \cup D^{t-1}, and \ D^* := \bigcup_{t \in I\!N} D^t,$$

where $pset(S)$ denotes the powerset of a set S, i.e., D^t is the set of all relations (of any arity a) over D^{t-1}, and D^* is the union of all these sets. An *interpretation* is a function

$$I : \mathcal{C} \cup \mathcal{P} \rightarrow D^*$$

from the constants and predicates of $\Re$ to D^* with the following properties:

$I(c) \in D$ for all $c \in \mathcal{C}$, $I(c_1) = I(c_2)$ only if $c_1 = c_2$ and
$I(p^{t,a}) \in pset((D^{t-1})^a) \subseteq D^t$ for all $p^{t,a} \in \mathcal{P}$.

In other words, each constant is mapped to a distinct element of the domain (the "unique names assumption"), and each predicate of type t and arity a is mapped to a relation of the same arity over D^{t-1}.

---

[3] See section 3.3.7 for an alternative, multi-valued semantics for $\Re$.

We can now define what it means for an $\Re$-statement to be true. A positive ground literal (fact) $L = p^{t,a}(T_1, \ldots, T_a)$ is true in an interpretation I if and only if

$$(I(T_1), \ldots, I(T_a)) \in I(p^{t,a}),$$

i.e., if the objects or relations that correspond to the fact's arguments are indeed in the relation that corresponds to the fact's predicate. Similarly, a negated ground literal (fact) $L = not((p^{t,a}(T_1, \ldots, T_a))$, is true in I if and only if

$$(I(T_1), \ldots, I(T_a)) \notin I(p^{t,a}).$$

To define truth for rules, we need to define how domain values can be substituted for variables in a rule. A *domain substitution* δ (for an interpretation I) is a function $\delta : \mathcal{C} \cup \mathcal{P} \cup \mathcal{V} \to D^*$ with the following properties:

$$\delta(v) \in D^t \text{ if } \tau(v) = t \text{ for all } v \in \mathcal{V}, \text{ and } \delta(s) = I(s) \text{ for all } s \notin \mathcal{V}.$$

In other words, δ substitutes for each variable a domain object of the fitting type, and is equal to I for all non-variables. Using domain substitutions, we can define truth in δ for (ground or nonground) literals in the obvious way: a positive literal $L = p^{t,a}(T_1, \ldots, T_a)$ is true in δ if and only if $(\delta(T_1), \ldots, \delta(T_a)) \in \delta(p^{t,a})$, and a negated literal $L = not((p^{t,a}(T_1, \ldots, T_a))$, is true in δ if and only if $(\delta(T_1), \ldots, \delta(T_a)) \notin \delta(p^{t,a})$.

We can now define when a rule is true. A rule $R = L_1 \& \ldots \& L_n \to L_{n+1}$ is true in an interpretation I if and only if for all domain substitutions δ for I, either there exists $i \in \{1, \ldots, n\}$ such that L_i is not true in δ, or L_{n+1} is true in δ. This defines the meaning of $\&$ and $\to$ in the usual fashion: an implication is true if one of its antecedents is false, or its conclusion is true (or both).

Finally, we have to define truth for metapredicates. A metapredicate $MP = L : RS$ is true in an interpretation I if and only if for all domain substitutions δ for I, the following holds: whenever L is true in δ, RS is true in δ as well. In other words, a metapredicate is true if for any true fact using the metapredicate, the rule defined by the metapredicate is true as well.

Whenever a formula of $\Re$ is not true (in I) it is *false* (in I). An interpretation I is called a logical *model* of a set of $\Re$-formulae Γ if all formulae in Γ are true in I. A formula F is *logically implied* by Γ (written $\Gamma \models F$) if and only if F is true in all models of Γ. This definition of $\models$ specifies the set of inferences that we would like to get from an inference engine for $\Re$. In the next section, we will therefore describe the basic inference rules that are implemented in IM-2, and then discuss whether they are correct and complete with respect to $\models$.

3.3.3 Inference Rules for $\Re$

To define the inference rules we want to use for $\Re$, we need to define a notion of substitution that respects the types of variables, and thus differs a little from the usual definition of substitution in first-order logic. A *substitution* in our context is a (usually partial) function $\sigma : V \to T$ with the following property:

$$\tau(\sigma(v)) = \tau(v) \text{ for all } v \in V \text{ on which } \sigma \text{ is defined.}$$

In other words, a substitution always replaces a variable by a term of the appropriate type, which in $\Re$ may be a variable or a predicate or constant. Following standard logical practice, we write the application of a substitution σ to a term t as $t\sigma$. We will often write $\{V_1/t_1, \ldots, V_n/t_n\}$ for a substitution that replaces V_i by t_i (for $1 \leq i \leq n$).

Following the description of IM-2 in [Emde, 1991], and matching its implementation in MOBAL, we can now define the inference rules for $\Re$ as follows. They define the *one-step derivation operator* $\vdash_1$.

(I) Let Γ be an $\Re$-theory, $R = L_1 \& \ldots \& L_n \to L_{n+1}$ is a rule in Γ, and $F_1, \ldots, F_n$ facts in Γ. If σ is a substitution such that

$$L_i\sigma = F_i \text{ for all } i \in \{1, \ldots, n\},$$

then

$$\Gamma \vdash_1 L_{n+1}\sigma.$$

(II) Let Γ be an $\Re$-theory, $MP = L : RS$ a metapredicate in Γ, and F a fact in Γ. If σ is a substitution defined only on $vars(L)$ such that

$$L\sigma = F,$$

then

$$\Gamma \vdash_1 RS\sigma.$$

In inference rule (II), σ must be restricted to variables of L to avoid inferring rules that are more instantiated than necessary.

We can now define syntactical derivability as follows. Let Γ^* be the closure of Γ under $\vdash_1$. Then define that $\Gamma \vdash F$ if and only if $F \in \Gamma^*$.

The first inference rule given here is not very remarkable if we regard only the base level of the representation (facts and rules of type 1), and represents a typical forward chaining inference mechanism. Other inference rules, such as resolution, could have been used as well[4]. These inference rules are special only in their treatment of the higher-order constructs of $\Re$, as it is expressed by the second inference rule, which ensures that for every metafact, a corresponding rule is inferred.

3.3.4 Fact-correctness of ⊢ for $\Re^+$

Ideally, the inference rules that are used in a representation should define ⊢ in such a way that it derives all statements that are logically implied as defined by ⊨ (completeness), and none that are not logically implied (soundness). If a set of inference rules fulfills both of these requirements, we will call it *correct* for a representation. A quick look at the inference rules realized in MOBAL shows that this ideal goal is not met. Clearly, the above inference rules do not produce any rules that are logically implied by a knowledge base. If our knowledge base contains the rules

large(X) → heavy(X) and heavy(X) → stationary(X)

then the third rule

large(X) → stationary(X)

is logically implied, but not derived by ⊢. The second source of incompleteness is due to the use of explicit negation in $\Re$. Given the knowledge base

large(X) → heavy(X), not(heavy(a))

the additional fact

not(large(a))

is logically implied, but not derived.

Nonetheless, things are not quite as bad as they might seem. If we adopt a restriction often used in logic programming and deductive database theory, and limit ourselves to the subset $\Re^+ \subset \Re$ that admits only positive literals in facts and rules, we can show (and do so below), that inference rules (I) and (II) above guarantee that all true facts and no false facts are derived from a knowledge base containing statements of arbitrary types. Even though this still leaves out the inference of rules as in our first example above, it is an

---

[4]In section 3.3.6, we will discuss why resolution cannot be chosen if the representation system is to tolerate inconsistencies gracefully.

important property that proves how the higher-order statements of $\Re$ can be correctly handled in a knowledge representation system.

Fact-completeness also meets the requirements of a functional knowledge representation: it is easy for a user to see which queries will be answered correctly (all factual queries), and which ones will not (anything else). As we will see in section 3.3.6, fact completeness on the positive subset of $\Re$ also provides an important hint as to how negation should be interpreted in $\Re$ — our inference rules provide all factual inferences that are possible if a fact and its negation are treated as if they were independent, i.e., as if they were expressed with separate predicates, because under this view, any $\Re$ theory can be regarded as consisting of positive literals only. Moreover, as we will discuss in section 3.3.7, it is possible even to capture this intuition formally by providing an alternative (albeit non-standard, multi-valued) semantics for all of $\Re$ according to which our inference rules are complete. First, however, we will prove the fact correctness of $\vdash$ for $\Re^+$ by showing that it is sound and complete.

Theorem 3.1 $\vdash$ *is sound and fact complete for* $\Re^+$, *i.e. for any* $\Re^+$-*theory* Γ, *if* $\Gamma \vdash S$ *for any statement S, then* $\Gamma \models S$, *and if* $\Gamma \models F$ *for any fact F, then* $\Gamma \vdash F$.

Proof:

Soundness. It is obvious that $\vdash$ will not derive any incorrect theorems when we compare inference rules (I) and (II) with the semantic definition of rules and metapredicates; we therefore omit the proof for this lemma.

Completeness. To prove the completeness of $\vdash$ for $\Re^+$, we will show that every $\Re^+$ theory Γ has a model in which a fact F is true only if $\Gamma \vdash F$, i.e., the only true facts are the ones in Γ^*. Knowing that such a model exists, we know that for any fact not $\vdash$-derivable from Γ, there is a model in which that fact is false, so the fact cannot be implied logically ($\models$) either, which means that $\vdash$ indeed produces all true facts.

We now prove the existence of such a model by constructing, for a given theory Γ, an interpretation called I in which only the facts in Γ^* are true, and then showing that indeed I is a model of Γ.

Let Γ^* be the transitive inferential closure of Γ as defined above. With a given vocabulary, only finitely many facts are expressible in $\Re^+$, so Γ^* must be finite also. Let $F_1, \ldots, F_f$ be a fixed enumeration of the facts in Γ^* such that

$$for\ all\ i, j\ :\ if\ 1 \leq i < j \leq f\ then\ \tau(F_i) \leq \tau(F_j),$$

i.e., the facts are enumerated beginning with the domain level (type 1), and then proceeding to higher levels.

Then let $D := \mathcal{C} \cup \mathcal{P}$ be the base domain for the interpretation we want to construct, where $\mathcal{C} \cap \mathcal{P} = \emptyset$. For every predicate $p \in \mathcal{P}$ of arity a, define $\hat{p}$ as:

$$\hat{p} := \{\underbrace{(p, \ldots, p)}_{a}\}.$$

Now we define a sequence of interpretations $I_j, j \in \{0, \ldots, f\}$ as follows, for $F_j = p'(A_1, \ldots, A_a)$:

$$I_j(c) \quad := \quad c\ for\ all\ c \in \mathcal{C}, j \in \{0, \ldots, f\}$$

$$I_0(p) \quad := \quad \hat{p}\ for\ all\ p \in \mathcal{P}$$
$$I_j(p) \quad := \quad \begin{cases} I_{j-1}(p) & if\ p \neq p' \\ I_{j-1}(p) \cup \{(I_{j-1}(A_1), \ldots, I_{j-1}(A_a))\} & if\ p = p'. \end{cases}$$

We are thus extending the interpretation in parallel with our enumeration of Γ^*. Since the type of a fact's arguments is required to be less than the type of its functor, $\tau(A_i) < \tau(p')$ for all $i \in \{1, \ldots, a\}$ for all facts F_j. This ensures that all A_i appear before p' in our enumeration, so their interpretation is fixed when it is used, and so the recursive part of the definition is well-defined. The inclusion of a special tuple $\hat{p}$ in I_0 for predicates is necessary to guarantee the uniqueness of interpretations for predicates (constants map to themselves anyway, but several predicates could share, say, the empty relation as their interpretation). Note that $\hat{p}$ is a legal interpretation for p according to the definition in section 3.3.2, and that for all terms T, $I(T) \neq p$, so the addition of $\hat{p}$ does not influence the truth of statements in $\Re^+$.

We define our target interpretation as the last element of the above sequence, i.e.,

$$I := I_f,$$

and note as an important property that I is invertible, i.e., if $I(s_1) = I(s_2)$, then $s_1 = s_2$.

This concludes the construction of I. We now show that a fact $F = p(T_1, \ldots, T_a)$ is true in I only if it is in Γ^*. So assume F is true in I. By definition, this means that $(I(T_1), \ldots, I(T_a)) \in I(p)$. Since for all terms T, $I(T) \neq p$, $(I(T_1), \ldots, I(T_a))$ cannot be equal to $\hat{p}$. Thus for $(I(T_1), \ldots, I(T_a))$ to be in

$I(p)$, by the construction of I, there must be a fact $F' = p(T'_1, \ldots, T'_a) \in \Gamma^*$ such that for all $i \in \{1, \ldots, a\}$, $I(T'_i) = I(T_i)$. Since I is invertible, however, this means $T'_i = T_i$, and therefore $F = F' \in \Gamma^*$.

As required, I thus makes only the facts in Γ^* true. We now need to show that $I = I_f$ is indeed a model of Γ, i.e., we need to show that all statements in Γ are true in I. By the construction of I, all facts in $\Gamma \subseteq \Gamma^*$ must be true in I. So it remains to be shown that all rules in Γ are true as well.

So, let $R = L_1 \& \ldots \& L_n \to L_{n+1}$ be a rule in Γ, where

$$L_i = p_i(T_{1,i}, \ldots, T_{a,i}) \ for \ all \ i \in \{1, \ldots, n+1\}.$$

Let δ be a domain substitution. According to the definition of truth for rules (see section 3.3.2), R is true if any antecedent literal is not true in δ; so assume that all antecedent literals are true in δ, i.e.,

$$(\delta(T_{1,i}), \ldots, \delta(T_{a,i})) \in I(p_i)^5 \ for \ all \ i \in \{1, \ldots, n\}.$$

By the construction of the model I, this means that for all $i \in \{1, \ldots, n\}$, there must be a fact $F_i = p_i(A_{1,i}, \ldots, A_{a,i}) \in \Gamma^*$ such that

$$I(A_{k,i}) = \delta(T_{k,i}) \ for \ all \ k \in \{1, \ldots, a_i\}$$

because otherwise, $(\delta(T_{1,i}), \ldots, \delta(T_{a,i}))$ could not have been in $I(p_i)^6$. Since I is invertible, this is equivalent to

$$A_{k,i} = I^{-1}(\delta(T_{k,i})) \ for \ all \ k \in \{1, \ldots, a_i\}.$$

Having thus assumed that all premises are true in δ, we have to show that the conclusion is also true in δ, i.e., that

$$(\delta(T_{1,n+1}), \ldots, \delta(T_{a_{n+1},n+1})) \in I(p_{n+1}).$$

For this to be true, there must be a fact

$$F_{n+1} = p_{n+1}(A_{1,n+1}, \ldots, A_{a_{n+1},n+1}) \in \Gamma^*$$

such that $I(A_{k,n+1}) = \delta(T_{k,n+1})$ for all $k \in \{1, \ldots, a_{n+1}\}$ by the same argument as above. We now show that such a fact must indeed have been inferred with inference rule (I).

---

[5] Remember that δ is equal to I on all non-variables, so since p_i is not a variable, we can write either δ or I here.

[6] $(\delta(T_{1,i}), \ldots, \delta(T_{a,i}))$ cannot be the dummy tuple that was added to $I(p)$ because no term of $\Re$ is mapped to its elements, see above.

To this end, define a substitution σ on the variables of R such that

$$\sigma(V) := I^{-1}(\delta(V)),$$

i.e., apply the inverse of I on the domain object substituted by δ. Since I is invertible (see above), I^{-1} is defined. With σ defined this way, the following holds for all $i \in \{1, \ldots, n\}$:

$$
\begin{aligned}
L_i\sigma &= p_i(T_{1,i}\sigma, \ldots, T_{a_i,i}\sigma) \\
&= p_i(I^{-1}(\delta(T_{1,i})), \ldots, I^{-1}(\delta(T_{a_i,i}))) \\
&= p_i(A_{1,i}, \ldots, A_{a_i,i}) \\
&= F_i
\end{aligned}
$$

This means that inference rule (I) is applicable, and will derive the fact

$$
\begin{aligned}
L_{n+1}\sigma &= p_{n+1}(T_{1,n+1}\sigma, \ldots, T_{a_{n+1},n+1}\sigma) \\
&= p_{n+1}(I^{-1}(\delta(T_{1,n+1})), \ldots, I^{-1}(\delta(T_{a_{n+1},n+1}))) \\
&= p_{n+1}(A_{1,n+1}, \ldots, A_{a_{n+1},n+1}) \\
&= F_{n+1}
\end{aligned}
$$

if we define $A_{k,n+1} = I^{-1}(\delta(T_{k,n+1}))$ for all $k \in \{1, \ldots, a_{n+1}\}$. Now we must show that indeed $I(A_{k,n+1}) = \delta(T_{k,n+1})$ *for all* $k \in \{1, \ldots, a_{n+1}\}$, which is easy since for all $k \in \{1, \ldots, a_{n+1}\}$:

$$
\begin{aligned}
I(A_{k,n+1}) &= I(I^{-1}(\delta(T_{k,n+1}))) \\
&= \delta(T_{k,n+1})
\end{aligned}
$$

as required. Thus, $\delta(L_{n+1})$ is in I, and so the conclusion of the rule is true in δ, as was to be shown.

The proof for a metapredicate $MP = L : RS$ works along the same lines, so we will only sketch it here. If L is false in δ, MP is true anyway, so assume L is true in δ. We then need to show that RS is also true. If one of the premises of RS is false in δ, RS is true anyway, so assume all premises of RS are true. We then need to show that the conclusion of RS is also true, and this can be done very similarly to the construction for rules above. By defining substitutions just as above, we can show that using inference rule (II), Γ^* will contain a rule that will derive, using inference rule (I), the required conclusion.

We have thus shown that indeed there is a model for any theory Γ which makes only the facts in Γ^* true, thus showing completeness and completing our proof. $\square$

3.3.5 Computational Complexity

We now know that the two inference rules we have specified provide a natural and interesting set of inferences for $\Re^+$, namely all facts that logically follow from a given knowledge base. This meets the second requirement of the list we set up at the beginning of section 3.3, leaving only the third one open: in what time can $\vdash$ be computed? For a knowledge representation system to be functional, the minimal requirement is certainly that $\vdash$ be decidable, i.e., that any query be answered in finite time; in practice, however, we usually require a polynomial upper bound on the time it takes to answer a query.

Our goal in this section, then, is to show that such a bound exists for $\vdash$ in $\Re^+$. Since the subset of $\Re^+$ of type 1 corresponds to the well-known language of function-free Horn clauses, the most interesting aspect of $\Re$ is its inclusion of restricted higher-order statements. In order to see more clearly the effect of these statements on the complexity of answering a query, we will subdivide the complexity analysis into two parts. First, we will show that the use of statements of type higher than 1 does not add exponential effort to the cost of reasoning in the base representation. We will then show that reasoning in the base representation is possible in polynomial time, which together shows that $\Re^+$ queries can be answered in polynomial time.

Lemma 3.1 *Using a given base level inference procedure, and assuming that the maximal arity of predicates is A, and that rules have an arbitrary fixed maximal branching factor, any query regarding the full range of $\Re^+$ including higher-level statements up to level t_{max} in a knowledge base of size (in symbols) N can be answered in time*

$$t_{max} \cdot O(N^{A+2}) + t_{max} \cdot C_b(O(N^{A+1})),$$

where $C_b(M)$ denotes the time it takes to execute the base level inference procedure on a knowledge base of size M.

Proof: Since our goal is not to analyze the actual time complexity of the implementation of $\vdash$ in IM-2 with its various optimizations, we will simply use $\vdash$ forwards as a proof procedure to show that a polynomial bound exists. So, assume our proof procedure for answering a query Q about an $\Re^+$ knowledge base Γ is:

> *Metalevel proof procedure:* In order to answer a query about a (ground or nonground) literal Q, compute Γ^* as described below, and then check for each $F \in \Gamma^*$ whether F unifies with Q; if so, the required substitution is a solution to the query. To compute Γ^*, the transitive closure of Γ under $\vdash_1$, do the following. Let $t_{max} = max_{s\in\Gamma}\tau(s)$ be the highest level used in Γ. (In MOBAL, $t_{max} \leq 3$.) Beginning on level t_{max}, and proceeding down to the level of the query $\tau(Q)$, do the following for each level. First, use the base level inference technique

to infer all facts on the current level from the rules on the current level. Second, for every fact ultimately derived, try to match it with every metapredicate, and if successful, enter the resulting rule in the next lower level according to inference rule (II).

If the base level proof procedure is correct, the above proof procedure correctly implements ⊢. This can be seen through the following argument. Since no metapredicates are ever generated, only the existing metapredicates can generate new rules. Since every metapredicate generates rules only on the next lower level, and we begin with the highest level above which there are no metapredicates any more, we are always assured that all rules that can be inferred have already been inferred when we start using them on a level.

To analyze the complexity of this proof procedure, observe that for every fact generated by the base level inference procedure on a particular level, we have to check for every metapredicate whether it can be applied to generate a rule on the next lower level. Let $|F_t|$ denote the number of facts before the base level inference procedure was executed, $|F_t^*|$ the number of facts after application of the base level inference procedure, $|R_t|$ the number of rules, and $|MP_t|$ the number of metapredicates on the current level t. Now observe that certainly on every level, we cannot derive more facts than we can express with the given vocabulary. If the maximal arity of predicates is A, we have at most $|\mathcal{P} \cup \mathcal{C}|$ choices for the predicate and each of the A argument positions. Since each symbol must occur in the knowledge base somewhere,

$$|\mathcal{P} \cup \mathcal{C}| \leq N,$$

so the maximal number of facts F_{max} is:

$$F_{max} \leq N^{A+1}.$$

We therefore know that

$$|F_t^*| \leq F_{max} \leq N^{A+1}.$$

The total cost on a level is thus the cost of base level inference, plus the cost of applying all metapredicates. To determine the cost of the base level inference, observe that in the worst case, the next higher level was inferring all possible facts, each of which was translated into a rule. The length of each fact is at most $A + 1$ symbols. If B denotes the maximal branching factor of rules, the length of each rule is at most $(B + 1)(A + 1)$ symbols, so we know that the size of the knowledge base for base level inference at level t is at most

$$N_t \leq (B+1)(A+1)|R_t| + (A+1)|F_t| \leq (B+1)(A+1)N^{A+1} + N = O(N^{A+1}).$$

Consequently, if we let $C_b(M)$ denote the cost of executing the base level inference procedure on a knowledge base of size M, the total cost of inference on one level is

$$
\begin{aligned}
C_1 &\leq C_b(O(N^{A+1})) + |F_t^*| \cdot |M P_t| \\
&\leq C_b(O(N^{A+1})) + N^{A+1} \cdot N = C_b(O(N^{A+1})) + O(N^{A+2}).
\end{aligned}
$$

This cost is incurred for a constant number of levels t_{max}, and we finally need to examine every element of the so-generated closure to see if it matches the query, so the total cost of answering a query is at most:

$$
\begin{aligned}
C_{total} &= t_{max} \cdot C_1 + F_{max} \\
&\leq t_{max} \cdot C_b(O(N^{A+1})) + t_{max} \cdot O(N^{A+2}) + N^{A+1} \\
&= t_{max} \cdot C_b(O(N^{A+1})) + t_{max} \cdot O(N^{A+2}). \square
\end{aligned}
$$

Lemma 3.2 *There is a base level proof procedure that computes all inferences in a time that is polynomial in the size of the knowledge base in symbols when a fixed vocabulary is used, and the maximal branching factor of rules and maximal predicate arity are fixed.*

Proof: We essentially follow the proof procedure that we developed in [Wrobel, 1987]. It is equivalent to the forward inference method of [Ceri *et al.*, 1990] for DATALOG languages.

> *Base level proof procedure:* Use all rules for forward inferences by matching their first premise, then for each instantiation matching their second premise, etc. For every successful instantiation of all premises, add the instantiation of the conclusion according to inference rule (I). Once through with all rules, repeat with all of them unless no new fact was derived.

Since the inference operator (I) is monotonic, i.e., only adds new inference, the order in which rules are used for inference does not matter. Furthermore, since the set of statements is necessarily finite, termination of the process is guaranteed, so the above proof procedure correctly performs the base level inferences as required by $\vdash$.

We derive a generous bound on the time it takes to execute the above procedure, and show that it is polynomial in the size of the knowledge base. In the actual implementation of IM-2, various optimizations are made in forwards and in backwards mode that we do not take into account (this would be necessary only to analyze IM-2's actual time complexity which is not our goal here).

In this proof, let M denote the size of the knowledge base given to the base level inference procedure. Let $|R|$ denote the number of rules, and $|F_0|$ the number of facts when we start inferring. If the maximal branching factor (maximal number of premises) of a rule is B, then the cost of performing the first forward inference step is

$$C_1 \leq |R| \cdot |F_0|^B,$$

since for every rule, we must in the worst case match its first premise against all facts, and for each such instantiation, match the second premise against all facts, etc. for up to B premises[7]. Since the first step generated additional facts (but no additional rules), the number of facts that form the basis for the second step is $|F_1| > |F_0|$, so the cost of the second step is at most

$$C_2 := |R| \cdot |F_1|^B.$$

In any case, however, $|F_i|$ can never exceed the number of well-formed facts constructible from the available vocabulary, F_{max} that was developed in the previous proof. If we define $N \geq |\mathcal{C} \cup \mathcal{P}|$,

$$F_{max} \leq N^{A+1},$$

Therefore, the cost of any step is at most

$$C_i \leq |R|(N^{A+1})^B = |R|N^{(A+1)B}.$$

Now, how many rules can there be in a knowledge base of size M? Each rule has at least one symbol, so $|R| \leq M$, and thus the cost of any step is at most

$$C_i \leq M N^{(A+1)B}.$$

How often do we need to repeat this single step in the worst case? Since we terminate whenever a step does not generate a new fact, every step must generate at least one new fact, which means, since there can be at most F_{max} facts, that there can be no more than F_{max} steps, and so the total cost of forward chaining is at most

$$C := F_{max} C_i \leq N^{A+1} M N^{(A+1)B}.$$

Since $M > N$, this is polynomial in the size of the knowledge base M. (Please note that if this proof procedure is applied in the context of the metalevel proof procedure for $\Re$, N corresponds to the size of the original knowledge base.) □

We can now state the theorem we were looking for.

---

[7]Note that since the arity of predicates is at most A, and there are no function symbols, matching a premise against a fact can be regarded as a constant time operation.

Theorem 3.2 *A fact-correct set of inferences for $\Re^+$, as defined by $\vdash$, can be provided in time polynomial in the size of the knowledge base if the maximal number of levels, maximal arity, and maximal branching factor are fixed.*

Proof: From lemma 3.1, we know that answers can be provided in polynomial time if there is a polynomial proof procedure for the base level; this however was shown in lemma 3.2. □

The result shown above carries over to all of $\Re$, because our inference rules simply treat negated literals as if they belonged to a new predicate independent of the corresponding unnegated predicates (this notion is further explored below). To reason in all of $\Re$, we can thus simply transform the original knowledge base into one with twice as many predicates, which means that the above theorem continues to hold.

Corollary 3.1 *The set of inferences for $\Re$ as defined by $\vdash$ can be provided in time polynomial in the size of the knowledge base if the maximal number of levels, maximal arity, and maximal branching factor are fixed.*

3.3.6 Reasoning with Inconsistencies

In section 3.3.4, we were able to show that $\vdash$ correctly provides all factual inferences for $\Re$, albeit only if we restricted the representation to statements without negated literals. In this section, we briefly discuss the difficulties involved in properly handling negation in the inference rules for $\Re$. Since the problem of negation is independent of whether metalevel statements are used or not, we refer to the base level only.

At first sight, specifying a proof procedure that will provide a complete set of inferences for $\Re$, including negation, seems to present no problem. The semantics in section 3.3.2 clearly defines what it means for an $\Re$ fact or rule with negated literals to be true or false. Furthermore, there are known inference procedures such as resolution [Lloyd, 1987] that will work properly when negation is used, and derive all facts, positive or negated, that follow from a knowledge base. For example, resolution will correctly infer:

$$\{p(X) \rightarrow not(q(X)), p(a), q(b)\} \vdash_{resolution} \{not(q(a)), not(p(b))\}$$

whereas the inference rule (I) we have specified will only produce

$$\{p(X) \rightarrow not(q(X)), p(a), q(b)\} \vdash_i \{not(q(a))\}$$

Resolution will even correctly infer from apparently useless rules such as:

$\{p(X) \rightarrow not(p(X))\} \vdash_{resolution} \{not(p(a)), not(p(b)), \ldots\}$

So why was resolution not used as a proof procedure in the inference engine of MOBAL, and why were the rules of section 3.3.3 used instead even though they are incomplete when negation is used? The reason for this choice is in the intended behavior of the inference system on *inconsistent* knowledge bases. According to the standard logical semantics defined in section 3.3.2, a knowledge base logically implies all statements that are true in all models. A knowledge base with a contradiction has no models, so this condition is vacuously true, and consequently, all statements are logically implied by an inconsistent theory. Indeed, resolution will also use contradictory information for inferences, and will be able to derive any query from a knowledge base containing contradictory information:

$\{p(a), not(p(a))\} \vdash_{resolution} \{q(a), q(b), not(q(c)), \ldots\}$

since the empty clause can be produced during the refutation proof simply by resolving the two literals in the original knowledge base. This can of course be prevented by requiring resolution only between the goal clause and clauses in the original theory, but then resolution is no longer complete according to our semantics.

In a learning system, it is very important to avoid this inference behavior on inconsistent knowledge bases, as during a learning process it is quite likely that the knowledge base will be in a transient inconsistent state, e.g. because a learned rule contradicts a new example input by the user. If we want to avoid producing *all* statements as inferences in such a situation, we *must* by definition give up completeness, which is exactly what has been done in MOBAL. The inference rules specified in section 3.3.3 allow us to work properly with inconsistent knowledge bases by treating a statement and its negation independently, i.e., using these inference rules, $p \vee \neg p$ is not a tautology.

There are two conceptually different approaches to characterizing the power of these inference rules formally. The first approach, which we have taken in the preceding sections, is to use a standard logical semantics for the representation, specify a set of incomplete inference rules for this representation which can handle inconsistencies gracefully, and characterize in which ways the inferences realized by the inference rules differ from the ones to be expected from the standard logical semantics. The advantage of this strategy is that a well-known semantics can be used, which should be easier to follow for most readers, and that only the differences need to be explained. This is precisely why we have chosen a standard two-valued semantics as our main reference point in the preceding sections.

The second approach, also chosen by many authors, is to use a non-standard semantics that is fitted exactly to the set of inferences we want to produce. The advantage of this strategy is that a nice completeness result can be obtained; the price to pay is that these semantics are usually more difficult to understand, e.g. because they rely on multiple truth values and fixpoint constructions. To allow the reader this alternative view of our representation as well, we will now provide such a multi-valued semantics for $\Re$.

3.3.7 A Multi-valued Semantics for $\Re$

As pointed out above, the basic intuition behind the multi-valued semantics for $\Re$ is to treat a statement and its negation independently, i.e., as if the negation of a fact were expressed by an independent predicate, i.e., reading not(p(a)) as not_p(a). Doing this means that the truth of a statement S is independent of the presence or absence of $\neg S$. To capture this intuition formally, we can use the semantics defined by Blair and Subrahmanian [Blair and Subrahmanian, 1989] in their work on paraconsistent logic programming with generally Horn programs (GHPs)[8].

Definition 3.4 (Generally Horn) *Let* $T_{\sqsubseteq}$ *be the set of truth values* $unknown$, $false$, $true$, $both$. *A generally Horn clause* is a statement of the form, for $n \geq 0$,

$$L_1 : T_1 \& \cdots \& L_n : T_n \rightarrow L_{n+1} : T_{n+1},$$

where the L_i *are positive literals[9], and the* $T_i \in T_{\sqsubseteq}$ *for all* i.

This means that our language $\Re$ can easily be mapped to a particular subset of GHPs.

Definition 3.5 ($\Re$-GHP) *The subset of generally Horn programs corresponding to statements from* $\Re$ *(*$\Re$-GHP*) is defined as follows. Let* Γ *be an* $\Re$ *theory. The corresponding* GHP *G is defined as follows:*

- *If* $f \in \Gamma$ *is a positive fact, and* $not(f) \in \Gamma$, *then* $f : both \in G$.

- *If* $f \in \Gamma$ *is a positive fact, and* $not(f) \notin \Gamma$, *then* $f : true \in G$.

---

[8] We will use a slightly different syntax, however, and omit parts that we do not need for $\Re$.
[9] As shown in [Blair and Subrahmanian, 1989], negated literals are unnecessary as they can be represented by letting $T_i = false$.

- *If $not(f) \in \Gamma$ is a negated fact, and $f \notin \Gamma$ then $f : false \in G$.*

- *If $L_1 \& \cdots L_n \to L_{n+1}$ is a rule in Γ, then $(\forall)P_1 : T_1 \& \cdots P_n : T_n \to P_{n+1} : T_{n+1}$ is in G, where for all i, $P_i : T_i = L_i : true$ if L_i is a positive literal, and $P_i : T_i = L_i' : false$ if $L_i = not(L_i')$ is a negated literal.*

$\Re$-GHP *is the union of all G for any $\Re$-theory Γ.*

In the terminology of Blair and Subrahmanian, $\Re$ corresponds to GHPs where all unit clauses must be ground (facts), and all non-unit clauses are well-annotated, universally quantified implications[10].

The meaning of the truth values used as literal annotations must be defined such that it captures the above intuitions about the use of inconsistent information. Following Blair and Subrahmanian, we therefore define the following ordering on truth values:

$$both \geq_{\mathcal{T}_\sqsubseteq} true \geq_{\mathcal{T}_\sqsubseteq} unknown; both \geq_{\mathcal{T}_\sqsubseteq} false \geq_{\mathcal{T}_\sqsubseteq} unknown.$$

We can now define a multi-valued semantics for $\Re$ (in the syntactical form of GHPs)[11]. We follow standard practice for the definition of nonstandard semantics and regard an interpretation I as a function from the Herbrand base of the language, i.e., the facts of $\Re$, to truth values.

Definition 3.6 (Satisfaction according to multi-valued semantics) *An interpretation I satisfies an $\Re$-GHP formula F ($I \models F$) under the following conditions.*

1. *I satisfies the ground annotated atom $F : T$ iff $I(F) \geq_{\mathcal{T}_\sqsubseteq} T$.*

2. *I satisfies the rule $R = (\forall)P_1 : T_1 \& \ldots P_n : T_n \to P_{n+1} : T_{n+1}$ iff for every instance of R (where ground terms have been substituted for variables using a substitution δ), there is some $1 \leq i \leq n$ such that I does not satisfy $P_i \delta : T_i$, or $I \models P_{n+1}\delta : T_{n+1}$.*

The reader will notice that the crucial difference to our two-valued semantics is the requirement that $I(F) \geq_{\mathcal{T}_\sqsubseteq} T$ to satisfy a fact; this immediately implies

---

[10]Well-annotated means that only *true* and *false* are used as annotations. MOBAL's inference engine actually uses a similar annotated format internally, i.e., stores only positive literals, and attaches an *evidence point* to each of them, see [Emde, 1991].

[11]We omit the semantics for GHP statements that do not correspond to statements in $\Re$; the complete semantics can be found in [Blair and Subrahmanian, 1989].

that the meaning of → is not material implication, but corresponds to the inferences made by our inference rules. In particular, contraposition inferences are no longer admitted under these semantics. The theory

p(x) → q(x), not(q(a))

no longer logically entails not(p(a)), since q(a) could simply have the truth value *both*. Thus, this semantics *a priori* excludes the inferences we had identified as "missing" above. We can formally prove that under these semantics, our inference rules are indeed complete and correct[12].

Theorem 3.3 *Under the multi-valued semantics defined above, the inference rules specified in section 3.3.3 are sound and complete.*

Proof: To prove this theorem, we use a result from [Blair and Subrahmanian, 1989] who show that the least model of a GHP G is the least fixpoint of the following operator T_G:

$T_G(I)(A) = lub \{T \mid (\forall)P_1 : T_1 \& \ldots P_n : T_n \to A : T$ is a ground instance of a statement in G, and $I \models P_i : T_i$ for all $1 \leq i \leq n\}$,

where *lub* refers to the least upper bound in the lattice defined by $\geq_{T_\sqsubseteq}$. Comparing T_G with our inference rule (I), we see that using the correspondence of $\Re$ theories to GHPs put forth in definition 3.5, this inference rule does exactly the same as T_G: if some of the inference rules that match A in G have a positive conclusion, A will be inferred; if some have a negative conclusion, $not(A)$ will be inferred. Given that our correspondence from definition 3.5 realizes a least upper bound operation on $T_\sqsubseteq$, we thus know that a single application of $\vdash_1$, i.e., all possible single step applications of inference rule (I), corresponds to a single application of T_G.

This is so because in the case where all rules concluding about a particular predicate have the same conclusion "sign" (all positive or all negated), the resulting fact will have the corresponding "sign" (truth value). If there are rules with both positive and negated conclusions for a particular predicate,

---

[12]We should point out that MOBAL's inference engine [Emde, 1989] also implements a mechanism that allows inferences with inconsistent statements to be blocked; this blocking roughly corresponds to requiring that $I(F) =_{T_\sqsubseteq} T$ to satisfy a fact, and leads to a nonmonotonic effect. At Universität Dortmund, work is presently under way to understand the exact interrelationship between blocking and the paraconsistent semantics presented here [Weber and Bell, 1994]. For our discussions in this and subsequent chapters, we assume blocking is not used.

both positive and negated instances will be derived and added to the closure of the theory. According to our translation, this corresponds to a truth value of both, which is exactly the least upper bound of the two values.

We thus only need to note that the semantics defined here are monotonic, i.e., the truth value of a statement can only increase, so that once a statement (in the $\Re$ formulation) has been inferred, it never needs to be taken back. Thus, the closure of our inference rules computes the smallest fixed point of T_G, and thus the least model of a theory under the four-valued semantics given here. □

We thus have two semantics available for our representation $\Re$, a standard two-valued one where our inferences are fact complete for the positive subset, and a four-valued one for which our inference rules are complete[13]. Depending on the preferences of the reader, each can be used to understand the properties of our representation.

3.4   RELATED WORK

The language and proof theory described here are based on our original description published in [Wrobel, 1987]. In the deductive database community, the language $\Re^+$ defined here has acquired the name DATALOG, and its properties have been investigated. A very relevant book is the one by Ceri, Gottlob, and Tanca [Ceri *et al.*, 1990], where a proof theory that is almost identical to ours is developed, but based on a minimal Herbrand model semantics. They also use a forward inference procedure as proof procedure, and arrive at similar statements about the size of the proof tree as were given in section 3.3.5. The book also contains chapters on optimizing the query answering process for DATALOG.

Higher-order statements have been used relatively rarely in other knowledge representation or learning systems, but have recently been picked up by a number of researchers. Silverstein and Pazzani [1991] use *relational cliches*, which are almost identical to metapredicates, for learning, but do not introduce them into their representation. Similarly, DeRaedt and Bruynooghe [1992] have used rule schemata for learning by analogy, but again without introducing them into the representation. Muggleton and Feng [1992] try to integrate higher-order schemata fully into a representation for a learning system by using a restricted variant of *lambda-calculus*.

---

[13]Even though we have not actually defined the four-valued semantics for higher-order statements and metapredicates, the definitions given here can be extended in analogy to the path taken for the two-valued semantics.

3.5 SUMMARY

In this chapter, we have laid the foundation for our computational model of concept formation by specifying exactly upon which knowledge representation language it is to be based. Through informal description and a formal definition, we have identified an extended Horn clause representation ("$\Re$") which includes restricted higher-order statements as a language that permits the representation of most of the concept properties that we had identified in chapter 2. Furthermore, we proved that this language has good formal properties by specifying both a standard two-valued and a multi-valued semantics, and defining inference rules that are fact correct (sound and complete) for $\Re$ (under the multi-valued semantics) and can be computed in polynomial time if the maximal arity and branching factor are fixed. This means our representation can be the basis for an effective concept formation method. In the next chapter, we will use our representation to describe the knowledge revision problem, which will be the context for our concept formation method.

4

KNOWLEDGE REVISION AS A
CONCEPT FORMATION CONTEXT

After discussing the technical aspects of what concepts are and how they are represented in the preceding chapter, let us now return to the issue of how concepts are formed. In chapter 2, we had concluded that one of the most important sources of constraints on concept formation is its embedding in a particular context. Based on those psychological arguments, our choice was to examine a *demand-driven* concept formation approach, i.e., an approach that forms concepts only when there is a specific need for a new concept arising out of the problem solving activities of the system.

From the work of Barsalou and Nelson described in chapter 2, we know what can be seen as a problem-solving context for human concept formation. Since these descriptions do not transfer immediately into the technical domain, however, this leaves us with the question of what is meant by a problem-solving context in a computer system such as MOBAL. In this chapter, we provide an operational answer to this question by describing problem solving as inference, and identifying the *knowledge revision* activities of the system as a relevant system-internal problem solving context that can trigger concept formation. We begin with a discussion of problem-solving in MOBAL in relation to the two basic notions of problem solving as they have been employed in Artificial Intelligence (section 4.1). We will then formally define the knowledge revision problem (section 4.2), and discuss which properties are to be required from a revision operation (section 4.3). Based on these results, section 4.4 develops a *minimal base revision* (MBR) operator for $\Re$, and discusses its theoretical properties with respect to the base revision postulates developed in section 4.3. Section 4.5 is devoted to ways of actually computing the preferred revisions among all possible minimal base revisions, and specifies both a two-tiered confidence model for selecting revisions as well as an algorithm for computing them. This is followed by an extension of the basic revision operation to perform further specializations in a rule reformulation process (section 4.6); it is during this reformulation process that concept formation can be triggered. A brief section (4.7) summarizes the interactive use of the operators in the knowledge revision tool KRT. We conclude with a discussion of related work (section 4.9) and a summary (section 4.10).

4.1 PROBLEM SOLVING IN MOBAL

In AI work on problem solving, two general paradigms are being used: problem solving as operator-based search, and problem solving as rule-based inference. In the operator based paradigm, the search space for problem solving is defined by a number of *operators* that are mappings from a given world state, or rather a description thereof, to the description of the world state that results from applying the operator. In this context, a *problem* to be solved consists of descriptions of the start and the desired goal state, and a solution is an operator sequence that reaches the goal state from the start state. The operator based paradigm has been very popular ever since the beginning of AI work; an early example is the General Problem Solver GPS [Newell and Simon, 1963]. It has also formed the basis for classical work on *planning*.

The second AI problem solving paradigm regards problem solving as a process of inference in a given theory or knowledge base. In this context, a problem is a goal clause or query to be proved, and a solution is an instantiation of the query, perhaps along with a proof tree. This paradigm is the traditional basis for work on automated theorem proving [Chang and Lee, 1973], and more recently, for work on rule-based expert systems, where the inference process is realized with forward-chaining production systems; an early example is MYCIN [Shortliffe, 1976]. Today, the inference based paradigm still underlies current expert system work.

From the description given in chapters 1 and 3, it is clear that the MOBAL system is an instance of the inference based approach to problem solving. MOBAL's inference engine IM-2 [Emde, 1989] is capable of storing a knowledge base of facts and rules in the representation $\Re$ defined in the preceding chapter, and of performing forward and backward inferences with it. In addition, MOBAL offers a knowledge structure called *topology* [Morik, 1993; Klingspor, 1991] that can be used to represent the overall task structure of the inference process. Problem solving in MOBAL then consists of asking a query to the system, which performs the necessary backward or forward inferences in $\Re$ to find an answer. As a simple example, consider the traffic law domain that we have been using all along: in this domain, the goal of problem solving is a decision about who is responsible for a traffic violation, and whether this person will have to pay a fine or go to court.

This is reflected in the traffic law topology, shown in figure 4.1, where we can see that from the base level information in the domain (bottom nodes), the system first derives a classification of the traffic violation along with a judgment about responsibilities (middle node), and then infers facts about fines and court citations based on this information (top node). In prototypical domain models, MOBAL has been used to solve the problems of diagnosing infant diseases (together with ICS FORTH, Crete), determining access rights for telecommunications networks (together with Alcatel Alsthom Recherche, Paris [Morik *et al.*, 1993]), and for deducing which parts should be removed from a design for easier assembly (with British Aerospace, Bristol).

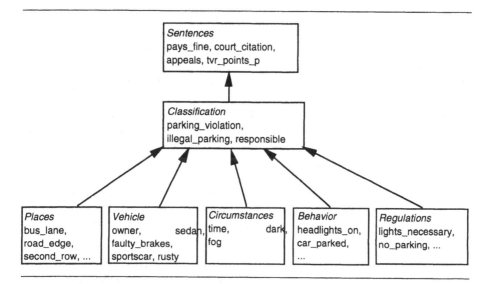

Figure 4.1 Traffic law domain topology

The concept formation approach to be described in chapter 5 makes use of the above problem solving context to constrain its search: as we will see, it introduces new concepts for sets of objects that have appeared in the same context during the problem solving activities of the system (the instances and exceptions of one inference rule). In addition to this problem-solving context towards an external goal, however, we also exploit constraints that derive from "system-internal" problem solving. By such system-internal problem solving, we are referring to goals that need to be reached in order to properly perform the external task of the system. This distinction is a pragmatic one of course, since ultimately, the system's activities are always triggered by externally set goals.

In MOBAL, the system-internal problem solving activity that we exploit for concept formation consists of the *knowledge revision* activities of the system. Knowledge revision is a subtask that arises as part of the general goal of correctly solving given external problems: if the knowledge base has become incorrect, it needs to be modified to prevent erroneous inferences. In the next section, we describe and formally define the knowledge revision problem.

4.2   THE KNOWLEDGE REVISION PROBLEM

4.2.1   Informal description

In an incremental, learning knowledge acquisition system such as MOBAL, the knowledge base (theory) of the system is subject to permanent changes. During the construction of the knowledge base, new statements will be added, either by the user, or as the result of a learning process in RDT. In the simple case, these new statements just extend existing knowledge, and do not contradict it. These additive changes are referred to as *monotonic*. Unfortunately, we just as commonly have to make *non-monotonic* changes to the evolving knowledge base, i.e., changes that do not leave existing knowledge untouched. This can be attributed to several factors:

Changing world. During the construction, and even more during the use of a knowledge base, the world or application domain that the knowledge base is intended to model has changed, so that existing entries in the knowledge base are no longer correct.

Sloppy modeling. Research on the nature of the knowledge acquisition process [Morik, 1987; Morik, 1989b; Morik, 1989a; Morik, 1990; Morik, 1991; Morik, 1993] has shown that knowledge acquisition is not a linear activity that follows a well-developed plan, but rather a cyclic process of construction and revision that starts out with an incorrect or sloppy domain model, and gradually revises and extends it until the desired degree of coverage and correctness is reached. As a consequence, this means that initial inputs may need to be retracted, or new inputs are added that are inconsistent with existing knowledge.

Selection bias & incremental learning. If an inductive, learning-from-examples procedure such as RDT is employed to add to the knowledge base, anything that is learned (any rules) will reflect the examples or cases entered into the system up to the time of testing a rule hypothesis, and entering it into the knowledge base. If the user advertently or inadvertently selects examples that do not cover the full space of cases that the system may see, the learned rules may be overly general, or even entirely incorrect. Thus, future inputs may contradict learned (or user-input) rules, which then need to be modified. A similar situation may arise in an incremental system that learns from observations [Emde, 1991]. Such a system receives inputs from an environment, and maintains one current learning hypothesis. Depending on the observations that are received, the system's early theories may be incorrect, requiring revision to make it consistent with new observations.

So how does a learning system find out that its knowledge base is no longer correct? Returning to the model-based semantics we defined in chapter 3, an *incorrect* knowledge base is one that does not admit the intended domain of interpretation as a model, i.e., that contains statements in its inferential closure that are not true in the intended interpretation. This can be contrasted with the case of an *incomplete* knowledge base, which admits too many models because its inferential closure does not contain the necessary statements that would sufficiently limit the possible models of the theory. While it is a matter of further knowledge acquisition or inductive generalization to extend incomplete knowledge bases until they are strong enough to sufficiently constrain their possible models, we want to find computational methods to deal with the incorrect knowledge base problem, i.e., methods to ensure that an incorrect statement is removed from the inferential closure. This is the knowledge revision problem.

4.2.2 Formal definition of the required operations

More precisely, there are three possible operations that a user may want a knowledge revision component to perform on an $\Re$-knowledge base Γ. We can define these operations as follows[1]:

I. Removal The user points the system at a member f of the inferential closure Γ^* that is incorrect and is to be removed. We are thus looking for a function:

$$\hat{-} : \Gamma, f \mapsto \Gamma'$$

that maps a knowledge base Γ and a fact f to a new knowledge base Γ' such that

$$\Gamma' \not\vdash f.$$

---

[1] Here, we define the revision operations with respect to single fact revisions; in section 4.5.3, we generalize them to perform multiple revisions at the same time.

We will often use infix (operator) notation and write $\Gamma' = \Gamma \dot{-} f$. In the context of work on the logic of theory change ([Gärdenfors, 1988], see below), this operation is called *theory contraction*.

II. Consistent Addition The user inputs a statement that causes the closure of the knowledge base to become inconsistent, and requires sufficient modifications to the existing knowledge base to prevent this. We are thus looking for a function:

$$\dot{+} : \Gamma, f \mapsto \Gamma'$$

that maps a knowledge base Γ and a fact f to a new knowledge base Γ' such that

$$\Gamma' \vdash f \text{ and } \Gamma' \text{ is consistent.}$$

We will often use infix notation and write $\Gamma' = \Gamma \dot{+} f$. In the context of work on the logic of theory change ([Gärdenfors, 1988], see below), this operation is called *theory revision*.

III. Inconsistency Resolution The user or the learning component inputs a statement that causes the closure of the knowledge base to become inconsistent, and requires sufficient modifications to the existing knowledge base to prevent this; the new statement may also be removed. We are thus looking for a function:

$$\dot{\pm} : \Gamma, f \mapsto \Gamma'$$

that maps a knowledge base Γ and a fact f to a new knowledge base Γ' such that

$$\Gamma' \vdash f \oplus \Gamma' \vdash not(f).$$

In other words, $\Gamma \dot{\pm} f$ is ensured to derive one of f or $not(f)$, but not both[2].

The three operations described above are not unrelated to each other. The second operation, consistent addition, can be performed by first removing the negation of the new statement from the inferential closure, and then simply adding the new statement without further ado, since it cannot be inconsistent any more. Thus we can define:

$$\Gamma \dot{+} f := \Gamma \dot{-} \neg f \cup \{f\},$$

where $\neg f = f_0$ if $f = not(f_0)$, and $\neg f = not(f)$ otherwise[3]. Furthermore, the third operation, inconsistency resolution, can be understood as the composition of a choice function

$$\phi : f \mapsto \phi(f) \in \{f, \neg f\}$$

---

[2] $\oplus$ is to be read as "exclusive or". This third operation is necessary because MOBAL permits additions which are inconsistent at first and are resolved later on, see below.

[3] This is a simplified version of the *Levi identity* known from theory change work ([Levi, 1977] foll. [Nebel, 1989]).

and a consistent addition operation if we define:

$$\Gamma \hat{\pm} f := \Gamma \hat{+} \phi(f),$$

i.e., we first decide which "side" of the contradiction we want to keep, and then consistently add this side of the contradiction to the knowledge base. Since this in turn can be reduced to a removal operation, all three operations can be based on the first one (plus a choice function ϕ).

Before proceeding, let us briefly illustrate the above operations in the practical context of MOBAL. The first operation, removal, is needed whenever the user detects among the facts derived by the system one that does not correspond to his or her intentions. The second operation, consistent addition, is basically required on every user input, since in general we do not want an inconsistent theory. In MOBAL, however, it is also possible to perform an inconsistent addition, which means that the system derives and simply stores a contradiction in the knowledge base. With the inference rules specified in section 3.3.3, this presents no problem. The contradiction can then later be handled by invoking the third operation, which is also necessary e.g. whenever the learning module RDT has induced two rules which produce inconsistent conclusions, since in these cases, we may resolve the contradiction by either removing the positive or the negated statement. Following the relationships spelled out above, MOBAL's knowledge revision tool KRT implements these operations by providing a basic removal operation $\hat{-}$, and defining a choice function ϕ for the cases where it is not clear which side of a contradiction is to be removed. What properties are we to require from the basic revision operation $\hat{-}$?

4.3 REQUIRED PROPERTIES OF REVISION OPERATIONS

After identifying the set of knowledge revision operations that we are interested in, we now need to decide how to define them. The problem, of course, is that the above definitions severely underconstrain the operators, since many theories Γ' will meet the conditions we have imposed. A very reasonable additional constraint is that the operators should produce theories Γ' that differ *minimally* from the original theory Γ. Such a *conservative* strategy [Salzberg, 1985] can be motivated by the human response to information that contradicts one's own perception of the world: we usually make the minimal change that is necessary to fix the inconsistency. Such a strategy minimizes the loss of knowledge, and thus maintains a maximal inferential power of the modified theory. The following discussion is therefore based on the assumption that a theory is to be changed minimally; as we will see below, however, the notion of minimality must be properly instantiated to make sense.

The goal of this section thus is to find a set of required properties of revision operations that adequately capture this notion of minimality. Since what we have to say in this section (4.3) applies to revisions of first-order logical theories in general, and not just to our representation $\Re$ in particular, we will assume a standard first-order logical language as our representation throughout section 4.3. In particular, we will assume that the full set of logical connectives $\wedge, \vee, \neg, \rightarrow, \leftrightarrow$ are available, and that Cn denotes the standard logical consequence operation, i.e., among others, we know that Cn monotonically produces the closure of a theory:

1. $\Gamma \subseteq Cn(\Gamma)$ (inclusion),

2. $Cn(\Gamma) = Cn(Cn(\Gamma))$ (closure),

3. $Cn(\Gamma_1) \subseteq Cn(\Gamma_2)$ if $\Gamma_1 \subseteq \Gamma_2$ (monotonicity).

The first-order part of the language $\Re$, i.e., considering only statements on level 1 (see section 3.3.1), is thus a sublanguage of the language considered in this section, and the derivability operator $\vdash$ defined for $\Re$ produces a subset of the inferences produced by Cn.

To develop the requirements we want to postulate of knowledge revision operators, we can build upon some well-known results from work on closed theory contraction [Alchourron and Makinson, 1982; Alchourron *et al.*, 1985; Makinson, 1985; Gärdenfors, 1988]. In the following, we will briefly summarize some important results, following the exposition in [Nebel, 1989, ch. 6].

4.3.1   Closed theory contraction

The goal of work on closed theory contraction was the examination of theory change operations independent of any concrete representation of the theory as a knowledge base, i.e., at the *knowledge level* in the sense of Newell [1982]. Consequently, in this work, it is generally assumed that the theories under consideration are *closed*. We can define a *closed theory* as any theory Γ such that

$$Cn(\Gamma) = \Gamma.$$

We further define a *base* of a closed theory Γ as any set B such that

$$Cn(B) = \Gamma.$$

As a simple example, consider the knowledge base

$$\Gamma_1 = \{p(a), \forall x : p(x) \rightarrow q(x)\}.$$

Assuming that the underlying alphabet contains the predicate symbols p and q, no function symbols, and the constants a and b, we find that

$$\Gamma_2 := Cn(\Gamma_1) = \{p(a), \forall x : p(x) \rightarrow q(x), q(a), p(a) \vee p(b), p(a) \vee \neg p(b), \ldots\}.$$

Γ_1 is a base of Γ_2, and Γ_2 is a closed theory. *Theory contraction* then refers to the operation that maps a given closed theory into another closed theory, removing a particular offending statement in the process; we will denote such operations by $\dot{-}$ in the following.

One of the best-known results from theory contraction work is the set of *Gärdenfors postulates* [Gärdenfors, 1988] (also known as *AGM postulates*, after [Alchourron *et al.*, 1985]) which are a minimal set of constraints claimed to be necessary for every sensible revision operation. The six major postulates are summarized in table 4.1, for a closed theory Γ and a fact f to be removed[4]. These postulates are mostly unspectacular and describe reasonable properties

---

1. $\Gamma \dot{-} f$ is a closed theory (*closure*).

2. $\Gamma \dot{-} f \subseteq \Gamma$ (*inclusion*).

3. If $f \notin \Gamma$, then $\Gamma \dot{-} f = \Gamma$ (*vacuity*).

4. If $f \notin Cn(\emptyset)$, then $f \notin \Gamma \dot{-} f$ (*success*).

5. If $Cn(f) = Cn(g)$, then $\Gamma \dot{-} f = \Gamma \dot{-} g$ (*preservation*).

6. $\Gamma \subseteq Cn(\Gamma \dot{-} f \cup \{f\})$ (*recovery*).

Table 4.1   The main Gärdenfors postulates for closed theory contraction

one would expect from a revised theory. Postulate 1 simply requires the revised theory to be closed, which if necessary can be ensured by applying Cn. The second postulate sets an upper bound for a removal operation by requiring that nothing new can enter into the results, thus ruling out revision operations that generalize or strengthen some part of the theory. Postulates (3) and (4) prescribe that nothing is to be done when a statement to be removed is already not in the closure, and that the removal operation must be guaranteed to be a success if the statement f to be removed is not a tautology (which is always the case if f is a fact). The fifth postulate requires the removal result

---

[4] Two less important supplementary postulates that deal with the properties of conjunction under removal are also sometimes used.

to be independent of the syntactical form of the statement to be removed, i.e., the preservation of semantic equivalence.

The final postulate, recovery, is the most interesting one from the standpoint of machine learning, as it addresses a likely scenario for an incremental learning system. The recovery postulate requires that if we modify a theory to exclude an inference f, and later find out that f was true after all, we should be able to obtain at least the same set of inferences again that we used to have before removing f in the first place. It thus acts as a lower bound on the revisions we may perform, and excludes for instance the trivial empty theory as a revision result.

Interestingly, as pointed out in [Nebel, 1989; Nebel, 1992], all possible revision operations that meet the above postulates can be defined with respect to the set of maximal correct subsets of a closed theory.

Definition 4.1 (Maximal correct subsets) *If Γ is a theory, and f a statement to be removed, the set of maximal subsets of Γ not implying f, denoted $\Gamma \downarrow f$ (pronounced "Γ down f" or "Γ less f") is defined by:*

$$\Gamma \downarrow f := \{\Gamma' \subseteq \Gamma | f \notin Cn(\Gamma') \text{ and for all } \Gamma'' : \text{if } \Gamma' \subset \Gamma'' \subseteq \Gamma \text{ then } f \in Cn(\Gamma'')\}.$$

As an example, consider the closed theory Γ_2 from the example in section 4.3.1 above, i.e.,

$$\Gamma_2 = \{p(a), \forall x : p(x) \rightarrow q(x), q(a), p(a) \vee p(b), p(a) \vee \neg p(b), \ldots\}.$$

If we want to remove $q(a)$ from this theory, some of the maximally correct subsets are:

$$\Gamma_2 \downarrow q(a) = \left\{ \begin{array}{l} \{p(a), p(a) \vee p(b), p(a) \vee \neg p(b), \ldots\} \\ \{\forall x : p(x) \rightarrow q(x), p(a) \vee p(b), \ldots\} \\ \{\forall x : p(x) \rightarrow q(x), p(a) \vee \neg p(b), \ldots\} \\ \ldots \end{array} \right\}$$

The following so-called "representation theorem" (first shown in [Alchourron et al., 1985]) allows us to express any revision operation on closed theories that meets the Gärdenfors postulates in one common form.

Theorem 4.1 — *is a revision operation that meets the Gärdenfors postulates 1›6 if and only if there is a selection function γ, mapping a set to one of its subsets, such that*

$$\Gamma \dot{-} f = \left\{ \begin{array}{ll} \bigcap \gamma(\Gamma \downarrow f) & \text{if } f \notin Cn(\emptyset) \\ \Gamma & \text{otherwise}. \end{array} \right.$$

In other words, any revision operation meeting postulates 1 through 6 can be defined by specifying a function γ that returns a subset of $\Gamma \downarrow f$, the set of all maximally correct subsets of Γ, and computing the intersection of these sets. Depending on the size of the set returned by γ, the resulting operations are given different names:

Definition 4.2 (Partial meet, full meet, maxi-choice contractions) *All revision operations of the form defined in theorem 4.1 are called* partial meet contractions. *If γ returns a singleton, the operation is called a* maxi-choice contraction, *if γ simply returns $\Gamma \downarrow f$, the operation is called* full-meet contraction.

4.3.2 Minimal specialization and its undesirable properties

The above Gärdenfors postulates, while providing reasonable upper and lower bounds on theory contraction operations, still leave a large space of possibilities for the definition of such operations. Depending on whether γ returns one, several, or all elements of $\Gamma \downarrow f$, very different contraction operations can be realized, so still further constraints are needed. In this subsection, we will examine one such constraint which has recently been proposed by some authors in Machine Learning [Bain and Muggleton, 1992; Ling, 1991a], who argue that *minimal specializations* should be performed. Interestingly, this additional constraint maps directly into the contraction operation framework presented above. To see this, consider the logical definition of generalization/specialization as it is commonly used in Machine Learning.

Definition 4.3 (Generality) *A theory Γ_1 is said to be* more general *than a theory Γ_2, written $\Gamma_1 \geq_g \Gamma_2$ iff*

$$\Gamma_1 \vdash \Gamma_2{}^5.$$

By the definition of Cn, this is equivalent to $\Gamma_1 \geq_g \Gamma_2 \Leftrightarrow Cn(\Gamma_1) \supseteq Cn(\Gamma_2)$. Given this definition of generality, we can define a minimal specialization, or *maximally general correct specialization*, as follows [Bain and Muggleton, 1992].

Definition 4.4 (mgcs) *Let f be an incorrect statement derived by a theory Γ. A maximally general correct specialization (mgcs) of Γ with respect to f is any theory Γ' such that*

---

[5] For two sets A and B, we simply write "$A \vdash B$" instead of "$A \vdash b$ for all $b \in B$".

1. $\Gamma \geq_g \Gamma'$

2. $\Gamma' \not\vdash f$

3. For all Γ''*: If* $\Gamma \geq_g \Gamma'' >_g \Gamma'$*, then* $\Gamma'' \vdash f$.

In other words, a *mgcs* is any theory that is a specialization of the original theory, and does not have any correct supersets, i.e., supersets that do not imply the fact to be removed. We will often refer to the *mgcs* simply as the *minimal specialization* of Γ with respect to f.

Looking at this definition, we can see that such minimal specializations correspond precisely to maxi-choice contractions on the closure of the given theory.

Theorem 4.2 *Given a (not necessarily closed) theory* Γ*, and statement to be removed* f*, the* mgcs *of* Γ *with respect to* f *are exactly the results of all possible maxi-choice contractions on* $Cn(\Gamma)$*, i.e., the members of the set* $Cn(\Gamma) \downarrow f$.

Proof: The proof follows trivially from definition 4.1, according to which $Cn(\Gamma) \downarrow f =$

$$\{\Gamma' \subseteq Cn(\Gamma) | f \notin Cn(\Gamma') \text{ and for all } \Gamma'' : if \Gamma' \subset \Gamma'' \subseteq Cn(\Gamma) \text{ then } x \in Cn(\Gamma'')\},$$

which is a reformulation of the definition of *mgcs*. Since maxi-choice contractions are exactly the ones that select a single element from this set as the result of the contraction, they are the only operations that produce maximally general correct specializations.□

This correspondence, unfortunately, means that minimal specializations inherit all the known undesirable properties of maxi-choice contractions as revision operations, as pointed out by [Nebel, 1989; Nebel, 1992] and others. The first of these is common to all operations that produce closed theories, while the second and third are unique to maxi-choice contractions:

Nonfinite representation. Since minimal specialization revisions are equivalent to maxi-choice operations on closed theories, they also produce closed theories. In general, it is impossible to determine whether a closed theory has a finite axiomatization, which is a necessary prerequisite for the use of minimal specialization for practical theory revision. This of course is true for all closed-theory contraction operations, which are thus impractical as computational methods.

Loss of reason maintenance. An operation on the closure of a theory does not take into account which statements were derived from which others. For instance, if from Γ_1 (section 4.3.1), we were to remove $p(a)$ by minimal specialization, the possible minimal specializations would be

$$mgcs(\Gamma_1, p(a)) = Cn(\Gamma_1) \downarrow p(a)$$
$$= \{\{\forall x : p(x) \rightarrow q(x), q(a), p(a) \vee p(b), \ldots\}, \ldots\},$$

i.e., we would remove the antecedent $p(a)$, but keep statements that were derived from it such as $q(a)$.

Besserwissers. Last, for a maxi-choice contraction $\dot{-}$, we know (theorem 6.2 from [Nebel, 1989] foll. [Alchourron and Makinson, 1982]) that for any proposition g:

$$(f \vee g) \in \Gamma \dot{-} f, \; or \; (f \vee \neg g) \in \Gamma \dot{-} f.$$

Now imagine that the learning system used to believe f, and now finds out that $\neg f$ is correct instead. To keep the theory consistent, the learner would first minimally specialize it not to derive f any more using a maxi-choice contraction, and then add $\neg f$. From the above, we see that all of a sudden, for any statement g,

$$\text{either } g \in Cn(\Gamma \dot{-} f \cup \neg f), \text{ or } \neg g \in Cn(\Gamma \dot{-} f \cup \neg f),$$

since obviously $(\{f \vee g\} \cup \{\neg f\}) \vdash g$. Our minimal specialization operation would thus have served to miraculously complete our theory Đ hardly what we want from a revision operation[6].

4.3.3 A new set of revision postulates

We can thus conclude that in general it is not desirable for a revision operation to produce closed theories as its results, and that in particular, interpreting minimality of revision as minimal specialization in the sense defined above means using maxi-choice contractions which in addition to producing closed theories have undesirable properties of their own. Based on the base contraction postulates in [Nebel, 1989], we have therefore developed a revised set of revision postulates that applies to revision operations on non-closed first-order theories; these postulates are shown in table 4.2.

---

[6]The term *besserwisser* is due to [Gärdenfors, 1988].

1. $\Gamma \dot{-} f \subseteq \Gamma \cup \{g' | \exists g \in \Gamma \text{ such that } g >_g g'\}$ (*minimal syntactic distance*).

2. $Cn(\Gamma \dot{-} f) \subseteq Cn(\Gamma)$ (*inclusion*).

3. If $f \notin Cn(\Gamma)$, then $\Gamma \dot{-} f = \Gamma$ (*vacuity*).

4. If $f \notin Cn(\emptyset)$, then $f \notin Cn(\Gamma \dot{-} f)$ (*success*).

5. If $Cn(f) = Cn(g)$, then $Cn(\Gamma \dot{-} f) = Cn(\Gamma \dot{-} g)$ (*preservation*).

6. $Cn(\Gamma) \subseteq Cn(\Gamma \dot{-} f \cup \{f\})$ (*recovery*).

Table 4.2   Postulates for minimal base revision

The most important difference between the closed theory postulates (resp. Nebel's base revision postulates) and the ones defined here is the first postulate, which together with the recovery postulate, expresses a new notion of minimal revision for theory bases based on the syntactic form of the theory. According to the first postulate, a revision is minimal if the new theory contains only statements that had been in the old theory, and perhaps other statements that are specializations of statements in the original theory, and are thus "close variants" of statements that were in the original theory. Note that minimal specialization revisions in general do not meet this new first postulate, as their results will contain elements from the closure of Γ that were not originally in Γ nor are specializations of single statements in Γ.

Nonetheless, the degree of specialization can be used to compare the results of different base revision operations that meet the new set of postulates, and a reasonable requirement would be that within the restrictions of these postulates, such operations should produce maximally general results, i.e., give up as little as possible. Since the new postulates require the new theory to be a subset of the old theory plus some specializations of statements in the old theory, we are assured that there is a finite representation[7], and that the "loss of reason maintenance" problem discussed above does not occur. Furthermore, as we will see in the next section, each subset of a theory base corresponds to several maximal subsets of a closed theory, so that base revision operations are always partial meet, and never maxi-choice, and thus do not exhibit the strange Besserwisser effect mentioned above.

---

[7] Strictly speaking, this is true only if we assume that clauses are reduced, i.e., that $a \vee a \vee a \vee \ldots$ is not permitted.

4.4 MINIMAL BASE REVISION IN ℜ

Concluding the general discussion of required properties of revision operations, let us now return to the revision problem in our representation ℜ, i.e., from now, we will again assume that our representation is in the clausal form as defined by facts and rules of ℜ, that facts are ground, and that the language contains no function symbols. While simplifying our discussion, these restrictions are not strictly necessary, so whenever appropriate, we will point out how the results of this section can be used in clausal representations without these restrictions. As before, Γ will now again denote a non-closed theory base.

4.4.1 Base contraction operators

To develop our base revision operator, we can build upon the work by Nebel [Nebel, 1989, ch. 6] about *base contraction* operators, i.e., operators that start out with a non-closed theory base, but produce a closed theory as their result. The idea of these base contraction operators is simply to apply a choice function γ not to the set of correct subsets of the closed theory, but directly to the original theory base. As Nebel points out, however, care must be taken to ensure that the recovery postulate is still met by adding in some replacements for the statements that are removed.

In particular, all such base contraction operations can be defined as follows[8].

Definition 4.5 (Base contraction) *Let* Γ *be a theory,* f *a fact to be removed, and* γ *a choice function that returns a subset of its argument. The operation* $\dot{\sim}$ *defined by*

$$B \dot{\sim} f := \begin{cases} Cn([\bigcap_{S \in \gamma(\Gamma \downarrow f)} Cn(S)] \cup [Cn(\Gamma) \cap Cn(\neg f)]) & iff \notin Cn(\emptyset) \\ Cn(B) & otherwise \end{cases}$$

is called a base contraction *operation on* Γ *with respect to* f.

Again note that if f is a fact to be removed, f is never in $Cn(\emptyset)$ (not a tautology).

To show that all such base contraction operations meet the Gärdenfors postulates, we will now show how a base contraction operation induces a partial meet contraction operation on closed theories by defining a particular choice function to be used in the partial meet contraction. Slightly generalizing Nebel's original function, we can define this choice function γ_B as follows:

$$\gamma_B(Cn(\Gamma) \downarrow f) := \{C \in (Cn(\Gamma) \downarrow f) \mid \exists S \in \gamma(\Gamma \downarrow f) \text{ such that } S \subseteq C\} ,$$

---

[8]Nebel's original definition did not include a choice function and instead assumed that *all* elements of Γ ↓ f would be used (full meet base contraction).

i.e., selecting from $Cn(\Gamma) \downarrow f$ exactly those elements that contain an element of $\gamma(\Gamma \downarrow f)$. This defines a partial meet contraction as follows:

$$Cn(\Gamma) -_B f := \begin{cases} \bigcap \gamma_B(Cn(\Gamma) \downarrow f) & \text{if } f \notin Cn(\emptyset) \\ Cn(\Gamma) & \text{otherwise} \end{cases}$$

The above defines a proper partial meet contraction, because γ_B returns a subset of $Cn(\Gamma) \downarrow f$, i.e., chooses some of the maximal correct subsets of $Cn(B)$. Now we must only show that the so-defined partial meet contraction is identical to $\dot{\sim}$.

Theorem 4.3 *Let Γ be a theory, $\dot{-}_B$ the partial meet contraction with choice function γ_B as defined above, and $\dot{\sim}$ the base contraction defined above. Then it holds that*

$$Cn(\Gamma) \dot{-}_B f = \Gamma \dot{\sim} f.$$

Proof: For the exceptional cases where $f \notin Cn(\Gamma)$, or where f is a tautology the two are immediately equal. For the main case, we need to note that for any $S \subseteq \Gamma$ that does not imply $f \in Cn(\Gamma)$:

$$\bigcap \{C \in (Cn(\Gamma) \downarrow f) \mid S \subseteq C\} = Cn(S \cup (Cn(\Gamma) \cap Cn(\{\neg f\}))), \qquad (4.1)$$

the proof of which can be found in [Nebel, 1989]. Using this equation, we see that:

$$
\begin{aligned}
Cn(\Gamma) -_B f &= \bigcap \gamma_B(Cn(\Gamma) \downarrow f) \\
&= \bigcap \{C \in (Cn(\Gamma) \downarrow f) \mid \exists S \in \gamma(\Gamma \downarrow f) : S \subseteq C\} \\
&\stackrel{4.1}{=} \bigcap_{S \in \gamma(\Gamma \downarrow f)} Cn(\gamma(\Gamma \downarrow f) \cup (Cn(\Gamma) \cap Cn(\{\neg f\}))) \\
&= Cn([\bigcap_{S \in \gamma(\Gamma \downarrow f)} Cn(S)] \cup [Cn(\Gamma) \cap Cn(\neg f)]) \\
&= \Gamma \dot{\sim} f. \square
\end{aligned}
$$

4.4.2 From base contraction to base revision

If we base our revision operation on a base contraction operation, we thus know that all of the Gärdenfors postulates, and thus our base revision postulates (2) through (6), will be met. Unfortunately, base contractions still produce closed theories, so we have to check whether the result of a base contraction can be expressed in terms of the original theory so that our base revision postulate (1) is met. As Nebel points out, a finite representation of $\Gamma \dot{\sim} f$ can be derived using the properties of Cn by noting that for $f \notin Cn(\emptyset)$,

$$\Gamma \dot{\sim} f = Cn([\bigvee_{C \in \Gamma \downarrow f} C] \wedge [\Gamma \vee \neg f]),$$

the inner part of which is a finite disjunction. This disjunction represents all possible outcomes of a revision operation, i.e., each disjunct is a possible maximally correct subset of the theory. An alternative way of imagining this strategy is to think of the system performing a breadth-first search of revisions, at any point maintaining in parallel a large number of theories representing all possible outcomes.

In an incremental system such as MOBAL, this is not a strategy we would like to consider, since we want the system to maintain one current theory that is incrementally modified. This means that in MOBAL, we actually want to commit to one of the possible revision results. In technical terms, this means that we want to restrict γ to a singleton choice. If this is done, the above expression indeed can be represented in $\Re$: If we assume $\gamma(\Gamma \downarrow f) = \{\hat{\Gamma}\}$, and let $\bar{\Gamma} := \Gamma \backslash \hat{\Gamma}$ denote the set of removed elements of Γ, we see that the result of the base contraction can be represented by:

$$
\begin{aligned}
\Gamma \dot{\sim} f &= Cn(\hat{\Gamma} \wedge (\Gamma \vee \neg f)) \\
&= \hat{\Gamma} \wedge ((\hat{\Gamma} \wedge \bar{\Gamma}) \vee \neg f)) \\
&= \hat{\Gamma} \wedge (\bar{\Gamma} \vee \neg f) \\
&= \hat{\Gamma} \wedge \bigwedge_{C \in \bar{\Gamma}} (C \vee \neg f).
\end{aligned}
$$

In the last line above, C is a clause of the original theory, so in order to represent the result of the revision in clausal form, we must only make sure that $C \vee \neg f$ can be represented as a clause. This, however, is clearly the case. Assume C has the form

$$
L_1 \& \ldots \& L_n \rightarrow L_{n+1},
$$

(where $n = 0$ for a fact and $n > 0$ for a rule), $C \vee \neg f$ corresponds to

$$
L_1 \& \ldots \& L_n \& f \rightarrow L_{n+1},
$$

which is a specialization of the existing clause C, and thus is an allowed addition to the theory according to our postulate (1). To emphasize this fact we introduce the abbreviation $f \diamond C$ for $C \vee \neg f$, to be read as "add premise f to C". As a first definition of our revision operation, we can thus use:

$$
\Gamma \dot{-} f := \left\{
\begin{array}{ll}
\hat{\Gamma} \cup \{f \diamond C \mid C \in \bar{\Gamma}\} & \text{if } f \in Cn(\Gamma) \\
\Gamma & \text{otherwise.}
\end{array}
\right.
$$

For $\Re$, the relevant consequence operation is $\vdash$, so that $Cn(\Gamma) = \Gamma^*$ as defined in section 3.3.3.

Note that the restriction of γ to a singleton choice does not produce the Besserwisser effect observed for maxi-choice contractions on closed theories, since $\dot{-}_B$, and thus $\dot{\sim}$ define a true partial meet contraction even if γ_B returns only a single element: For any language which allows at least two statements, and a non-empty knowledge base Γ, $\gamma_B(Cn(\Gamma) \downarrow f)$ will always contain more than one element. As an example, let $\Gamma = \{a\}$, then $B \downarrow a = \{\emptyset\}$, and necessarily $\gamma(\Gamma \downarrow a) = \emptyset$. Now, since

$$Cn(\Gamma) = \{a, a \vee b, a \vee \neg b, \ldots\},$$

we see that

$$Cn(\Gamma) \downarrow a = \{\{a \vee b, \ldots\}, \{a \vee \neg b, \ldots\}\},$$

since having both $a \vee b$ and $a \vee \neg b$ would allow the derivation of a. Our revision operation thus does not have the undesirable properties of maxi-choice contractions.

4.4.3   Ensuring minimality: support sets

The above preliminary definition meets all of our base revision postulates, since it is directly based on a base contraction operation, and its result meets postulate (1). But how does it fare on the requirement that the resulting theory should be maximally general? The answer depends on which specializations of individual clauses are available to us in our representation, i.e., which statements we can add under our base revision postulate (1). If all we can do is to add a new atomic literal in the form defined in section 3.3.1, then the above preliminary definition is indeed the best we can do — we have to remove entire clauses from our theory, which seems drastic if we consider that we actually only want to prevent the use of a clause in the proof of an offending statement.

To do this, we introduce a representational construct that allows individual *substitutions* to be excluded from a clause by defining a predicate $\in_\sigma$ as follows:

$(T_1, \ldots, T_n) \in_\sigma S$ iff there exists $T \in S$ and a substitution σ such that $T\sigma = (T_1, \ldots, T_n)$. Otherwise, $(T_1, \ldots, T_n) \notin_\sigma S$.

The =-sign in this definition refers to syntactic equality, i.e., as defined in chapter 3 (section 3.3.2), we assume that different constants represent different objects (unique names assumption). As an example, $(a) \in_\sigma \{(a), (b)\}$ will evaluate to true[9], as well as $(a, b) \in_\sigma \{(X, b)\}$. By adding this construct to a clause as a premise, we can now block individual substitutions on the clause's variables. Such premises are actually represented in MOBAL

---

[9] For unary tuples, we usually omit the parentheses.

using a slightly more powerful form called a *support set* [Emde *et al.*, 1983; Wrobel, 1989], which is an additional data structure attached to a rule, but is interpreted as an additional premise.

Definition 4.6 (Support set) *Each rule R (with variables $vars(R) := \{X_1, \ldots, X_n\}$) has an attached* support set $S(R)$, *which is an expression of the form*

$$(p_1 \backslash LE_1) \times \cdots \times (p_n \backslash LE_n) \setminus GE.$$

The p_i are predicate symbols or the special symbol all, *the LE_i are sets of constant symbols and called* local exception sets, *and GE, the set of* global exceptions, *has the form*

$$\{(c_{1,1}, \ldots c_{1,n}), \ldots, (c_{m,1}, \ldots c_{m,n})\},$$

where the $c_{j,i}$ are constant symbols, and $m \geq 0$. The meaning of a support set is defined by the following set of rule premises:

$$p_1(X_1)\& \ldots \& p_n(X_n)\& X_1 \not\in_\sigma LE_1 \& \ldots \& X_n \not\in_\sigma LE_n \& (X_1, \ldots, X_n) \not\in_\sigma GE.$$

The meaning of the special symbol all *is defined by:*

$$all(X) \equiv true.$$

In the following, we will use both the $\in_\sigma$ and the support set notation depending which is more convenient. For a rule R with variables $\{X_1, \ldots, X_n\}$, the correspondence between the two is:

$$(X_1, \ldots, X_n) \not\in_\sigma S \equiv all \times \cdots \times all \setminus S.$$

When the support set notation is used, we will often simply append the support set to the rule, separated by a dash, i.e.,

$$R - S(R).$$

We can easily add the so-defined support sets to our representation $\Re$ by extending rules with a support set part in the syntax described above, and defining the semantics of this support set part to be the same as the semantics of the list of additional premises as defined above. In addition, we need to allow support sets to be attached to metafacts, so that metapredicates can generate rules with supports sets as well. We omit the details of this construction, and simply point out that the results derived about the formal and computational properties of $\Re$ in section 3.3 continue to hold.

Given support sets, the idea behind a more general revision operation is to "split" (or "factorize") each clause participating in the derivation of the offending fact f into one clause representing all the substitutions that were not used in any proof of f, and other clauses each of which represents one substitution used to derive f. As an example, consider the theory

$$\Gamma_1 = \{p(a), p(X) \rightarrow q(X)\}$$

from section 4.3.1, shown here in the clausal notation of $\Re$ with capitalized variables. If we want to remove $q(a)$ from this theory, we can either remove $p(a)$ or the entire clause $p(X) \rightarrow q(X)$. If, however, we first transform Γ_1 into the equivalent theory

$$\begin{aligned} \Gamma_1' &= \{p(a), (X) \notin_\sigma \{(a)\} \& p(X) \rightarrow q(X), (X) \in_\sigma \{(a)\} \& p(X) \rightarrow q(X)\} \\ &= \{p(a), (X) \notin_\sigma \{(a)\} \& p(X) \rightarrow q(X), p(a) \rightarrow q(a)\}, \end{aligned}$$

we can now remove $p(a)$, or simply the particular rule instance $p(a) \rightarrow q(a)$, keeping our original rule with the added restriction as $(X) \notin_\sigma \{(a)\} \& p(X) \rightarrow q(X)$. Using this general idea of blocking individual substitutions, we can show that our revision operator produces the logically maximally general revision results that meets our base revision postulates. First, however, we need to get into some technicalities to properly define this more sophisticated version of the operator.

4.4.4   The minimal base revision operator $\overset{\wedge}{-}$

As a first step, we must make precise what we mean by splitting a clause into parts that cover the substitutions not used in any proof of the offending statement f, and into parts that represent the substitutions used in proofs of f. To this end, we need the notion of a *derivation*.

Definition 4.7 (Derivation) *Let Γ be a theory, and $f \in Cn(\Gamma)$ a factual query provable from Γ by a finite resolution refutation proof. The* derivation *of f in Γ, $\Delta(f, \Gamma)$, is the pair*

$$\Delta(f, \Gamma) := (f, S),$$

where S, the set of supports *of f, is the following set of triples:*

$$S := \{(C, \sigma, A) | \exists C \in \Gamma \wedge \exists g_1, \ldots, g_n \in Cn(\Gamma) : C \text{ resolves with} \\ \{g_1, \ldots, g_n\} \text{ using substitution } \sigma \text{ to produce } f\}.$$

A, the set of antecedents *of S, are recursively defined as follows:*

$$A := \{\Delta(g_1, \Gamma), \ldots, \Delta(g_n, \Gamma)\}.$$

Wherever Γ is clear from context, we will simply write $\Delta(f)$ instead of $\Delta(f, \Gamma)$.

Since different refutation proofs of f may share the same clauses and sub-stitutions, the (C, σ, A) triples representing clause applications may repeat in a derivation structure, meaning that a derivation is best understood as a directed acyclic graph. This is also the format that we will be using when we display derivations graphically (see figure 4.2, page 110). Also note that in $\Re$, derivations are guaranteed to be finite due to the absence of function symbols; if function symbols are allowed, one can construct proofs where a clause can be used with an infinite number of substitutions to prove f. If we want to use our method on representations with function symbols, we thus must at least assume that Δ is finite for the fact to be removed.

From a derivation, the set of standard *proof trees* it represents can be obtained by beginning at the root, choosing one of its supports, and then repeating this recursively for the derivation subbranches rooted at the antecedents of these supports. By varying the choices in all possible ways, the set of all proof trees can be obtained.

As an example of a derivation, consider again the theory

$$\Gamma_1 = \{p(a), p(X) \rightarrow q(X)\}. \quad \cdot$$

Let us assume that q(a) is to be removed from this theory. There is only one way of proving q(a), so

$$\Delta(q(a), \Gamma_1) = \quad (q(a),$$
$$\{(p(X) \rightarrow q(X), \{X/a\},$$
$$\{(p(a),$$
$$\{(p(a), \emptyset, \emptyset)\}) \}) \}),$$

Given this definition of a derivation, we can now define what it means to "split" a clause so that different substitutions can be blocked individually. As it turns out, it is simpler not to produce a transformed theory Γ' as we did in the preceding section, but to work with structures that directly represent individual rule applications. As we will see, the transformed theories can be defined based on these application sets.

Definition 4.8 (Application set) *Let Γ be a theory and $f \in Cn(\Gamma)$ a fact. The* clause application set *of Γ with respect to f is defined as:*

$$\Pi(f, \Gamma) := \{(C, \sigma) | \exists S = (C, \sigma, A) \text{ somewhere in } \Delta(f, \Gamma)\}.$$

Instead of $(C, \emptyset)$ (where $\emptyset$ in this context is the empty substitution), we often simply write C in $\Pi(f, \Gamma)$. In our example, the clause application set is

$$\Pi(q(a), \Gamma_1) = \{(p(a), \emptyset), (p(X) \rightarrow q(X), \{X/a\})\},$$

and we define for later use abbreviations for the two nonempty subsets of this application set:
$$P_1 := \{(p(a), \emptyset)\}$$
$$P_2 := \{(p(X) \rightarrow q(X), \{X/a\})\}$$

In order to define the theory corresponding to an application set, we need to define substitution and instance sets.

Definition 4.9 (Substitution and Instance sets) *Let C be a clause in a theory Γ, with variables $vars(C) = \{X_1, \ldots, X_n\}$, let $f \in Cn(\Gamma)$ be a fact, and $P \subseteq \Pi(f, \Gamma)$. The substitution set of C with respect to P is defined as follows. We say that one substitution is more general than another, $\sigma_1 \geq_g \sigma_2$, iff there is a substitution θ such that $\sigma_1 \theta = \sigma_2$. Let*

$$\Sigma_0(C, P) := \{\sigma | (C, \sigma) \in P\}$$

denote all substitutions used with C in P. Then

$$\Sigma(C, P) \subseteq \Sigma_0(C, P)$$

is any set such that:

- *for any $\sigma \in \Sigma_0(C, P)$, there is a $\sigma' \in \Sigma(C, P)$ such that $\sigma' \geq_g \sigma$.*

- *for no $\sigma \in \Sigma(C, P)$, there is a $\sigma' \neq \sigma$ in $\Sigma(C, P)$ such that $\sigma' \geq_g \sigma$.*

For non-ground clauses ($n \geq 1$), the instance set *of C with respect to P is defined as*
$$I(C, P) := \{(X_1, \ldots, X_n)\sigma | \sigma \in \Sigma(C, P)\}.$$

We should note that for $\Re$-theories, all substitutions are ground substitutions, so $\Sigma(C, P) = \Sigma_0(C, P)$. For non-$\Re$ clausal theories, the construction of $\Sigma(C, P)$ ensures that there are no redundant substitutions in this set. Continuing with our example, we see that

$$\Sigma(p(a), P_1) = \{\emptyset\}$$
$$\Sigma(p(X) \rightarrow q(X), P_2) = \{\{X/a\}\}$$
$$\Sigma(p(a), P_2) = \Sigma(p(X) \rightarrow q(X), P_1) = \emptyset$$
$$I(p(X) \rightarrow q(X), P_1) = \emptyset$$
$$I(p(X) \rightarrow q(X), P_2) = \{(a)\}.$$

We can now define which theory corresponds to an application set:

Definition 4.10 (Corresponding theory) *Let* Γ *be a theory and* $f \in Cn(\Gamma)$ *a fact, and* $P \subseteq \Pi(f,\Gamma)$. *The* clauses occurring in P *are defined as*

$$C(P) := \{C|(C,\sigma) \in P\},$$

and the theory corresponding to P *is defined as:*

$$
\begin{aligned}
\Gamma_\Pi(P) := \quad & (\Gamma \backslash C(\Pi(f,\Gamma))) \\
& \cup \{vars(C) \not\in_\sigma I(C,\Pi(f,\Gamma)) \diamond C \mid C \in C(\Pi(f,\Gamma)) \text{ and } C \text{ nonground}\} \\
& \cup \{C\sigma | (C,\sigma) \in P\}.
\end{aligned}
$$

Here again, $L_0 \diamond C$ *is a shorthand notation for the addition of a premise, i.e., if* C *is a clause of the form* $L_1 \& \cdots \& L_n \rightarrow L_{n+1}$, *then*

$$L_0 \diamond C := L_0 \& L_1 \& \cdots \& L_n \rightarrow L_{n+1}.$$

The expression $vars(C)$ *denotes the ordered tuple of variables of the clause* C. *As a shorthand notation, we define*

$$\Gamma \times_\Pi f := \Gamma_\Pi(\Pi(f,\Gamma))$$

and call this theory the f-factorization *of* Γ.

For our example theory Γ_1, we can see that its $q(a)$-factorization is

$$
\begin{aligned}
\Gamma_1 \times_\Pi q(a) \ &= \ \{p(a), (X) \not\in_\sigma \{(a)\} \& p(X) \rightarrow q(X), p(a) \rightarrow q(a)\} \\
&= \ \Gamma'
\end{aligned}
$$

i.e., just the replacement theory we had produced in the preceding section. We note that the factorization of a theory is equivalent to the theory.

Lemma 4.1 *For any theory* Γ *and fact* $f \in Cn(\Gamma)$,

$$Cn(\Gamma \times_\Pi f) = Cn(\Gamma).$$

Proof: All statements not occurring in proofs of f remain unchanged by this construction; the same holds for ground statements. Each non-ground statement is replaced by a specialization that excludes exactly the substitutions in $\Sigma(C,\Pi(f,\Gamma))$; for each of these substitutions, however, there is a new statement $C\sigma$ which makes up for the loss. $\square$

To complete the definition of our minimal base revision operator, remember that the idea behind the more sophisticated version of the operator was to make it operate on the factorized theory instead of on the original one so that it could choose for each individual clause application whether to keep it or to remove it. For each maximal correct subset of the factorized theory that might be chosen, i.e., for each element of $(\Gamma \times_\Pi f) \downarrow f$, there actually is a corresponding set of clause applications, i.e., a subset of $\Pi(f, \Gamma)$ that must be removed. Thus instead of choosing maximal correct subsets of the factorized theory for keeping, we can also choose minimal subsets of the clause application set for removal.

Definition 4.11 (Minimal removal sets) *Let Γ be a theory, and f a fact to be removed. The* set of maximal application sets *of Γ with respect to f is defined as:*

$$\Gamma \downarrow_\Pi f := \Pi(f, \Gamma) \downarrow f := \{P \subseteq \Pi(f, \Gamma) | f \notin Cn(\Gamma_\Pi(P)) \text{ and for all } P' : \\ \text{if } P \subset P' \subseteq \Pi(f, \Gamma) \text{ then } f \in Cn(\Gamma_\Pi(P'))\}.$$

The complement of $\Gamma \downarrow_\Pi f$ is called the set of minimal removal sets, *and defined by*

$$\overline{\Gamma \downarrow_\Pi f} := \overline{\Pi(f, \Gamma) \downarrow f} := \{\Pi(f, \Gamma) \backslash P | P \in \Gamma \downarrow_\Pi f\}.$$

It is easy to see that the maximal application sets are isomorphic to the maximal correct subsets of the factorized theory.

Lemma 4.2 *For any theory Γ, and any fact f,*

$$(\Gamma \times_\Pi f) \downarrow f = \{\Gamma_\Pi(P) \mid P \in \Gamma \downarrow_\Pi f\}.$$

From now on, we will therefore simply assume that the maximal correct subset, or the minimal removal set, is chosen from $\Pi(f, \Gamma)$, and not from the factorized theory $\Gamma \times_\Pi f$.

In our example, there are two maximal correct application subsets, which are each other's complement, so

$$\Gamma_1 \downarrow_\Pi q(a) = \overline{\Gamma_1 \downarrow_\Pi q(a)} = \{P_1, P_2\}.$$

As our last preliminary, we now define sets of clauses that are added to a theory to replace each clause, or more precisely, each application of a clause, that needs to be removed.

Definition 4.12 (Add set) *For a clause C with the ordered set of variables $vars(C) = \{X_1, \ldots, X_n\}$, $n \geq 1$, in a theory Γ, a fact f to be removed, and $P \subseteq \Pi(f, \Gamma)$ such that $C \in C(P)$, i.e. occurs in P, define*

$$add(C, f, P) := \{(X_1, \ldots, X_n) \notin_\sigma I(C, P) \diamond C\} \cup \{(f \diamond C)\sigma | \sigma \in \Sigma(C, P)\}.^{[10]}$$

---

[10] Instead of the set $\{(f \diamond C)\sigma | \sigma \in \Sigma(C, P)\}$, it would be possible to simply use $(f\sigma \diamond C)$, but this would produce redundancy in the revised theory.

For ground clauses C (where $n = 0$ and $\Sigma(C, P) = \{\emptyset\}$), we define

$$add(C, f, P) := \{f \diamond C\}.$$

This definition thus uses the support set premises that we have defined in the preceding section. In our example, the add sets for our two statements in Γ_1 would be:

$$add(p(a), q(a), P_1) = \{q(a) \rightarrow p(a)\},$$
$$add(p(X) \rightarrow q(X), q(a), P_2)$$
$$= \{(X) \not\in_\sigma \{(a)\} \& p(X) \rightarrow q(X), q(a) \& p(a) \rightarrow q(a)\}$$
$$= \{(X) \not\in_\sigma \{(a)\} \& p(X) \rightarrow q(X)\}.$$

We can now define the minimal base revision (MBR) operator $\hat{-}$.

Definition 4.13 (MBR **operator** $\hat{-}$) *Let Γ be a knowledge base, f be a fact to be removed, and γ a selection function on $\Gamma \downarrow_\Pi f$. Let $\hat{P} := \gamma(\Gamma \downarrow_\Pi f)$ denote the chosen maximally correct application subset of $\Pi(f, \Gamma)$, and $\overline{P} := \Pi(f, \Gamma) \setminus \hat{P}$ its complement. The minimal base revision (MBR) operator $\hat{-}$ is defined as follows:*

$$\Gamma \hat{-} f := \begin{cases} \Gamma \backslash C(\overline{P}) \ \cup \ \bigcup_{C \in C(\overline{P})} add(C, f, \overline{P}) & \text{if } f \in Cn(\Gamma) \\ \Gamma & \text{otherwise.} \end{cases}$$

In the above example, the MBR operation would produce the following results. If the first element of $\Gamma_1 \downarrow_\Pi q(a)$, P_1, is chosen by γ, we have to remove P_2, so the resulting new theory is

$$\Gamma_1 \hat{-} q(a) = \{p(a), (X) \not\in_\sigma \{(a)\} \& p(X) \rightarrow q(X), q(a) \& p(a) \rightarrow q(a)\}$$
$$= \{p(a), (X) \not\in_\sigma \{(a)\} \& p(X) \rightarrow q(X)\};$$

if the second element, P_2 is chosen, we remove P_1, resulting in

$$\Gamma_1 \hat{-} q(a) = \{q(a) \rightarrow p(a), p(X) \rightarrow q(X)\}.$$

At this point, let us illustrate that the just defined $\hat{-}$ operator can indeed be applied to clausal theories with functions and non-ground facts, provided, as pointed out above, that $\Delta(f, \Gamma)$ is finite for the statement f to be removed. As an example involving a non-ground fact to be removed, consider the theory (shown in rule form with capitalized variables for readability)

$$\Gamma_3 = \begin{cases} f1: & p(X) \\ r1: & p(X) \rightarrow q(X) \\ r2: & q(X) \rightarrow r(X) \end{cases}$$

from which we want to remove q(f(Y)). In this example, we see that the minimal removal sets are

$$\overline{\Gamma_3 \downarrow_\Pi q(f(Y))} = \{\{(r1, \{X/f(Y)\}\}, \{(f1, \{X/f(Y)\}\}\}.$$

The two theories that result from these choices are:

$$\Gamma_3 \hat{-} q(f(Y)) = \left\{ \begin{array}{ll} f1: & p(X) \\ r11: & X \notin_\sigma \{f(Y)\} \& p(X) \rightarrow q(X) \\ [r12: & q(f(Y)) \& p(f(Y)) \rightarrow q(f(Y))] \\ r2: & q(X) \rightarrow r(X) \end{array} \right\}$$

where $r12$ is vacuous and can be omitted, and

$$\Gamma_3 \hat{-} q(f(Y)) = \left\{ \begin{array}{ll} f11: & X \notin_\sigma \{f(Y)\} \rightarrow p(X) \\ f12: & q(f(Y)) \rightarrow p(f(Y)) \\ r1: & p(X) \rightarrow q(X) \\ r2: & q(X) \rightarrow r(X) \end{array} \right\}$$

respectively. To see why the revision operator must consider individual clause applications in deciding about minimal removal sets, consider the example of

$$\Gamma_4 = \left\{ \begin{array}{l} p(X) \\ p(a) \& p(b) \rightarrow r(a) \end{array} \right\}$$

from which we want to remove r(a). If we choose to modify p(X) (or rather, one or more of its applications), $\hat{-}$ will correctly produce either one of

$$\left\{ \begin{array}{l} (X) \notin_\sigma \{(a)\} \rightarrow p(X) \\ r(a) \rightarrow p(a) \\ p(a) \& p(b) \rightarrow r(a) \end{array} \right\} \ or \ \left\{ \begin{array}{l} (X) \notin_\sigma \{(b)\} \rightarrow p(X) \\ r(a) \rightarrow p(b) \\ p(a) \& p(b) \rightarrow r(a) \end{array} \right\}$$

whereas a revision operation not based on individual clause applications would have to produce the overly specific

$$\left\{ \begin{array}{l} (X) \notin_\sigma \{(a), (b)\} \rightarrow p(X) \\ r(a) \rightarrow p(a) \\ r(a) \rightarrow p(b) \\ p(a) \& p(b) \rightarrow r(a) \end{array} \right\}$$

4.4.5   The properties of $\hat{-}$

We now prove that $\hat{-}$ meets the set of postulates for base revision operations defined in table 4.2, and after this, that it is the most general such operator.

Theorem 4.4 *The minimal base revision operator* $\hat{-}$ *meets the base revision postulates (1) through (6) from table 4.2.*

Proof: For the exceptional case where $f \notin Cn(\Gamma)$, the postulates are trivially true, so in the following we will assume $f \in Cn(\Gamma)$, and verify each postulate in turn.

(1). Since $\Gamma \backslash C(\overline{P}) \subseteq \Gamma$ anyway, we only need to show that for any removed clause $C \in C(\overline{P})$, $add(C, f, \overline{P})$ only contains statements that are subsumed (implied) by elements of Γ. Looking at the definition of add, we see that new statements are defined by adding literals to and/or instantiating existing statements, so this is indeed true.

(2). True as an immediate consequence of (1).

(3). True by definition of $\hat{-}$.

(4). By the definition of $\Gamma \downarrow_{\Pi} f$, f is not derivable from the theories corresponding to its members. It thus remains to verify that this is not changed by the additional statements from add. This is easy to see, because the additional premises added to removed statements ensure that all substitutions which could be used to prove f are excluded; the other additional statements can be used only if f is present. Since the derivation operator Cn is monotonic, this means that f cannot be derived any more after the revision.

(5). Trivially true since for factual queries, $Cn(f) = Cn(g)$ implies $f = g$.

(6). We can easily show that $\Gamma \subseteq Cn(\Gamma \hat{-} f \cup \{f\})$. For non-removed statements, this is trivially true. For each nonground removed statement C, we find that

$$
\begin{aligned}
& Cn(add(C, f, \overline{P}) \cup \{f\}) \\
= \ & Cn(\{(X_1, \ldots, X_n) \notin_{\sigma} I(C, \overline{P}) \diamond C\} \cup \{(f \diamond C)\sigma | \sigma \in \Sigma(C, \overline{P})\} \cup \{f\}) \\
= \ & Cn(\{(X_1, \ldots, X_n) \notin_{\sigma} I(C, \overline{P}) \diamond C\} \cup \{C\sigma | \sigma \in \Sigma(C, \overline{P})\}) \\
= \ & Cn(C),
\end{aligned}
$$

and similarly for ground statements. $\square$

Knowing that $\hat{-}$ meets the set of revision postulates from table 4.2, the remaining open question is whether it truly captures the essence of minimality as expressed by these postulates, i.e., whether it produces the maximally general base revisions consistent with these postulates. Indeed this is the case.

Theorem 4.5 (Minimality) *Let* $\hat{-}'$ *be any base revision operation that also meets the base revision postulates. Then for any theory* Γ, *and any fact* f, *there is a maximal application set* $\hat{P} \in \Gamma \downarrow_{\Pi} f$ *such that if* γ *chooses* $\hat{P}$ *for* $\hat{-}$,

$g \in Cn(\Gamma \hat{-}' f)$ *implies* $g \in Cn(\Gamma \hat{-} f)$.

for any fact g.

Proof: From postulate (1), we know that $\Gamma \hat{-}' f$ consists of a subset of Γ, plus perhaps some added statements. With a proper selection function, we can make $\hat{-}$ choose the same subset. As for the added statements, we likewise know they are specializations of existing statements. To complete the proof, we thus only need to show that $add(C, f, \overline{P})$, where $\overline{P} = \gamma(\Gamma \downarrow_\Pi f)$, is a minimal specialization of C. So assume that there is a statement C' such that $C \geq_g C' >_g add(C, f, \overline{P})$. This means that there is some substitution (inference) possible with both C and C', and not admitted by $add(C, f, \overline{P})$. Since $add(C, f, \overline{P})$ excludes precisely the substitutions mentioned in the minimal removal set $\overline{P}$, however, we know that none of them may be readmitted without rederiving f again. Thus C' is not a correct specialization of C. □

We thus know that $\hat{-}$ produces the maximally general revision that meets the base revision postulates from table 4.2. In some case, this revision actually corresponds to the minimal specialization revision.

Corollary 4.1 *If Γ is a theory, and $f \in Cn(\Gamma)$ is a fact to be removed, $\Gamma \hat{-} f$ is a minimal specialization of Γ if and only if*

1. *all statements in $Cn(\Gamma)$ except f have proofs that do not use f, and*

2. *γ has selected for removal exactly the clauses of Γ that resolved with f in the proof of f from Γ, or clauses that resolved with intermediate results in the proof of f that were not used for proving any $g \in Cn(\Gamma) \backslash \{f\}$.*

Proof: The definition of add ensures that the modified versions of removed statements in $\Gamma \hat{-} f$ will continue to derive anything that was derived previously, except f. Thus, if the intermediate results in the proof tree derived with the modified statements were not used to prove any other statement than $f \in Cn(\Gamma)$, then in $Cn(\Gamma) \backslash Cn(\Gamma \hat{-} f)$ we find only statements that can be used to prove f, so they cannot be added, and so $\Gamma \hat{-} f$ really is a minimal specialization. To prove the reverse, note that if any other statements were derived, we can just add these to obtain a more general theory that still does not derive f. □

As an example of a removal problem that does not meet these conditions, consider the theory Γ_3 at the end of section 4.4.4:

$$\Gamma_3 = \left\{ \begin{array}{ll} f1: & p(X) \\ r1: & p(X) \rightarrow q(X) \\ r2: & q(X) \rightarrow r(X) \end{array} \right\}$$

If we are to remove q(a) from this theory, we will necessarily also lose the inference r(a). Interestingly, this result also applies to the minimal specialization algorithm given in [Bain and Muggleton, 1992], and means that the algorithm does not always correctly produce a minimal specialization (see section 4.9 for details).

4.5 COMPUTING PREFERRED MINIMAL BASE REVISIONS

In the preceding sections, we have developed the theoretical definition of our minimal base revision operator $\doteq$, but in order to make this definition practical in a computer system, we need two more things. First of all, we must specify just how the choice function γ which selects among the possible minimal revisions in $\Gamma \downarrow_\Pi f$ is to be defined. Second, the definition of $\Gamma \downarrow_\Pi f$ does provide a way of computing this set, but only a very inefficient one that needs to look at all possible subsets, so we need a better algorithm for computing $\Gamma \downarrow_\Pi f$. In this section, we will first develop a general, two-tiered confidence model for defining γ, then proceed to describing an algorithm for computing $\Gamma \downarrow_\Pi f$ based on the derivation trace information of the inference engine. After showing how this algorithm can be extended to multiple simultaneous revisions, we give a description of the concrete instantiation of the two-tiered confidence model in MOBAL, and conclude with an assessment of the computational complexity of the revision problem.

4.5.1 The two-tiered confidence model

As we have seen in the preceding sections, the theoretical properties of $\doteq$ as a revision operation are independent of the particular choice function γ that is used. As long as γ selects any element of the set $\Gamma \downarrow_\Pi f$, i.e., the set of maximal subsets of $\Pi(f, \Gamma)$ whose corresponding theories do not imply f, we showed that $\doteq$ meets our minimal base revision postulates. We thus must resort to pragmatical considerations to decide which choice function γ to use.

In essence, the question we need to answer is which statements of our theory, i.e., which entries in our knowledge base we are most willing to modify or delete, and which entries we are most interested in keeping. We are thus interested in some measure of *confidence* in the statements in our knowledge base such that we are more likely to change or delete statements in which we are less confident. So let χ be a confidence function that assigns each statement s in our knowledge base a confidence value $\chi(s)$. What kinds of values are to be used as the range of χ?

The answer to this question depends on how we want to use $\chi(s)$ in our choice function γ, which we can do in basically two ways. The first one, proposed in [Nebel, 1989], and further developed in [Nebel, 1992], is to regard the confidence values (which are called *epistemic relevance* values there) as indexes of confidence *classes*. In this case, γ is defined such that a statement of a higher confidence class is modified or deleted only if revisions of statements in lower confidence classes are insufficient to prevent the derivation of the offending statement. With this interpretation of confidence values, we would thus rather delete any number of lower-confidence statements than a single higher confidence statement.

The other possible interpretation of confidence regards $\chi(s)$ as a continuously varying measure, and requires γ to select the element of $\Gamma \downarrow_\Pi f$ that minimizes the sum (or some other combination) of the confidence values of the statements that are to be modified or removed. In this case, it is thus well possible that the system will prefer to delete one statement with high confidence in order to keep a large number of statements with lower confidence.

Both approaches can be justified pragmatically in the context of a learning knowledge acquisition system such as MOBAL. The first interpretation, confidence classes, is very appropriate to distinguish between statements of different origin, for example between user inputs and learning results. Indeed in many situations we would probably rather modify a large number of learning results than a single user input. Due to their discrete nature, the effect of assigning a confidence class to a statement is easy to foresee, so confidence classes are likely to be easier to handle for users. The second model, on the other hand, seems more appropriate to deal with revisions in sets of statements from the same source, e.g. to select which among a set of learned rules to modify. Each such rule has been verified during learning with a certain confidence, and it would not be appropriate to delete many rules that were confirmed at 60 percent to keep one that was confirmed at 70 percent.

In sum, the choice between the two interpretations again boils down to pragmatics, and cannot be decided once and for all on theoretical grounds. We have therefore decided to allow for both a discrete and a continuous confidence model in KRT. To this end, we will interpret χ as the continuous confidence function, i.e.,

$$\chi : \Gamma \to [0, 1] \subseteq I\!R,$$

and add a second, discrete confidence class function

$$\kappa : \Gamma \to \{0, \ldots, \kappa_{max}\} \subseteq I\!N,$$

which corresponds to the extended epistemic relevance function of [Nebel, 1989][11].

We can now define an ordering $\geq_\gamma$ on subsets of Γ as follows.

Definition 4.14 ($\geq_\gamma$) *For any set $S \subseteq \Gamma$, let $S_{\kappa=n} := \{s \in S \mid \kappa(s) = n\}$. For two sets $X, Y \subseteq \Gamma$, let*

$$i := max\{j \in \{0, \ldots, \kappa_{max}\} \mid X_{\kappa=j} \neq Y_{\kappa=j}\},$$

i.e., the index of the highest confidence class where X and Y differ. Then define

$$X \geq_\gamma Y \Leftrightarrow \left\{ \begin{array}{l} X_{\kappa=i} \supset Y_{\kappa=i} \\ or \quad \left(\begin{array}{l} X_{\kappa=i} \not\supset Y_{\kappa=i} \wedge Y_{\kappa=i} \not\supset X_{\kappa=i} \\ \wedge \sum_{s \in X} \chi(s) \geq \sum_{s \in Y} \chi(s) \end{array} \right) \end{array} \right.$$

Based on $\geq_\gamma$, we define a choice function γ for $\overset{\frown}{-}$ as follows.

Definition 4.15 (Choice function for $\overset{\frown}{-}$) *Let Γ be a theory, and f a fact to be removed. Let $M_{\geq_\gamma}(\Gamma, f)$ denote the following set:*

$$M_{\geq_\gamma}(\Gamma, f) :=$$
$$\{P \in \Gamma \downarrow_\Pi f \mid for\ all\ P' \in \Gamma \downarrow_\Pi f : if\ C(P') \geq_\gamma C(P)\ then\ C(P) \geq_\gamma C(P')\}.$$

The choice function γ for the minimal base revision operator $\overset{\frown}{-}$ is defined as any function that, given Γ and f, returns an arbitrarily chosen element of $M_{\geq_\gamma}(\Gamma, f)$.

In other words, γ selects among the maximal application sets of Γ with respect to f an arbitrarily chosen set whose corresponding theory is maximal according to $\geq_\gamma$. Instead of choosing arbitrarily among the maximal sets, it is also imaginable that additional application-specific criteria are used to make a choice.

We have thus completed the definition of the removal operator $\overset{\frown}{-}$. Before proceeding to implementational issues, let us return to the other two revision operators introduced in section 4.2.2, i.e., $\overset{\frown}{+}$ and $\overset{\frown}{\pm}$. As we pointed out above, they can be defined in terms of $\overset{\frown}{-}$ as follows:

$$\Gamma \overset{\frown}{+} f := (\Gamma \overset{\frown}{-} \neg f) \cup \{f\}$$
$$\Gamma \overset{\frown}{\pm} f := \Gamma \overset{\frown}{+} \phi(f),$$

---

[11]Note that χ and κ differ greatly in their effect on the computational complexity of choosing an optimal revision; see section 4.5.5 for details.

Chapter 4

i.e., to complete the definition of these operations, we only need to specify the choice function

$$\phi : f \mapsto \phi(f) \in \{f, \neg f\}$$

that decides which "side" of a contradiction to keep.

Here again, we want to keep the side that we have more confidence in, so we need to extend our basic confidence function χ to elements of $Cn(\Gamma)$. The intuitive idea that underlies this extension is that derived facts somehow inherit confidence from the statements in Γ that they were derived from. More precisely, if $\Delta(f)$ again denotes the derivation of f in Γ (definition 4.7), we can define

$$\chi(f) := f_{or}(\{\chi(s) \mid \Delta(f) = (f, S) \wedge s \in S\}),$$

where f_{or} is a function that combines the confidence of the different supports of the derivation into a confidence level for the resulting fact. One reasonable choice for f_{or} is

$$f_{or}(S) := max(S),$$

i.e., simply taking the maximum confidence of all proofs that support f.

We can now define the confidence of a support s as follows:

$$\chi(s) := \begin{cases} \chi(g) & if \ s = (g, \sigma, \emptyset) \ (g \ is \ a \ fact) \\ f_{and}(\chi(g), \{\chi(g_i) \mid (g_i, S_i) \in A\}) \\ & if \ s = (g, \sigma, A) \ (g \ is \ a \ rule) \end{cases}$$

Here, f_{and} is a function that computes the confidence level of the rule conclusion based on the confidence level of the antecedents and the confidence in the rule itself. One reasonable choice for f_{and} is

$$f_{and}(\chi(r), S) := \chi(r) \cdot min(S),$$

which uses the confidence value of the rule as a discounting factor on the minimum premise confidence[12]. Given this definition of χ for facts in $Cn(\Gamma)$, we can define ϕ as follows.

Definition 4.16 *If χ is a confidence function defined on the elements of $Cn(\Gamma)$, define*

$$\phi(f) := \begin{array}{ll} f & if \ \chi(f) \geq \chi(\neg f) \\ \neg f & otherwise. \end{array}$$

---

[12]The confidence computation is thus similar to the evidence point computations performed by the inference engine. There also, an evidence transfer function is used to compute the conclusion evidence of a rule, and a multiple-derivation combination function is used to compute the evidence point for a fact. Given this similarity, it seems an attractive possibility to simply identify χ with the evidence functions — this however, would not accurately reflect the meaning of the two: it is well possible for a derivation to contribute a lot of evidence with little confidence, as well as little evidence with perfect confidence, so the two must be kept separate.

This completes our definition of the three knowledge revision operators $\hat{-}$, $\hat{+}$, and $\hat{\pm}$. We will now describe how they are computed and used in KRT.

4.5.2   An algorithm for computing minimal removal sets

Given the above definition of $\hat{-}$, and the other operators based on it, how can we compute $\Gamma \hat{-} f$ for a knowledge base Γ and a fact f? The simplest approach would be to follow the definitions directly, i.e., first compute $\Gamma \downarrow_\Pi f$ by looking at all possible subsets of $\Pi(f, \Gamma)$ (perhaps in a top-down fashion) and checking whether their corresponding theories imply f, and then comparing the elements of $\Gamma \downarrow_\Pi f$ using $\geq_\gamma$ to select the best one. Unfortunately, such a simple-minded approach, in the worst case, would require us to look at the exponential number of $2^{|\Pi(f,\Gamma)|}$ subsets of $\Pi(f, \Gamma)$, and for each one, to check whether f is implied by its corresponding theory.

Fortunately, $\Gamma \downarrow_\Pi f$ can be computed much more cheaply from the derivation trace information stored in the inference engine [Emde, 1989]. In an actual MOBAL knowledge base, we do not simply find the base of the theory, i.e., the set that we have been referring to as Γ, but, depending on the settings of inference engine parameters, a more or less complete record of Γ^*, i.e., the set of consequences of Γ with respect to $\vdash$ as defined in chapter 3, section 3.3.3. In any case, asking a query from the inference engine triggers a Prolog-style backward chaining proof that is also recorded in the knowledge base. When performing a removal operation $\Gamma \hat{-} f$, we can thus ask the inference engine to prove f. If this is impossible, the knowledge base remains unchanged anyway; if the query succeeds, we can obtain from the inference engine the derivation $\Delta(f)$.

Figure 4.2 shows Δ for the fact $q(a)$ in the knowledge base

$$\Gamma = \left\{ \begin{array}{ll} f11: & r(a) \\ f12: & p(a) \\ f13: & s(a) \\ f14: & t(a) \\ r1: & p(X) \to r(X) \\ r2: & p(X)\ \&\ t(X) \to s(X) \\ r3: & r(X) \to q(X) \\ r4: & s(X) \to q(X) \end{array} \right\}$$

In the figure, rectangular nodes depict elements of Γ^*, whereas oval nodes represent elements of $\Pi(q(a), \Gamma)$, i.e., clause applications. The drawing shows the derivation, i.e., the set of all proofs, as an *or-and* DAG (directed acyclic graph), i.e., the arcs below a rectangular node represent alternative proofs,

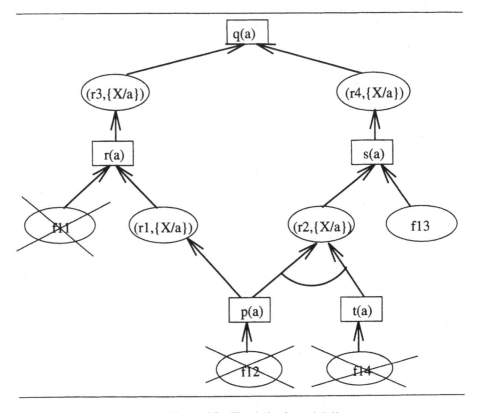

Figure 4.2   The derivation $\Delta(q(a))$

whereas the arcs below an oval rule node (linked by a curve) represent the set of premises that need to be present conjunctively. Based on such a graphical representation, it is clear that to prevent the derivation of the root of the derivation, we need to "cut" each of the disjunctive proofs; to cut an individual proof, we either need to modify the element at the root of the proof, or need to cut one of the conjunctive antecedents. Thus, for example, if the clause applications {f11, f12, f13}[13] were deleted as marked in figure 4.2, this would be sufficient to prevent the derivation of $q(a)$, so the remaining clause applications would be an element of $\Gamma \downarrow_\Pi f$.

Table 4.3 presents an algorithm for computing minimal removal sets that uses the general steps described above.

---

[13]Remember that instead of $(c, \emptyset)$, we usually simply write c when writing down application sets.

minimal_removal_sets(Γ, f)
    1. retrieve $\Delta(f, \Gamma) = (f, \{S_1, \ldots, S_m\})$ from the inference engine
    2. for i from 1 to m
        assuming $S_i = (g, \sigma, A)$
        if $A = \emptyset$ (g is a leaf node)
        then let $\overline{\Gamma \downarrow_\Pi S_i} := \{\{(g, \sigma)\}\}$
        else
            recursively compute $U := \bigcup_{(g_j, S) \in A} \overline{\Gamma \downarrow_\Pi g_j}$
            let $\overline{\Gamma \downarrow_\Pi S_i} := \{\{(g, \sigma)\}\} \cup U$
    3. compute

$$\overline{\Gamma \downarrow_\Pi f}^+ := \{s \mid \exists s_1, \ldots, s_m : (\forall i \in \{1, \ldots, m\} : s_i \in \overline{\Gamma \downarrow_\Pi S_i})$$
$$\wedge \ s = \bigcup_{i \in \{1, \ldots, m\}} s_i\}.$$

    4. return as result

$$\overline{\Gamma \downarrow_\Pi f} := \{s \in \overline{\Gamma \downarrow_\Pi f}^+ \mid \not\exists s' \in \overline{\Gamma \downarrow_\Pi f}^+ : s' \subset s\}.$$

Table 4.3   Computing minimal removal sets

The last step (4), the removal of non-minimal sets, is necessary because the different supports of a fact may share elements of Γ: if in one subbranch, the shared element is selected for removal, the other subbranch must select the same, because anything else would not need to be removed since the shared element already prevents the derivation. Note that in the general case where our operator is applied to theories with non-ground facts and function symbols, there may be elements of $\overline{\Gamma \downarrow_\Pi f}^+$ which have the same clause, but substitutions where one is a specialization of the other. We do not need to check for this here, because such redundant substitutions are removed in the computation of Σ upon which the actual modifications made by $\hat{-}$ are based.

Before we show that the above algorithm actually computes the complement of $\Gamma \downarrow_\Pi f$, let us illustrate its operation on the example derivation shown above (figure 4.2). The subbranches give rise to the following sets (where we abbreviate $\sigma_a := \{X/a\}$):

$$
\begin{aligned}
\overline{\Gamma \downarrow_\Pi p(a)} &= \{\{f12\}\} \\
\overline{\Gamma \downarrow_\Pi t(a)} &= \{\{f14\}\} \\
\overline{\Gamma \downarrow_\Pi r(a)} &= \{\{f11, (r1, \sigma_a)\}, \{f11, f12\}\} \\
\overline{\Gamma \downarrow_\Pi s(a)} &= \{\{f13, (r2, \sigma_a)\}, \{f13, f12\}, \{f13, f14\}\}.
\end{aligned}
$$

If we number the supports from the left, this means that

$$\overline{\Gamma \downarrow_\Pi S_1} = \{\{(r3, \sigma_a)\}, \{f11, (r1, \sigma_a)\}, \{f11, f12\}\}$$
$$\overline{\Gamma \downarrow_\Pi S_2} = \{\{(r4, \sigma_a)\}, \{f13, (r2, \sigma_a)\}, \{f12, f13\}, \{f13, f14\}\}$$

Here we can clearly see that simply performing the pairwise join of these sets will produce non-minimal answers (marked with a $*$):

$$\overline{\Gamma \downarrow_\Pi q(a)}^+ = \{\{(r3, \sigma_a), (r4, \sigma_a)\}, \{f13, (r2, \sigma_a), (r3, \sigma_a)\}, \{f12, f13, (r3, \sigma_a)\},$$
$$\{f13, f14, (r3, \sigma_a)\}, \{f11, (r1, \sigma_a), (r4, \sigma_a)\}, \{f11, f12, (r4, \sigma_a)\},$$
$$\{f11, f13, (r1, \sigma_a), (r2, \sigma_a)\}, \{f11, f12, f13, (r1, \sigma_a)\}^*, \{f11, f13, f14, (r1, \sigma_a)\},$$
$$\{f11, f12, f13, (r2, \sigma_a)\}^*, \{f11, f12, f13\}, \{f11, f12, f13, f14\}^*\}.$$

Since the minimal subsets of all the marked sets are in $\overline{\Gamma \downarrow_\Pi q(a)}^+$ also, however, the subset check removes these as required, and:

$$\overline{\Gamma \downarrow_\Pi q(a)} = \{\{(r3, \sigma_a), (r4, \sigma_a)\}, \{f13, (r2, \sigma_a), (r3, \sigma_a)\}, \{f12, f13, (r3, \sigma_a)\},$$
$$\{f13, f14, (r3, \sigma_a)\}, \{f11, (r1, \sigma_a), (r4, \sigma_a)\}, \{f11, f12, (r4, \sigma_a)\},$$
$$\{f11, f13, (r1, \sigma_a), (r2, \sigma_a)\}, \{f11, f13, f14, (r1, \sigma_a)\},$$
$$\{f11, f12, f13\}\}.$$

We can now show our theorem.

Theorem 4.6 *The above recursive procedure correctly computes $\overline{\Gamma \downarrow_\Pi f}$, i.e., the complement of $\Gamma \downarrow_\Pi f$.*

Proof: We show the theorem by complete induction.

Base case. We are starting with derivations of depth 1, i.e., for a query f that was answered by resolving only with facts in Γ. Note that since the derivation is finite and non-circular, the leaves of the derivation must be such statements, so this is a proper base case. Let

$$\Delta(f) = (f, \{S_1, \ldots, S_n\})$$

be the derivation of f. If all supports of f are from facts in Γ, we know that:

$$S_i = (g_i, \sigma_i, \emptyset) \ for \ all \ i \in \{1, \ldots, n\},$$

since there are no further antecedents. For such a derivation, according to step 2 in the algorithm in table 4.3,

$$\overline{\Gamma \downarrow_\Pi S_i} := \{\{(g_i, \sigma_i)\}\},$$

so that we have only one choice for each support, and consequently

$$\overline{\Gamma \downarrow_\Pi f} = \{\{(g_1, \sigma_1), \ldots, (g_n, \sigma_n)\}\}.$$

Call the single member of this set s, and note that s removes all applications of facts in Δ. Since furthermore $\vdash$ is monotonic, and Δ contains all possible proofs of f, $\Gamma_\Pi(\Pi(f, \Gamma) \backslash s)$, the theory corresponding to the remaining clause applications, does not derive f. Since failing to remove any of the members of s allows the derivation of f, $\Pi(f, \Gamma) \backslash s$ is also maximal and thus an element of $\Gamma \downarrow_\Pi f$. Since $g_1, \ldots, g_n$ are the only facts used in derivations of f, and all of them must be removed, there can be no other elements of $\Gamma \downarrow_\Pi f$. Thus, for the base case, we have shown that $\overline{\Gamma \downarrow_\Pi S_i}$ and $\overline{\Gamma \downarrow_\Pi f}$ contain all and only the minimal removal sets.

Inductive step. Let

$$\Delta(f) = (f, \{S_1, \ldots, S_n\}),$$

where

$$S_i = (g_i, \sigma_i, A_i) \ for \ all \ i \in \{1, \ldots, n\}.$$

We first show that $\overline{\Gamma \downarrow_\Pi S_i}$ contains all and only the minimal removal sets. For $A_i = \emptyset$, we already showed this in the base case. So assume

$$A_i = \{(g_{i,1}, S_{i,1}), \ldots, (g_{i,m_i}, S_{i,m_i})\}.$$

According to the definition,

$$\overline{\Gamma \downarrow_\Pi S_i} := \{\{(g_i, \sigma_i)\}\} \cup \overline{\Gamma \downarrow_\Pi g_{i,1}} \cup \cdots \cup \overline{\Gamma \downarrow_\Pi g_{i,m_i}}.$$

By the inductive assumption, we know for all $i \in \{1, \ldots, n\}$ that $\overline{\Gamma \downarrow_\Pi g_{i,j}}$, $j \in \{1, \ldots, m_i\}$, contains exactly the minimal removal sets of the antecedents. Thus, if one of the member sets of $\overline{\Gamma \downarrow_\Pi S_i}$ is removed, f cannot be derived any more, since we remove the rule g_i or one of the antecedents $g_{i,j}$, $\vdash$ is monotonic, and Δ contains all possible derivations. The first set is minimal since if g_i is left in, the rest will derive f again. Since the other sets remove just what is necessary to remove one premise (by inductive hypothesis), they are minimal also. There cannot be any other minimal removal sets, because if such a set removes either g_i or one of the premises, it must be a superset of $\{g\}$ or of a member of one of the $\overline{\Gamma \downarrow_\Pi g_{i,j}}$; if it doesn't remove any of these, f can still be derived.

It thus remains to be shown that the combination of all the S_i produces exactly the minimal removal sets for $\overline{\Gamma \downarrow_\Pi f}$. We again show this by complete induction on the number of supports.

Base case. If there is only one support,

$$\overline{\Gamma\downarrow_\Pi f} = \overline{\Gamma\downarrow_\Pi S_1},$$

which we just showed to be exactly the minimal removal set.

Inductive step. For a simpler notation, in the definition of $\overline{\Gamma\downarrow_\Pi f}^+$ based on $n+1$ supports, let us rewrite $\bigcup_{i\in\{1,\dots,n\}} s_i =: s_{1\dots n}$, i.e.,

$$\overline{\Gamma\downarrow_\Pi f}^+ := \{s|\exists s_1,\dots,s_n,s_{n+1} : \quad (\forall i \in \{1,\dots,n\}s_i \in \overline{\Gamma\downarrow_\Pi f_n}) \wedge s_{n+1} \in \overline{\Gamma\downarrow_\Pi S_{n+1}}$$
$$\wedge\, s = s_{1\dots n} \cup s_{n+1}\},$$

where $\overline{\Gamma\downarrow_\Pi f_n}$ stands for the minimal removal set based on the first n supports. Let $s_{1\dots n} \in \overline{\Gamma\downarrow_\Pi f_n}$, and $s_{n+1} \in \overline{\Gamma\downarrow_\Pi S_{n+1}}$. The set $s_{1\dots n}$ is minimal by the inductive hypothesis, and s_{n+1} was shown to be minimal for S_{n+1}. Let $t_2 \subseteq s_{n+1}$ be the maximal set with the property that $\exists t_1 \subseteq s_{1\dots n}$ such that t_2 can be replaced by t_1 in s_{n+1} while still removing S_{n+1}. Thus,

$$s = (s_{n+1}\setminus t_2) \cup t_1$$

would be sufficient for removing S_{n+1}, and t_2 would be superfluous in the union of $s_{1\dots n}$ and s_{n+1}, resulting in the non-minimal removal set

$$u = s_{1\dots n} \cup (s_{n+1}\setminus t_2) \cup t_2.$$

However, this is not a problem: Since $\overline{\Gamma\downarrow_\Pi S_{n+1}}$ was shown to contain all minimal removal sets, and s removes S_{n+1}, there must be a set

$$t_2' \in \overline{\Gamma\downarrow_\Pi S_{n+1}} : t_2' \subseteq s.$$

The union

$$u' = s_{1\dots n} \cup t_2' \in \overline{\Gamma\downarrow_\Pi f}^+$$

is minimal, since no part of t_2' can be replaced any more. Since

$$u' \subseteq u,$$

u will be removed when computing $\overline{\Gamma\downarrow_\Pi f}$ from $\overline{\Gamma\downarrow_\Pi f}^+$. To complete the proof, it remains to be shown that there can be no other minimal sets except those in $\overline{\Gamma\downarrow_\Pi f}^+$; this is clear, however, since the sets $\overline{\Gamma\downarrow_\Pi S_i}$ are complete as shown above, and not removing any support would allow the derivation of f.□

4.5.3 Multiple revisions

In many situations, an incorrect entry in a knowledge base is the basis for inferring several incorrect facts in the closure, so an interesting question is whether this set of incorrect elements of the closure can be removed at the same time. Obviously, it is possible to define an extended removal operation on sets of facts as follows:

$$\Gamma \hat{-} \{f_1, \ldots f_n\} := (\ldots ((\Gamma \hat{-} f_1) \hat{-} f_2) \cdots \hat{-} f_n),$$

i.e., by the repeated application of the single fact removal operation. Unfortunately, this may not lead to the best overall revision, as a simple example shows. If

$$\Gamma = \{p(a), p(X) \rightarrow r(X), p(X) \rightarrow s(X)\},$$

then assuming that $\chi(p(a)) = 0.6$, $\chi(p(X) \rightarrow r(X)) = 0.5$, and $\chi(p(X) \rightarrow s(X)) = 0.5$ as well, γ will select to remove $p(X) \rightarrow r(X)$ from the knowledge base. If we now remove $s(a)$, we will select $p(X) \rightarrow s(X)$, keeping only $p(a)$. If γ had been applied to $\Gamma \downarrow_\Pi \{r(a), s(a)\}$ directly, however, $p(a)$ would have been chosen for modification according to $\geq_\gamma$.

This order dependency of revisions is a typical characteristic of any incremental method, since each of the incremental steps must make a choice and commit to it. If we want to avoid this for multiple revisions, we must avoid serializing them, and thus need to find a way to compute $\Gamma \downarrow_\Pi \{f_1, \ldots, f_n\}$, again without looking at the powerset of Γ, but based on the derivations of $f_1, \ldots, f_n$. To this end, we first extend the notion of derivation to multiple facts.

Definition 4.17 (Derivation, multiple facts) *Let Γ be a theory, and $F = \{f_1, \ldots f_n\}$ a set of facts such that $f_i \in Cn(\Gamma)$ for all $i \in \{1, \ldots, n\}$. Based on the derivation of individual facts, the derivation of the fact set F with respect to Γ is defined as:*

$$\Delta(F, \Gamma) := (F, \bigcup_{i \in \{1, \ldots, n\}} \Delta(f_i, \Gamma)).$$

Using this definition of a derivation for multiple facts, we can extend the remaining definitions from section 4.4.4 in the obvious fashion.

Definition 4.18 (Application set,multiple facts) *Let Γ be a theory and $F = \{f_1, \ldots f_n\}$ a set of facts such that $f_i \in Cn(\Gamma)$ for all $i \in \{1, \ldots, n\}$. The clause application set of Γ with respect to F is defined as:*

$$\Pi(F, \Gamma) := \{(C, \sigma) | \exists S = (C, \sigma, A) \text{ somewhere in } \Delta(F, \Gamma)\}.$$

Definition 4.19 (Minimal removal sets, multiple revisions) *Let Γ be a theory, and $F = \{f_1, \ldots f_n\}$ a set of facts to be removed. The* set *of maximal application sets of Γ with respect to the set of facts F is defined as:*

$$\Gamma \downarrow_\Pi F := \Pi(F, \Gamma) \downarrow f := \{P \subseteq \Pi(F, \Gamma) | F \cap Cn(\Gamma_\Pi(P)) = \emptyset \text{ and } for \text{ } all \text{ } P' :$$
$$if \text{ } P \subset P' \subseteq \Pi(F, \Gamma) \text{ } then \text{ } F \cap Cn(\Gamma_\Pi(P')) \neq \emptyset\}.$$

The complement of $\Gamma \downarrow_\Pi F$ is called the set of minimal removal sets *for multiple revisions, and defined by*

$$\overline{\Gamma \downarrow_\Pi F} := \overline{\Pi(F, \Gamma) \downarrow F} := \{\Pi(F, \Gamma) \backslash P | P \in \Gamma \downarrow_\Pi F\}.$$

Given these definitions, the procedure for computing $\Gamma \downarrow_\Pi f$ can easily be adapted to the multiple revision case; the resulting modified procedure is shown in table 4.4. In fact, the only difference is in step 1, where we need to retrieve the multiple fact derivation from the inference engine.

---

minimal_removal_sets_multi(Γ, F)
    1. retrieve $\Delta(F, \Gamma) = (F, \{S_1, \ldots, S_m\})$ from the inference engine
    2. for i from 1 to m
        assuming $S_i = (g, \sigma, A)$
        if A=$\emptyset$ (g is a leaf node)
        then let $\overline{\Gamma \downarrow_\Pi S_i} := \{\{(g, \sigma)\}\}$
        else
            recursively compute $U := \bigcup_{(g_j, S) \in A} \overline{\Gamma \downarrow_\Pi g_j}$
            let $\overline{\Gamma \downarrow_\Pi S_i} := \{\{(g, \sigma)\}\} \cup U$
    3. compute
        $\overline{\Gamma \downarrow_\Pi f}^+ := \{s \mid \exists s_1, \ldots, s_m : (\forall i \in \{1, \ldots, m\} : s_i \in \overline{\Gamma \downarrow_\Pi S_i})$
                    $\wedge s = \bigcup_{i \in \{1, \ldots, m\}} s_i\}.$
    4. return as result
        $\overline{\Gamma \downarrow_\Pi f} := \{s \in \overline{\Gamma \downarrow_\Pi f}^+ \mid \not\exists s' \in \overline{\Gamma \downarrow_\Pi f}^+ : s' \subset s\}.$

Table 4.4 Computing minimal removal sets for multiple revisions

The correctness proof of the procedure for single fact revisions (theorem 4.6) does not depend on the fact that all supports derive the same conclusion, so it carries over directly to the above multiple revision procedure. We can thus state the following corollary without separate proof.

Corollary 4.2 *Given a theory* Γ *and a set of facts* $F = \{f_1, \ldots f_n\}$ *to remove, the procedure in table 4.4 correctly computes the set of minimal removal sets* $\overline{\Gamma \downarrow_\Pi F}$.

4.5.4   Instantiating the two-tiered confidence model

Once the set $\overline{\Gamma \downarrow_\Pi f}$ has thus been computed based on the derivation of f, we need to select one of its maximal elements according to $\geq_\gamma$, which requires particular instantiations of the functions χ, κ, f_{or}, and f_{and} introduced in section 4.5.1. As we already pointed out above, χ and κ could directly be assigned by the user, thus providing extra control over the revision process, but requiring additional work. In KRT, we have therefore chosen to define χ and κ based on general heuristics. For χ, we assume that we can have perfect confidence in all user input facts, and that the confidence of a rule depends on its ratio of successful applications to exceptions as recorded in the rule's support set[14].

The latter measure is precisely defined as follows. Let R be a clause (rule) with a non-ground conclusion, let

$$X_{i_1}, \ldots, X_{i_m} \subseteq vars(R)$$

be the variables occurring in the conclusion of the rule, and

$$S(R) = D_1 \times \cdots \times D_n \backslash GE,$$

be the support set of R. If $\pi_{i_1, \ldots, i_m}$ denotes the projection operation on dimensions i_1 through i_m, we can define the instance and exception sets as follows. P is a set of clause applications (namely, the clause applications we want to remove).

$$Exc(R, P, \Gamma) := \pi_{i_1, \ldots, i_m}(GE \cup I(R, P))$$
$$Inst(R, P, \Gamma) := \pi_{i_1, \ldots, i_m}(I(R, \Pi(\Gamma^*, \Gamma))) \backslash Exc(R, P, \Gamma).$$

We have thus defined the exception set to be the previously known exceptions from the support set, plus all instances of the rule in applications we want to remove. The reason for including the latter is that it permits us to define the confidence of a rule as the *loss* of confidence when the rule is modified (see below). Correspondingly, the instance set of the rule is defined as all instances

---

[14]Clearly, this measure is not without problems, as the number of applications of a rule directly depends on what other rules are in the theory. Thus a rule that appears very strong before revision may end up very weak if another rule that produced the former rule's antecedents is removed.

of the rule in Γ, i.e., the instance tuples of all applications of R in the derivation of any fact in Γ^*, minus the exceptions. Computing the global instance set may seem like an expensive operation, but since the inference engine maintains a trace of all derivations in Γ^* anyway, finding these applications is a simple lookup operation. The reason for projecting these instance and exceptions sets on the conclusion variables is the undesirable effect that occurs if a rule contains existentially quantified variables, i.e., variables that do not occur in the conclusion: if there are several ways to derive a single conclusion, each of them is counted individually[15]. Since the quality of a rule really depends on how many correct conclusions it has produced, and not on how many ways of producing them, we project onto the conclusion variables to avoid this effect.

We can now define the confidence in a rule simply as the ratio of instances to exceptions. To ensure that rules with more total instances have a higher confidence than those with less, even if the ratio is the same, we add a penalty factor that decreases with the total number of instances[16]. If we let $Inst$ abbreviate for $Inst(R, P, \Gamma)$, and Exc abbreviate for $Exc(R, P, \Gamma)$, the definition of χ for a clause (rule) $R \in \Gamma$ with a non-ground conclusion is:

$$\chi(R, P) := \begin{cases} 0 & if \ |Inst| = 0 \\ \frac{|Inst| - 1}{|Inst| + |Exc|} & otherwise \end{cases}$$

If we let $P = \emptyset$, we obtain the confidence in the rule before the proposed modification is performed, if we let $P = \gamma(\Gamma \downarrow_\Pi f)$, we obtain the confidence after actually doing the removal. Instead of simply using the confidence of a rule before modification for γ, we could thus also use the difference, or "loss" of confidence as a comparison measure. In MOBAL, we presently use the former variant.

For clauses $f \in \Gamma$ with ground conclusions (which includes all facts), we simply let

$$\chi(f) := 1.$$

In addition, we want the system to always try modifying rules before deleting any input facts, so we subdivide Γ into two confidence classes for facts and rules, defining

$$\begin{aligned} \kappa(R) &:= 0 \quad for \ rules \ R \in \Gamma \\ \kappa(f) &:= 1 \quad for \ facts \ f \in \Gamma \end{aligned}$$

---

[15]Thanks to J.U. Kietz for pointing this out.
[16]This also implies that ϕ will always keep the side of a contradiction that is supported by an input fact, which corresponds well with our intentions.

Finally, for f_{and} and f_{or}, we use the definitions proposed above, i.e.,

$$\begin{aligned}
f_{or}(S) &:= max(S) \\
f_{and}(\chi(R), S) &:= \chi(R) \cdot min(S).
\end{aligned}$$

Using these definitions, we can compare the elements of $\overline{\Gamma{\downarrow_\Pi}f}$ by defining a comparison function $\overline{\geq_\gamma}$ in the obvious fashion based on the definition of $\geq_\gamma$:

$$X\overline{\geq_\gamma}Y \Leftrightarrow \left\{ \begin{array}{l} X_{\kappa=i} \subset Y_{\kappa=i} \\ or \quad X_{\kappa=i} \not\subset Y_{\kappa=i} \wedge Y_{\kappa=i} \not\subset X_{\kappa=i} \\ \wedge \sum_{s\in X} \chi(s) \leq \sum_{s\in Y} \chi(s) \end{array} \right.$$

We can thus select the set of statements for removal or modification. Since *add* can also be computed directly, this is all we need to effectively compute $\dot{-}$ in KRT.

4.5.5   Computational complexity of the revision problem

Given the above algorithm for computing preferred removal sets according to the minimal base revision operator $\dot{-}$, a natural question is how expensive (in terms of computation time) such an operation can be in the worst case. Such an analysis can be performed by characterizing the complexity of a particular algorithm, or by studying the problem characteristics independent of a particular algorithm. Since the former produces results that are potentially dependent on certain peculiarities of the chosen algorithm, only the latter can deliver general results about the difficulty of the problem as such.

Research in complexity theory (see [Garey and Johnson, 1979] for an introduction) has identified a number of important problem classes of different computational difficulty. A very basic and important distinction is expressed by the classes P and NP. Roughly speaking, P is the class of (decision) problems amenable to a polynomial-time solution with a deterministic algorithm, whereas NP is the class of (decision) problems that can be solved in polynomial time by a nondeterministic algorithm (see [Garey and Johnson, 1979] for precise definitions). Of particular interest within the latter class are problems referred to as *NP-complete*, meaning that given a polynomial time solution to one of these problems, *any* other problem in NP can be solved in polynomial time also. In a sense, these problems are thus the "hardest" problems in NP. All problems exhibiting the latter property are called *NP-hard* independent of whether they are in NP or not.

As of now, no polynomial time algorithm for any NP-complete or NP-hard problem is known despite long years of research. Therefore, although this has never been shown formally, it is universally believed that P≠NP, meaning that there cannot be a polynomial time solution to any NP-complete or NP-hard problem: if there were such a solution, all problems in NP could be solved in polynomial time, so P and NP would be the same. Thus, if we can prove our revision problem to be NP-complete or NP-hard, we know that there is no hope of finding a polynomial time algorithm (if indeed P≠NP).

To prove such a result, we must first phrase the revision problem as a *decision problem*, i.e., as a problem with a yes/no answer, and then show that assuming we had a polynomial time solution to the revision problem, we could solve some already known NP-complete problem in polynomial time. So let us first define a simplified decision problem associated with the revision problem.

Definition 4.20 (Revision decision problem) *The* revision decision problem *is defined by the following question. Given an $\Re$-theory Γ with $\kappa(s) = 0$ for all $s \in \Gamma$, a fact $f \in Cn(\Gamma)$ to be removed, and a real number R, is there a minimal removal set S such that*

$$\Sigma_{s \in S} \chi(s) \leq R?$$

It should be noted that this decision problem is indeed easier than the problem of computing $\dot{-}$, since κ is restricted: given a particular preferred minimal removal set chosen by $\geq_\gamma$, we know there cannot be a minimal removal set with a lower χ-sum (if there were, $\geq_\gamma$ would have chosen it since κ is equal for all statements). Therefore, we can answer "yes" to the above question if the χ-sum of the preferred minimal removal set is at most R, and "no" otherwise, thus solving the decision problem with the general $\dot{-}$ operator.

We can now prove that the revision decision problem is NP-hard.

Theorem 4.7 *The revision decision problem from definition 4.20 is NP-hard.*

Proof: We show that the "hitting set" decision problem, which is known to be NP-complete [Garey and Johnson, 1979, p. 64], transforms to the revision decision problem. An instance of the hitting set problem is characterized by a collection C of subsets of a set S, and a positive integer K, and the decision question is:

> "Does S contain a *hitting set* for C of size K or less, that is, a subset $S' \subseteq S$ with $|S'| \leq K$ and such that S' contains at least one element from each subset in C?"

The transformation is realized as follows. Assume S consists of elements $\{s_1, \ldots, s_m\}$ that are atomic constants (otherwise rename). Assume C contains the sets $S_1, \ldots, S_n$. Define a knowledge base Γ for C as follows. Γ contains the set of nullary facts $\{s_1, \ldots, s_m\}$. For each $S_i = \{s_{i,1}, \ldots, s_{i,|S_i|}\}$ ($i \in \{1, \ldots, n\}$), Γ contains the rule r_i

$$s_{i,1} \& \cdots \& s_{i,|S_i|} \rightarrow p,$$

where p does not occur in S. From this theory, p can be derived in n different ways corresponding to the different rules (see figure 4.3). Now let κ be 0 for

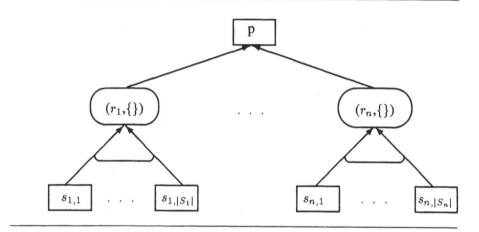

Figure 4.3 Derivation corresponding to hitting set instance

all elements of Γ, and let χ be $1/2m$ for all facts and 1 for all rules. Let the fact to be removed in the revision problem instance be p, and specify $R := K/2m$. This transformation can be computed in polynomial time, and produces a legal instance of the revision decision problem.

It remains to be shown that the answer for the hitting set instance is "yes" if and only if the answer to the revision instance is "yes". So assume there is a hitting set H of size at most K. Since all elements of S are facts in Γ, H can be considered as a removal set. By definition, it contains at least one element from each of the sets S_i ($i \in \{1, \ldots, n\}$), and thus at least one premise from each of the corresponding rules. This blocks all derivations of p, so H indeed is a removal set. Since each of its at most K members has a χ value of $1/2m$, the sum is indeed at most $K/2m$ as required. Note that H may not be minimal, but of course contains a minimal subset with even smaller χ-sum.

For the reverse direction, assume there is a minimal removal set with a χ-sum of at most $K/2m$. Since all rules have a χ value of 1, we know that only facts are in this minimal removal set. Furthermore, since p is removed, we know that for each rule, at least one premise must be in the removal set, which means that the minimal removal set is a hitting set for C. ◻

The removal set problem is thus at least as hard as any NP-complete problem, so we have no hope of finding a polynomial time algorithm for it (if P≠NP). Since in the general case[17] it is not possible to always check in polynomial time (in the size of a knowledge base) whether a proposed minimal removal set really prevents the derivation of the fact to be removed, the problem is not even in NP.

Indeed the algorithm presented in the preceding sections cannot be guaranteed to run in polynomial time in the number of knowledge base entries, since it needs to look at all possible removal sets, of which there can be exponentially many. The need to look at all these sets stems from the properties of χ. We cannot locally decide which removal set is best for each subbranch of the derivation, because different branches may share nodes, making an optimal local decision non-optimal globally (the shared elements contribute only once to the combined χ). To guarantee good answer times, the implemented version of the algorithm allows the specification of a maximal number of removal sets to be kept at each local choice point (beam search); if desired, completeness can thus be gradually sacrificed to gain speed.

Note that if we restrict our confidence model to κ, it is possible to compute preferred minimal revisions in time polynomial in the size of the given derivation. This is so because we can always choose a removal set with minimal κ locally, and then keep only this set for further processing. When combining different branches, shared elements do not lead to lower κ values (we only take the maximum), so locally optimal choices are globally optimal as well. Of course, when keeping only one removal set at each recursive choice point, the union of different branches may result in non-minimal sets, but these always contain minimal subsets which have the same κ value.

4.6 BEYOND MINIMAL BASE REVISION: RULE
REFORMULATION

In the preceding sections, we have specified a knowledge revision operation $\dot{-}$ that satisfied the base revision postulates while making revisions that were in a certain sense minimal (even though they are not the minimal specialization, which we have identified as undesirable, see section 4.3). If we look at the transformations that were used to achieve this, however, we find that there are

---

[17]Without assuming maximal predicate arities.

situations in which we actually *do* want to specialize beyond the results of the $\hat{-}$ operator.

In order to meet the recovery postulate, the $\hat{-}$ operator specializes each rule by adding explicit exceptions to its support set. From a logical point of view, there is no reason to question this method, as it always reaches the desired goal. Pragmatically however, can we justify adding exceptions and exceptions to a rule forever? Over time, the exception lists may become very long (a problem that has also been noted by [Ling, 1991b]). Certainly, in many situations it would be preferable to entirely delete a rule instead of keeping a rule that has many more exceptions than successful applications. If we do this we are no longer guaranteed to have a minimal special in the sense of the base revision postulates, but we are assured that the size of the knowledge base will remain plausibly small. As we will see below, the loss can actually be kept small by trying to *reformulate* rules instead of deleting them entirely.

4.6.1 The Plausibility Criterion

So let us try to find a more precise definition of the situations in which it might be useful or even necessary to specialize beyond the results of the $\hat{-}$ operation. Clearly, there can be no universal answer to this question, as it again depends largely on pragmatics, and thus on the intentions of the user, whether the emphasis is to be on minimizing inferential loss, tolerating many exceptions if necessary, or on maintaining a small knowledge base with easy-to-understand, short rules while tolerating a possible loss in inferential power. KRT therefore offers to the user a system parameter called the *plausibility criterion* which is evaluated whenever a rule has been modified by a minimal base revision operation. If this criterion is not met, KRT attempts to *reformulate* the support set by performing further specializations beyond the minimal one produced by the minimal base revision operator.

The plausibility criterion is a conditional expression in which pos denotes the number of instances of the rule R to which the criterion is being applied, and neg denotes the number of exceptions from R as defined above, i.e., if F is the set of incorrect facts that are to be removed,

$$pos := |Inst(R, \emptyset, \Gamma)|,$$

and

$$neg := |Exc(R, \emptyset, \Gamma)|,$$

where the second argument can be $\emptyset$ since all known exceptions have already been removed by adding them to the global exception list of the support set.

An example of a typical plausibility criterion (used e.g. in the traffic law domain) is

pos > 0 & (neg < 4 ; neg < 0.3*pos),

which requires at least one successful application, and less than 4 or less than 30% unsuccessful applications (explicitly listed exceptions) for a rule.

4.6.2 Reformulation Operators

The task of the process that reformulates a rule is to provide a rule that did not meet the plausibility criterion with a "more plausible" form. The plausibility concept in this context is primarily based on the extent to which a rule is universal: only rules that are universal, i.e. that do not have an explicit list of the valid and invalid applications, can be regarded as plausible. Consequently, the aim of the reformulation process must be to replace a very large *extensional* description of exceptions by an *intensional* description on the basis of a domain concept [Emde *et al.*, 1983]. To perform such reformulations, KRT possesses a small set of reformulation operators that are summarized in table 4.5[18]. In this table, $\pi_{i_1,...,i_m}(S)$ of a set S of n-tuples ($m \leq n$) denotes the projection of S on positions $i_1, ..., i_m$, i.e.,

$$\pi_{i_1,...,i_m}(S) := \{(c_1, ..., c_m) \mid \exists t \in S : c_1 = t[i_1], ..., c_m = t[i_m]\}.$$

For projections on a single dimension, we regard the result as a simple set, i.e., $\{(c_1), ..., (c_n)\}$ is regarded as $\{c_1, ..., c_n\}$. Where no confusion can arise, we have simply written $p(t)$ instead of $p(c_1, ..., c_n)$ where $t = (c_1, ..., c_n)$. Also, throughout the table we use the abbreviations *Inst* and *Exc* as defined in section 4.5.4. If $\dot{-}$ has been applied to remove all incorrect facts from the closure of Γ before applying the reformulation operators (this is the default in KRT), there are no incorrect facts to be removed any more, so at this point, $F = \emptyset$, and $Exc = E(R, \emptyset, \Gamma) = GE$.

We will briefly illustrate the effect of these operators with a few examples. As a starting point for the examples, we will use a knowledge base Γ which contains the rule R

involved_vehicle(Event,Car)
                     & owner(Person,Car) $\rightarrow$ responsible(Person,Event).

The initial support set $S(R)$ of this rule is assumed to be

---

[18]This table shows only the reformulation operators that use existing concepts. In chapter 5, we define additional operators that use CLT to introduce new concepts for reformulation.

(1) *localize(X_i)* : Localize exceptions to individual variable domains.
$X_i \in vars(R)$. Let $Int := \pi_i(Inst) \cap \pi_i(Exc)$. In $S(R)$, replace GE by
$\{t \in Exc \mid \pi_i(t) \in Int\}$, and replace LE_i by $LE_i \cup (\pi_i(Exc)\backslash Int)$.

(2) *add_ei(V', p)*: Add an existing predicate (instances).
$V' = [X_{i_1}, \ldots, X_{i_k}]$ is a sequence of elements of $vars(R)$, and p must be
an existing predicate of arity $|V'|$ such that $\forall t \in \pi_{i_1,\ldots,i_k}(Inst) : p(t) \in \Gamma$.
Add the additional premise $p(X_{i_1}, \ldots, X_{i_k})$ to R, and in $S(R)$, replace
GE by $\{t \in Exc \mid p(\pi_{i_1,\ldots,i_k}(t)) \in \Gamma\}$. If $V' = \{X_j\}$, replace LE_j by
$\{s \in LE_j \mid p(s) \in \Gamma\}$.

(3) *add_ee(V', p)*: Add an existing predicate (exceptions).
$V' = [X_{i_1}, \ldots, X_{i_k}]$ is a sequence of elements of $vars(R)$, and p must be an
existing predicate of arity $|V'|$ such that $\forall t \in \pi_{i_1,\ldots,i_k}(Inst) : not(p(t)) \in \Gamma$.
Add the additional premise $not(p(X_{i_1}, \ldots, X_{i_k}))$ to R, and in $S(R)$, replace
GE by $\{t \in Exc \mid not(p(\pi_{i_1,\ldots,i_k}(t))) \in \Gamma\}$. If $V' = \{X_j\}$, replace LE_j by
$\{s \in LE_j \mid not(p(s)) \in \Gamma\}$.

Table 4.5 KRT's reformulation operators using existing concepts

(Event, Car, Person) $\in$ all $\times$ all $\times$ all,

i.e., the unrestricted default support set where $GE = \emptyset$. Now assume that R
has the following instances and exceptions in Γ:

$Inst = \{$	(event1,b_au_6773,sw),	(event2,b_dx_1385,dj),	
	(event3,hh_mo_195,mo),	(event4,b_md_4321,md),	
	(event5,b_st_888,st),	(event6,b_ab_89,ab),	
	(event7,b_bc_90,bc),	(event8,b_cd_01,cd),	
	(event9,b_de_12,de),	(event10,b_ef_23,ef),	
	(event11,b_fg_34,fg),	(event12,b_gh_45,ef)	$\}$
$Exc =\{$	(cab_event,cab1,ace_cab_co),	(loan_event,b_xs_400,sw),	
	(stolen_event,b_dx_986,dx)		$\}$.

In this example, the removal operator $\hat{-}$ would produce a new support set,
replacing GE by $GE \cup Exc$[19]:

all $\times$ all $\times$ all $\backslash$ {(cab_event,cab1,ace_cab_co),
(loan_event,b_xs_400,sw), (stolen_event,b_dx_986,dx)}

---

[19] In the following, we omit the variable list of the support set.

This support set is the basis for the application of the reformulation operators. The *localize* operator moves exceptions from GE to one of the local exception lists. $localize(1)$ would produce:

(all \ {cab_event, loan_event, stolen_event}) × all × all

leaving no global exceptions, whereas $localize(3)$ would produce:

(all × all × (all \ {ace_cab_co, dx})) \ {(loan_event,b_xs_400,sw)}

since $Int := \pi_3(Inst) \cap \pi_3(Exc) = \{sw\}$. The reformulation operator add_ei adds an extra, positive premise to the rule, using an existing predicate that can be specified. Assuming that Γ contained a predicate sedan defined by the following facts:

sedan(b_au_6773),	sedan(b_dx_1385),	sedan(hh_mo_195),
sedan(b_md_4321),	sedan(b_st_888),	sedan(b_ab_89,ab),
sedan(b_bc_90)	sedan(b_cd_01)	sedan(b_de_12),
sedan(b_ef_23),	sedan(b_fg_34),	sedan(b_gh_45)
sedan(b_dx_986),	not(sedan(b_xs_400))	

the operator $add\_ei(\{Car\}, sedan)$ would produce the support set:

involved_vehicle(Event,Car) & owner(Person,Car)
                    & sedan(Car) → responsible(Person,Event).

with the new support set:

all × all × all \ {(stolen_event,b_dx_986,dx)}

since b_dx_986 is also a sedan, but an exception to the rule.

Similarly, the reformulation operator add_ee adds an extra, negative premise to the rule, again using an existing predicate that can be specified. Assuming that Γ contained a predicate motorcycle defined by the facts:

motorcycle(b_xs_400),   not(motorcycle(cab1))

then the application of the operator $add\_ee(\{Car\}, motorcycle)$ would result in the new rule:

involved_vehicle(Event,Car) & owner(Person,Car)
                    & not(motorcycle(Car)) → responsible(Person,Event).

with the new support set:

all $\times$ all $\times$ all $\setminus$ {(cab_event,cab1,ace_cab_co)},

since cab1 is not a motorcycle, and still an exception to the rule.

Let us briefly point out some properties of the reformulation operators. The operators are defined in such a way that the specialization they produce remains complete, i.e., the rules they produce are guaranteed to still cover *Inst*. For the *localize* operator, this is ensured by allowing only non-members of the set *Int* to be added to the local exception list; for the other operators, this is ensured by requiring that all instances (or rather, their appropriate projections) must match the new premise that is added. This means that any reformulation does not lose inferential power at the time that it is being performed, but may make inferences with future additions to the theory impossible. Operators (2) and (3) ensure that KRT's reformulation process will produce only rules that meet our postulate (1), since each of them does not remove any existing premises, and only adds one new premise. This does not exhaust the space of rules possible under postulate (1) (rules which require existential variables, variable instantiations, or several new premises are not considered), but rather comprises a heuristic selection of possible specializations to consider. If desired, any complete specialization operator, such as the one defined by [Shapiro, 1983], could be substituted for operators (1) to (3) without principled problems, albeit at the cost of enlarging the search space of the reformulation step.

As a small point, note that KRT uses the support set representation only to list explicit exceptions, i.e., the GE and LE_i parts of a support set; the domains themselves are not modified by KRT, and usually remain all. The reasons for choosing to add an extra premise instead of including a concept in the support set were uniformity and understandability: since the support set representation only allows unary positive concepts to specify domains, additional premises would have been necessary anyway in all cases where exception concepts or relational concepts are used. Furthermore, users generally find it easier to understand additional premises than complex support sets.

The disadvantage of this strategy is that new metapredicates are often needed to represent the rules that are the result of knowledge revision reformulations. If the new rule does not match any existing metapredicate, a new one will automatically be generated, but this new metapredicate is not integrated into the system's meta-metaknowledge, so the user would ultimately have to add meta-rules to express the properties of the new metapredicate, or its connections to other metapredicates. Supports sets were originally introduced to circumvent this problem by attaching support sets to metafacts as well, thus

Level	*Operators*	*Arguments*
1	$localize(i)$	$foralli : \pi_i(Inst) \cap \pi_i(Exc) = \emptyset$
2	$add\_ei(\{V_i\}, p)$	$foralli : \pi_i(Inst) \cap \pi_i(Exc) = \emptyset,$ all unary p in Γ
	$add\_ee(\{V_i\}, p)$	$foralli : \pi_i(Inst) \cap \pi_i(Exc) = \emptyset,$ all unary p in Γ

Table 4.6   Cost levels of reformulation operators 1 to 3

allowing the original metapredicate to be used[20]. In practice, it has turned out that metarules are used much less frequently than we had envisioned, so uniformity and understandability of KRT results took precedence. In any case, the results of the *localize* operator can still be expressed using the support set only; furthermore, the full support set format can be used for manual input.

4.6.3   Search strategy

The operators (1), (2), and (3) defined in table 4.5 can produce all specializations of a rule that do not involve new existential variables or instantiations of existing variables, i.e., they define a particular search space of possible KRT reformulations. They do not yet prescribe a particular search strategy. Since it would be much too expensive in practice to try all these reformulations, KRT employs a greedy, heuristic strategy that searches the space partially according to a fixed ordering of operators that reflects the costs of executing the operator. This ordering assigns each of the operators a search depth level as summarized in table 4.6[21].

As can be seen in this table, KRT's efforts are kept low on levels (1) and (2) by limiting the search to unary reformulations, and including only those variables for which a "perfect" reformulation can be found, i.e., where the lists of instances and exceptions do not overlap so that in principle, a predicate can be found that includes all instances, and excludes all exceptions.

The progression from one to the next higher search level is governed by a user settable parameter that specifies a default search depth up to which KRT will search. Within the specified search levels, the plausibility criterion introduced

---

[20] As pointed out in [Emde, 1991], using supports sets instead of premises also means that rules which have been revised are easy to find in the knowledge base if this should become necessary.

[21] In chapter 5, this table will be extended to include the concept formation operators.

in section 4.6.1 is used as a filter, i.e., only those reformulations that pass the the plausibility criterion are collected. In this context, the plausibility criterion is applied not to the global instance and exceptions sets, but to their projections on the variable X_i that was chosen as the argument for the reformulation operator. If no satisfactory reformulation was found within the allocated effort, the user is queried whether to proceed.

At the end of the search, KRT applies a heuristic evaluation metric to select one of the reformulations that were found. For m rules $R_1, \ldots, R_m$ to be compared, let

$$S(R_i) = D_{i,1} \times \cdots \times D_{i,n} \setminus GE_i,$$

be the support sets of the reformulated rules, where $D_j = all \setminus LE_{i,j}$ ($i \in \{1, \ldots, m\}, j \in \{1, \ldots, n\}$). The evaluation metric is defined as follows:

$$R_1 \geq_{ref} R_2 \; iff \; \begin{cases} |GE_1| < |GE_2| \\ or \quad |GE_1| = |GE_2| \wedge \Sigma_{j=1\ldots n} LE_{1,j} < \Sigma_{j=1\ldots n} LE_{2,j} \end{cases}$$

i.e., the evaluation metric orders all reformulations according to the number of explicitly remaining exceptions, and prefers those with less exceptions. Among reformulations that are equal according to $\geq_{ref}$, those that use existing concepts are preferred over reformulations with newly formed concepts, and concepts that cover the instances are preferred over those that cover the exceptions of a rule. In any case, the user is given a chance to modify the system's choice, or to specify a reformulation on his or her own.

When the above steps in the reformulation process have led to a plausible support set description, the knowledge revision process can be terminated successfully. Otherwise, the system will query the user for a reformulation, and if none is supplied, delete the rule entirely.

4.7 INTERACTIVE USE OF KRT

The knowledge revision methods described above are fully operational in KRT as a part of MOBAL. Since in a lot of situations, determining the best revision is possible only by taking pragmatic consideration into account, the above operators for minimal revisions and further reformulation are embedded into an interactive program that permits the user to make the final choice on practically all decisions. In the actual implementation, the second revision operator $\hat{+}$ is not used. Instead, the system if necessary adds a fact to the knowledge base, causing a contradiction, which is recorded on MOBAL's agenda of "open ends". The user can then at any point invoke the third operation $\hat{\pm}$, to resolve the inconsistency. If desired, he or she is given a chance to correct the choice made by the function ϕ.

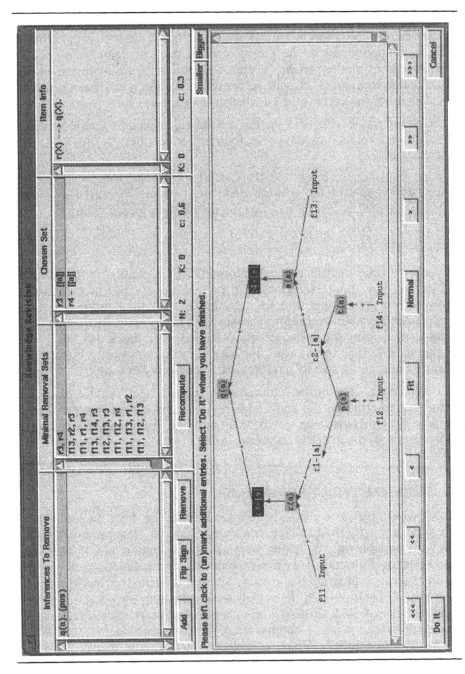

Figure 4.4   Interactive graphical KRT display

The basic revision operator $\dot{-}$ likewise can be called directly by the user by selecting a set of derived facts that is to be removed, or $\dot{-}$ is used in the course of resolving a contradiction with $\dot{\pm}$. In any case, the user is given a graphical display of the choices made by γ, and can thus very simply modify these choices. Figure 4.4 (page 130) shows the KRT panel for user interaction during the selection of a minimal removal set; the example shown is the same as in section 4.5.2. In the top half of the display, the system shows, from left to right,

- the set F of inferences to be removed,

- the set $\overline{\Gamma \downarrow_\Pi F}$ of minimal removal sets (showing only the clauses, and not the substitutions),

- the details of the currently selected minimal removal sets, showing the instance sets instead of the substitutions, and showing the χ and maximal κ values for the set below;

- and details on the currently chosen element of the removal set, including χ and κ.

In the bottom half of the panel, the derivation is presented graphically. The system's preferred revision (according to γ) is marked, but the user can just use the mouse to select other elements for removal. Once the user has committed to a removal set, KRT performs the minimal base revision. When the resulting support set is judged implausible, KRT proceeds to a search of its reformulation space, querying the user after each level whether to proceed. At the very end, after a successful or unsuccessful revision, the user can again choose to leave everything as before, to accept the system's proposal, or to supply a reformulation of his or her own. By setting the appropriate parameter, it is also possible to let KRT run completely non-interactively.

4.8   A SAMPLE APPLICATION IN TELECOMMUNICATIONS

To illustrate the practical use of the concepts and algorithms for knowledge revision described in this chapter, we will now briefly describe the application of MOBAL and KRT to a problem in telecommunications which has been developed in cooperation with Alcatel Alsthom Recherche, Paris, in the *Machine Learning Toolbox* (MLT) ESPRIT project. The problem addressed by this application prototype is the following [Fargier, 1991; Sommer *et al.*,

1994]. A telecommunications network generally consists of a number of regionally distributed switching systems that are responsible for allocating network resources and implementing the connections requested by end users. These switching computers may be installed on the premises of the network provider, or on the premises of customers needing local equipment. They may be owned and operated by the network provider, or owned, rented, and operated in whole or part by customer companies.

In such a complex environment, it is a serious problem to ensure that only personnel authorized to perform a particular class of operations can actually access the switching systems and perform the operations. Currently, this access control task is often addressed by manually established access control lists. These lists, however, are error-prone, and it is impossible to guarantee that a consistent *security policy* is being followed throughout. The goal of the project at Alcatel Alsthom Recherche was to develop an approach for formally specifying, validating, and using an explicit security policy that could replace the above-mentioned manual methods. By using formal methods, a security policy could be proved consistent, and it could be guaranteed that the policy is being followed in all cases. As a language for the expression of security policies, a Horn-clause-like representation was chosen that could easily be represented using MOBAL's facts and rules.

In a first step, background knowledge about the employees, systems, and companies and the manually assigned access permissions were represented as MOBAL facts [Sommer *et al.*, 1994] (see table 4.7 for some exemplary facts).

To see how the knowledge revision capabilities of KRT are used in such an application, consider the following scenario. Given the knowledge base illustrated in table 4.7, assume the security manager has entered two rules that are intended to express the correct access control policy[22]:

> r117: manages(X, Y) & works-in(Z, X) & manager(Z)
> & optype(U, log-create) → may-operate(Z, Y, U).
> r118: manages(X, Y) & works-in(Z, X) & operator(Z)
> & optype(U, status-read) → may-operate(Z, Y, U).

These rules, when applied to the background knowledge about operators, departments, and systems, infer additional access rights for certain employees:

> may-operate(collier,pabxb-17,op1).
> may-operate(fodor,pabxc-32,op1).
> may-operate(goreman,pabxd-44,op1).

---

[22]If desired, such rules can also be learned by letting RDT or some other learning algorithm analyze the manually assigned access rights.

manager(earlich).	has-dept(gross-kg,std).
works-for(earlich,gross-kg).	service_provider(std).
works-in(earlich,std).	manages(std,sabxb-01).
operator(bode).	has-dept(wichtig-co,tod).
works-for(bode,wichtig-co).	not(service_provider(tod)).
works-in(bode,tod).	manages(tod,pabxf-69).
operator(hosanna).	has-dept(winzigco,lilsmorg-dept).
works-for(hosanna,winzigco).	service_provider(lilsmorg-dept).
works-in(hosanna,lilsmorg-dept).	manages(lilsmorg-dept,sabxd-01).
. . .	. . .
sw(sabxb-01).	optype(op8,log-create).
stat(sabxb-01,op).	optype(op1,status-read).
sw(pabxf-69)	. . .
stat(pabxf-69,maintenance).	
sw(sabxd-01).	
stat(sabxd-01,op).	
. . .	
may-operate(earlich,sabxb-01,op8).	
may-operate(hosianna,sabxd-01,op1).	
. . .	

Table 4.7 Example background knowledge and access right facts

may-operate(bode,pabxf-69,op1).
. . .

If all these newly assigned permissions are correct and intended, the security manager working with the system need not do anything else — the system has automatically applied the new access control policy to all employees. If however, some of the assigned permissions are unwanted, or become unwanted after a while due to changes in policy or network structure, a revision of the access control rules is necessary to reflect this. It is at this point, of course, that the services of KRT can be used. In the graphical user interface, the security manager simply selects the incorrect access permissions:

may-operate(fodor,pabxc-32,op1).
may-operate(bode,pabxf-69,op1).

and calls KRT on them. KRT computes the possible minimal revisions necessary to remove these two inferences, and presents the user the corresponding

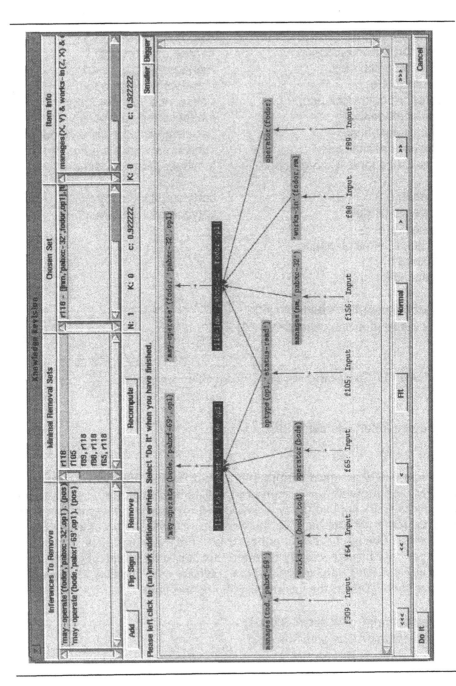

Figure 4.5   Revision interaction panel in telecommunications domain

interaction window (figure 4.5, see section 4.7 for an explanation of the parts of this panel).

This example nicely shows the effect of treating multiple revisions simultaneously: since both incorrect derivations involve the same rule (r118), KRT's heuristic preference criterion focuses immediately on the revision involving this rule. Of course, this choice may also happen to be incorrect in which case the security manager could select other rules or facts for modification. If we assume that indeed r118 is selected, its minimal revision with exception set will be:

manages(X, Y) & works-in(Z, X) & operator(Z) & optype(U, status-read)
$\rightarrow$ may-operate(Z, Y, U) – all $\times$ all $\times$ all $\times$ all
\ {(tod, pabxf-69, bode, op1),(nm, pabxc-32, fodor, op1)}

No recovery rules are added, since r118 had immediately resolved with the facts to be removed.

As described in section 4.6.2, if the user is unsatisfied with an explicit exception list, the reformulation step of KRT can be invoked to search for a more special rule using additional premises instead of the exception list. In this example, it turns out that both the departments tod and nm are not service providers, i.e., applying the operator *add_ei*, KRT then proposes the reformulated rule

manages(X, Y) & works-in(Z, X) & operator(Z) & optype(U, status-read)
& service_provider(X) $\rightarrow$ may-operate(Z, Y, U)

Alternatively, the user could have also let KRT search for a new concept on the other variables — chapter 5 provides a detailed example of a knowledge revision process involving concept formation in the traffic law domain.

4.9 RELATED WORK

The approach presented here is an elaboration of the knowledge revision method used in the knowledge acquisition and machine learning system BLIP, a predecessor of MOBAL. As described in [Wrobel, 1988; Wrobel, 1989], BLIP already used exception sets to produce minimal specializations of individual rules. As in MOBAL, these exception sets were represented as support sets, a simple form of which was first proposed in [Emde *et al.*, 1983]. In other respects, BLIP was seriously lacking in contrast to the method described here that is used by KRT/MOBAL. In particular, the computation of removal sets was incomplete in many cases, and no formal characterization was available. Furthermore, BLIP could not work on multiple revisions at the same time, and could not ensure recovery (postulate 6).

For the presentation of other related work below, we have chosen to begin with three specialization approaches that are closely related to the minimal-base revision approach of KRT. We will then discuss compression measures as alternatives to our current evaluation criteria. After this, we take a slightly more general view, and compare our work to work on logic program debugging and to current theory refinement systems, i.e., systems that handle both specialization and generalization of theories. We conclude with a discussion of the concept of paradigm changes, a philosphically motivated more radical view of theory revision.

4.9.1   Related specialization algorithms

Closed-world specialization

In section 4.3.2, we already discussed the problems of the minimal special-ization hypothesis that was proposed in [Bain and Muggleton, 1992]. In the same paper, the authors also present a specialization algorithm based on the introduction of non-monotonically interpreted premises with new predicates. Thus, for example, if the substitutions $\{\{X/a\}, \{X/b\}\}$ were to be excluded from $p(X) \to q(X)$, the basic CWS algorithm (see table 4.8)

Input: Set of clauses T and ground atom A such that $T \vdash A$ and A incorrect.

■   Let $C = (Body \to Head)$ be the clause in T which resolved with $\bar{A}$ in the SLDNF-resolution proof of $T \vdash A$ using substitution θ.

■   If there is a literal $not(B)$ in $Body$, then let $T' = T \cup \{B\theta\}$.

■   Else let $\{V_1, \ldots, V_n\}$ the domain of θ, and q a predicate symbol not found in T, $B = q(V_1, \ldots, V_n)$. Then

$$T' := T \backslash \{C\} \cup \{(Body \cup not(B)) \to Head\} \cup \{B\theta\}.$$

Output: T'.

Table 4.8   Specialization algorithm of Muggleton and Bain

would produce the theory

$$p(X) \wedge not(c1(X)) \rightarrow q(X)$$
$$c1(a)$$
$$c1(b)$$

where $c1$ is a new predicate, and *not* is interpreted as negation by failure. As can easily be seen, this is a notational variant of the exception set method used to specialize clauses used in BLIP and KRT/MOBAL. The advantage of representing exceptions with a new predicate and using negation by failure is that the standard logic program representation — which includes a negation by failure operator anyway — can be used. On the other hand, this representation might be more difficult to understand for a user since exceptions are not locally represented in the corresponding rule, and a new anonymous predicate is introduced. In KRT, this predicate introduction step is therefore performed only if the concept learning tool CLT can find an intensional characterization of the exceptions (see chapter 5).

The algorithm of [Bain and Muggleton, 1992] actually does not always meet its stated goal of producing maximally general correct specializations. It always selects to modify those clauses that have directly resolved with the fact that is to be removed, and thus ensures condition (2) of corollary 4.1 (page 104), albeit with a considerable loss of flexibility in choosing revisions. Since condition (1) cannot be guaranteed, however, the algorithm incorrectly produces a non-minimal specialization on removal problems where this condition is not met, e.g. in the example given right after corollary 4.1 (page 104).

The exception method of Ling

Our method of using exception lists to specialize individual clauses has also been adopted in the algorithm proposed in [Ling, 1991b]. This paper also introduces the important notion of learning in a growing language: specialization operations should be such that when a new constant is added to the language anything provable about the new constant with the original theory should also be provable from the specialization. As Ling points out, the exception method ensures that this is the case. He also points to an important problem that was also recognized in [Wrobel, 1988; Wrobel, 1989]: if exclusion is used as the only specialization operator on individual clauses, we may build up long exception lists. As we have seen, in KRT, this problem is addressed through the user specified plausibility criterion that defines when further specialization is necessary to get rid of an overly long exception list. KRT then applies a number of specialization operators that specialize further, essentially by introducing new premise literals on existing variables of the clause, where Ling instead uses a *complete* set of refinement operators, i.e., capable of producing all specializations of a clause, and simply replaces a clause by all of its specializations. This guarantees minimal specialization and thus identification in the limit, but brings with it the undesirable properties of minimal specializations as spelled out in section 4.3.2.

Factoring and exceptions vs. unfolding

In their recent work on SPECTRE, Boström and Idestam-Almquist [1994] have proposed a method for specialization that need not rely on exception lists nor on new predicates with negation by failure. Their method works by using unfolding on the original theory. Whenever a negative example is covered, the approach of SPECTRE picks the clause that resolved with the negative example as candidate for revision. In this respect, it thus makes the same assumption as CWS and limits its revision choices to top-level clauses, unlike KRT which considers all clauses in the derivation. If the chosen clause does not cover any positive examples, it is simply deleted. If it does cover positive examples, it is unfolded into different longer clauses until each of the new clauses covers only positive or only negative examples. At this point, all clauses covering only negative examples can then be deleted. SPECTRE thus does not need special representational constructs to represent the revised theory. In non-incremental operation, checking against all positive examples ensures that no interesting inferences are lost. Nonetheless, the revision that is produced is non-minimal, since as soon as unfolding has produced clauses special enough not to cover existing positive examples any more, they are removed. This cuts possible derivations that in an incremental setting might become relevant later on. In contrast, the factoring approach of the MBR operator (which can be seen as a kind of unfolding) unfolds the clause right down to the most specific clause corresponding to the substitution used in the offending derivation, and thus ensures minimality.

4.9.2 Compression measures for revision selection

In a continuation of the work on closed-world specialization, Srinivasan *et. al.* [1994] have augmented the general CWS algorithm described in the preceding section with compression-based evaluation criteria. The basic idea of such criteria is based on results from algorithmic information theory ("Kolmogorov complexity", see [Li and Vitanyi, 1993] for a comprehensive introduction). Roughly speaking, the description complexity of a string is interpreted as the minimal length of a program that when run outputs the string[23]. For a random string, this length is the length of string itself, since no regularities can be exploited. Furthermore, a simple argument [Li and Vitanyi, 1993, Theorem

---

[23]It can be shown that different programming languages change the size of this quantity only by an additive factor.

2.3, p. 96] shows that among all strings of length n, less than $2^{n-c} - 1$ are compressible by more than c bits. Therefore, if the encoding of a learned theory is c bits shorter than the encoding of the examples, there is only a $1/2^c$ probability that the learning result accidentally captures random noise in the examples, so ''shorter'' theories should be preferred by a learner. The quality of this evaluation measure strongly depends on the chosen encoding, and different encodings have been proposed for logical learning systems (e.g. [Muggleton, 1988],[Quinlan, 1990b], [Muggleton and De Raedt, 1994]).

In the context of closed-world specialization, a compression measure was applied as follows [Srinivasan *et al.*, 1994]. In a first step, the CWS algorithm (see table 4.8, page 136) is used to specialize all overly general clauses of the theory (again assuming that incorrect clauses directly resolve with the target predicate). From the set of clauses so obtained, clauses are first evaluated individually and then according to this ranking re-added one-by-one to the theory until the overall compression of the entire theory no longer increases[24]. In an empirical experiment in the KRK chess domain, it turned out that in this fashion, 98% accuracy could be achieved even on data with 40% noise.

In KRT, the problem of selecting revisions is different, so the above strategy cannot be directly applied. First of all, in KRT, we assume that incorrect inferences are made known incrementally, so we cannot evaluate different theories with respect to the entire dataset immediately. Second, the MBR operator treats multi-level theories, and thus as an additional choice point has to consider which clause in a derivation to revise. A compression measure could perhaps be applied to the problem of selecting removal sets, since each possible removal set results in a modified theory that could be evaluated. However, for single revisions, the differences in compression are likely to be small. Furthermore, we would no longer use the additional user knowledge that can be incorporated into the χ and κ functions. As in CWS, applying compression measures in KRT would therefore be most useful when including the clauses found when trying to characterize the exceptions during concept formation (see chapter 5).

4.9.3 Logic program debugging

MIS

Turning to related work from logic programming, we must first mention the early milestone, Shapiro's Model Inference System MIS [Shapiro, 1983].

---

[24][Srinivasan *et al.*, 1994] point out that equivalently this evaluation could be incorporated into the CWS specialization directly.

In MIS, the global property of program incorrectness is reduced to a local property on individual clauses in the program: a clause C is said to be incorrect if there is a goal $Q \notin M$ proved by C, and all subgoals invoked by C are in M. To decide clause incorrectness, we thus somehow need access to M, the intended model. In the case of MIS, the user is relied upon to answer queries about M, and Shapiro develops a query-optimal strategy called *contradiction backtracing* for finding incorrect clauses in the proof tree of an incorrect answer of P.

In terms of our results developed above, MIS thus relies on user queries to select among $\Gamma \downarrow_\Pi f$ by choosing to remove from Γ all clauses found to be incorrect. Since the user provides access to M, there is no need to resort to heuristic confidence functions such as χ or κ above. The strategy used in MIS would thus be an alternative to the graphical presentation of derivations that is currently used in KRT in interactive operation. The querying strategy of MIS is also used in the interactive learning programs MARVIN [Sammut and Banerji, 1986] and CLINT [DeRaedt, 1991] to recover from overgeneralizations that lead to incorrectly covered negative examples.

Since MIS and the above-cited systems entirely remove the chosen clauses, they typically remove more than the incorrect inference from the closure of the program. This contrasts with the strategy implemented in KRT, where the *add* operator inserts minimally modified versions of the removed clauses into the theory, thus avoiding the introduction of unnecessary new incompleteness errors into the theory. In MIS, MARVIN, and CLINT, such errors are introduced, and subsequently handled by the procedures for fixing incompleteness errors.

As an extension, Shapiro also proposes to use the removed clause as the basis for introducing a corrected version, which is searched for among an equivalence class of clauses induced by a set of typical programming error operators, such as misspelled variable, or missing (arithmetic) test. The *add* and reformulation operators we have described above can be seen as a particular instantiation of such operators, since they define a set of clauses to be considered as a replacement for the clause to be removed, along with a particular search strategy for selecting among them.

Inde+

A more recent logic program debugging system is INDE+ by Aben and van Someren [1990]. Like KRT, and unlike MIS, INDE+ does not rely on user queries to choose incorrect clauses in a program. Instead, it uses a heuristic strategy that is an interesting extension of the one we are using in KRT. The basis of the strategy is the same as in KRT, i.e., each clause is assigned a measure of confidence computed as the ratio of successful to unsuccessful applications in all proofs (*indirect empirical evidence*). This corresponds to the definition of χ given above. In addition, clause *types* indicating general confidence levels are used; they correspond to our function κ.

Instead of directly using the confidence in clauses to select what to remove, INDE+ uses the confidence of clauses to compute confidence factors for each path of variable bindings in the proof, where a path of a variable binding includes all previously instantiated variables in the proof. INDE+ then selects the variable path with the lowest total confidence, from this path the variable binding with the lowest confidence, and then considers as incorrect the clause that caused this variable binding. It is not clear from [Aben and van Someren, 1990] in which way this strategy actually differs from directly choosing the least confident clause for modification, but it appears to offer a finer grain, and is used heavily in fixing incompleteness bugs (by changing variable substitutions to complete proofs).

4.9.4 Theory refinement systems

Theory refinement systems, in contrast to revision systems, address both the issue of specializing an incorrect theory and the issue of generalizing an incomplete theory. In this respect, logic program debugging systems, and especially MIS, can be seen as theory refinement systems. Typically, a theory refinement system possesses a number of different operators for specializing and for generalizing individual clauses or the entire theory, and a control strategy that selects which operation to perform at which point. The various systems differ both in their set of operators, their control strategy, and in whether they are incremental or assume all examples to be present at once.

In the simplest scenario, a non-incremental refinement system consists of a learning algorithm that is used to induce an initial theory and a revision component that then modifies this theory. An example of this is KR-FOCL [Pazzani and Brunk, 1991] where FOCL is first used to induce a domain theory, and an interactive component then heuristically proposes revisions to the user based on the way clauses were learned, i.e., in contrast to KRT and most other approaches, revisions are neither triggered by the need to exclude incorrect inferences nor evaluated against examples. In MOBAL, the combination of RDT and KRT can be seen as a non-incremental refinement system, in which RDT (or any of the external learning algorithms available in MOBAL) is used to induce a set of rules which KRT may then revise. In fact, we have used this setting to perform empirical experiments on concept formation (see section 5.4.2).

Typically, however, refinement systems work on an existing theory and delete, add, or change clauses. In the simplest case, the only specialization operator is clause deletion, and the only generalization operator is one that can induce new clauses for uncovered examples. This approach is followed for example in MIS [Shapiro, 1983], MARVIN [Sammut and Banerji, 1986] and CLINT [DeRaedt, 1991]. As pointed out above, these three essentially share the backtracing strategy that leads to the selection of an incorrect clauses and its subsequent retraction. They differ greatly, on the other hand, in their generalization operators (e.g. top down refinement in MIS, bottom-up generalization from a starting clause in CLINT). These systems do not perform minimal specialization, but overspecialize using clause deletion and rely on subsequent generalization to recover.

More recent refinement systems have tried to avoid deleting entire clauses, and so their specialization operators are more closely related to what is done in KRT. In FORTE [Richards and Mooney, to appear], three operators are available for specializing clauses: clause deletion, antecedent addition in the manner of FOIL [Quinlan, 1990b], and relational pathfinding which adds multiple antecedents at once by following argument paths (cf. the LINK algorithm [Sommer, 1994] available as an external tool for MOBAL). As discussed above, all of these operators produce non-minimal revisions since by adding literals, they will usually exclude derivations other than the offending one. In FORTE, which is a non-incremental system, this problem is handled by checking each revision on the positive examples. If a specialized clause stops covering some positive examples, it is kept, but the system looks for additional alternate specializations until the resulting set covers all known positive examples. The specialization operators of FORTE thus are related to the non-minimal reformulation phase of KRT, which uses a simpler specialization operator (addition of single new literals), but in contrast to FORTE introduces new concepts when required.

Several other refinement systems with a relatively similar general structure have been proposed recently, but none of them has devoted particular attention to the specialization step, relying instead on non-minimal specialization by adding antecedents or deleting clauses. AUDREY [Wogulis, 1991] recovers from overspecializations with an abductive method. APT [Nedellec and Causse, 1992] is a refinement system with an interactive specialization algorithm under user control. WHY [Saitta *et al.*, 1993] is a multistrategy learning system including a revision component specialized towards diagnostic problem solving. RUTH [Ade *et al.*, 1993] is a refinement system that can handle not only simple examples, but also entire clauses that are treated as integrity constraints; it also performs non-minimal specializations.

4.9.5 Revision as paradigm changes

Finally, returning to a more general perspective, let us briefly describe Emde's arguments for radical revisions called *paradigm changes*. In a position similar to ours in section 4.3 above, Emde [Emde, 1991] has argued that in many situations, non-minimal changes to a theory are desirable or even necessary to allow learning to proceed. Whereas we have argued based on the difficult and unnatural properties of closed theories, Emde uses arguments from the philosophy of science, and in particular, the models of Kuhn [Kuhn, 1962] to support a similar conclusion. According to [Emde, 1991], a simple kind of "paradigm change" can be modeled by the revision of statements in a knowledge base that were held unchangeable before. As pointed out by Nebel [Nebel, 1989], and further supported by arguments from Quine [Quine, 1964] about analytic and synthetic statements, this means changing the importance or confidence of statements in our knowledge, and can thus be modeled in KRT by allowing changes in the assigned values of the χ and κ functions. In a similar fashion, Emde defines a *non-conservative* knowledge revision as any revision that causes the loss of a proposition that was marked as "relevant" by an (unspecified) relevance function.

The main point of [Emde, 1991] is the observation that an incremental learning system cannot rely only on specializing operations for theory revision, but must at some point also consider introducing totally new statements into the theory. This means that, as in a theory refinement system, the knowledge revision methods realized in KRT should always be combined with a generalization component (such as RDT) in a learning system. In Emde's framework, additional flexibility is gained by allowing the learning system to treat new inputs as "errors", permitting it to leave the theory inconsistent with these inputs for the moment, and reconsider them at a later stage in a global restructuring of the theory. The framework proposed in [Emde, 1991] is thus more general than the one examined here, but in turn had to leave open some of the details of how such revisions could actually be implemented. With $\hat{-}$, we now have a precisely defined minimal base revision operator, so it is now an interesting topic for future research to try and define the more general revision operations on the basis of this operator.

4.10 SUMMARY

In the course of our discussion of concept formation, the goal of this chapter was to describe the problem solving context in which the concept formation activities of CLT take place in MOBAL. To this end, we saw that problem solving in MOBAL generally consists of a process of goal-directed inference, in contrast to the operator-based search paradigms that are also frequently used to capture problem solving.

The rest of the chapter was then devoted to a more specific problem solving context that arises within MOBAL, namely the knowledge revision activities of the system. As we saw, knowledge revision is the task of repairing a knowledge base when it produces unwanted derivations, and is a necessary part of an incremental knowledge acquisition and learning system. Assuming that the revisions that are performed to remove an unwanted inference should be minimal in some sense, we evaluated different notions of minimality, and finally proposed a set of postulates for minimal base revision based on previous work on closed theory contraction. Along the way, we showed that interpreting minimal revision as minimal specialization, as is sometimes done in Machine Learning, is not appropriate.

We then defined a revision operator $\hat{-}$, and showed that it meets the minimal base revision postulates, and is the maximally general operator with this property. To choose among the possible revisions proposed by this operator, we have presented a two-tiered confidence model based on both a continuous and a discrete confidence function. We also showed how the preferred revisions according to this model can be computed from the derivation trace information in the inference engine, and how the basic operator $\hat{-}$ can be extended to multiple simultaneous revisions.

The last part of the chapter was then devoted to the issue of specializing beyond the results of $\hat{-}$, which we realized was necessary to prevent implausibly long exception lists that could be produced by $\hat{-}$. We defined a set of reformulation operators and a search strategy to carry out this specialization process. Finally, we briefly explained how the above results have been incorporated into KRT, a fully operational knowledge revision tool that can be used both autonomously and interactively.

In the next chapter, we will build on what we have discussed here, and show how a concept formation process can exploit the context of KRT to focus concept formation.

5

DEMAND-DRIVEN CONCEPT FORMATION

5.1 INTRODUCTION

With the discussion of KRT knowledge revision in the preceding chapter, we have finally assembled the three pillars upon which our model of computational concept formation is to be built:

- In chapter 2, we have discussed a number of psychological results as hints to the requirements for concept representation, and the possible mechanisms for concept formation.

- In chapter 3, we developed a logical representation language that meets most of the psychological requirements on concept representation, and showed that it has a well-defined semantics and is tractable.

- In chapter 4 finally, we discussed MOBAL's knowledge revision activities, which are to provide the context for concept formation.

In order to put all this together, recall from our discussions in chapter 1 that concept formation can be seen as a three step process of *aggregation*, *characterization*, and *utilization* [Easterlin and Langley, 1985]: aggregation means deciding which objects to group together to form the extension of a concept, characterization means finding an intensional definition for the so-chosen aggregate, and utilization means introducing the new concept into the representation. As we already discussed, the most problematic step in this process is aggregation, because in a set of n objects, 2^n possible aggregates can be formed, so that strong constraints are needed. Based on results from psychology, in chapter 2 we have identified the goals of the learning system, or rather the *context* in which concept formation takes place, as a very powerful constraint to be used as the basis for our computational model.

145

In this chapter, we will explore the practical and theoretical consequences of taking up this suggestion from psychology, and show how the context defined by the knowledge revision activities of the learning system can be used to constrain the aggregation step of concept formation, and how these aggregates are then characterized and used. In section 5.2, we define precisely how the knowledge revision module KRT can trigger and supply the aggregates for concept formation, and discuss how this relates to the psychological results about human concept formation. In section 5.3, we then describe CLT, the *concept learning tool* of MOBAL that implements the characterization, evaluation and utilization steps of concept formation. In particular, we will discuss how RDT, the first-order learning system incorporated into the MOBAL system, can be used to produce an intensional definition of a proposed aggregate (5.3.1), how new concepts are evaluated (5.3.2), and how they are used to restructure the knowledge base (5.3.3). After a detailed example (5.3.4), we proceed to a theoretical and empirical evaluation of the properties of our approach (section 5.4), and conclude with a discussion of related work (section 5.5) and a summary (section 5.6).

5.2 AGGREGATION BASED ON INSTANCES AND EXCEPTIONS

From the discussion of psychological results in chapter 2, the two central points about goal-driven concept formation are worth recalling here. The first, mentioned by Wygotski [Wygotski, 1964], and taken up in the models of Nelson [Nelson, 1983] and Barsalou [Barsalou, 1983], was that concepts are formed in response to a particular need, or demand, that requires the aggregation and common naming of a set of objects. The second, taken from the models of Nelson and Barsalou, was that concept formation consists of aggregating together a set of objects that occur in the same context in an event, or in Barsalou's words, that are "instrumental to achieving goal X".

If phrased this way, it is quite obvious how the activities of the knowledge revision tool KRT can give rise to aggregates for concept formation. One part of the task of KRT is to reformulate rules that have become implausible, and this is done by applying one of three reformulation operators. Two of these operators need an appropriate concept in the available representation to succeed, namely a concept that covers the instances of the offending rule and excludes the exceptions, or vice versa. If such a concept is not available, the reformulation goal cannot be met. Thus, it is here that a concept formation activity can be triggered by a precisely identified need for a new concept in the system.

Furthermore, this situation also identifies quite clearly what the extension of the new concept is to be, since the instances and exceptions of the rule have already been collected. If we stretch the notion of context a little bit, and regard problem solving as a rule-based inference process as described in the preceding chapter, it is quite reasonable to interpret individual rules as the common context in which objects may occur. The instances of a rule, then, are exactly those objects that can be used in this context to reach the goal of a successful inference, whereas the exceptions need to be avoided. Thus, in a remote sense, this way of triggering concept formation indeed takes up the psychological hints about human concept formation. Nonetheless, we should emphasize that due to the restricted interpretation of problem solving that underlies our computational system, this correspondence most likely is no more than an analogy; so let us now turn to the technical description of the process.

In order to have KRT trigger a concept formation attempt, all we need to do is to define two new reformulation operators that use new concepts instead of existing ones, and then incorporate these operators in KRT's reformulation search strategy after the existing operators. Table 5.1 defines the new operators; they differ from KRT's add_ei and add_ee operators only in that instead of using an existing concept they call CLT, the *concept formation tool* of MOBAL to be described below. In the definition of the operators, we have again used the abbreviations $Inst$ and Exc that denote the set of instances and exceptions of the rule (defined in section 4.6.2). Finally, table 5.2 shows the new search strategy of KRT for reformulation, now including the new CLT operators. During interactive use, the user can of course request to be queried before each individual application of the add_ni or add_ne operators, i.e., before each call to CLT. This is especially necessary for search on level 5 where all combinations of variables would otherwise be searched.

5.3 CHARACTERIZATION AND EVALUATION OF CONCEPTS IN CLT

Once the aggregation step of concept formation has been performed, the second step, characterization, is very similar to the task of concept learning from examples, and as we will see, it can be performed by suitable use of a learning from examples algorithm. Nonetheless, there are a number of differences to concept learning from examples that we will also need to address. First, the instances and exceptions that are given by the aggregation step are the extension of a *proposed* concept only, so that after concept characterization has been completed, it is necessary to assess the quality of the

(4) $add\_ni(V')$: Add newly formed predicate (instances).
$V' = [X_{i_1}, \ldots, X_{i_k}]$ is a sequence of elements of $vars(R)$. Call CLT to form a new concept c of arity k, specifying $\pi_{i_1,\ldots,i_k}(Inst)$) as instances and $\pi_{i_1,\ldots,i_k}(Exc)$ as non-instances. If CLT successfully forms a concept c (producing a knowledge base Γ') such that $\forall t \in \pi_{i_1,\ldots,i_k}(Inst) : c(t) \in \Gamma'$, add the additional premise $c(X_{i_1}, \ldots, X_{i_k})$ to R, and in $S(R)$, replace GE by $\{t \in Exc \mid c(\pi_{i_1,\ldots,i_k}(t)) \in \Gamma'\}$. If $V' = \{X_j\}$, replace LE_j by $\{s \in LE_j \mid c(s) \in \Gamma\}$.

(5) $add\_ne(V')$: Add newly formed predicate (exceptions).
$V' = [X_{i_1}, \ldots, X_{i_k}]$ is a sequence of elements of $vars(R)$. Call CLT to form a new concept c of arity k, specifying $\pi_{i_1,\ldots,i_k}(Exc)$ as instances and $\pi_{i_1,\ldots,i_k}(Inst)$ as non-instances. If CLT successfully forms a concept c (producing a knowledge base Γ') such that $\forall t \in \pi_{i_1,\ldots,i_k}(Inst) : not(c(t)) \in \Gamma'$, add the additional premise $not(c(X_{i_1}, \ldots, X_{i_k}))$ to R, and in $S(R)$, replace GE by $\{t \in Exc \mid not(c(\pi_{i_1,\ldots,i_k}(t))) \in \Gamma'\}$. If $V' = \{X_j\}$, replace LE_j by $\{s \in LE_j \mid not(c(s)) \in \Gamma\}$.

Table 5.1 KRT's reformulation operators using new concepts

Level	Operators	Arguments
1	$localize(i)$	$for\,all\,i : \pi_i(Inst) \cap \pi_i(Exc) = \emptyset$
2	$add\_ei(\{V_i\}, p)$	$for\,all\,i : \pi_i(Inst) \cap \pi_i(Exc) = \emptyset$, all unary p in Γ
	$add\_ee(\{V_i\}, p)$	$for\,all\,i : \pi_i(Inst) \cap \pi_i(Exc) = \emptyset$, all unary p in Γ
3	$add\_ne(\{V_i\})$	$for\,all\,i : \pi_i(Inst) \cap \pi_i(Exc) = \emptyset$
4	$add\_ni(\{V_i\})$	$for\,all\,i : \pi_i(Inst) \cap \pi_i(Exc) = \emptyset$
5	$add\_ni(\{V_i, V_j\})$	$for\,all (V_i, V_j) \in vars(R) \times vars(R), V_i \neq V_j$

Table 5.2 Cost levels of reformulation operators (all operators)

new concept, and decide whether it is to remain in the representation or not. This of course is unnecessary in a learning from examples situation. Second, and just as important, when a new concept is introduced into a representation, it is possible that existing knowledge can be reexpressed in a better form with the new concept, so the concept formation process must include an additional step that checks for this.

5.3.1 Concept characterization

Before describing the evaluation and restructuring steps, however, we will first describe the core of concept formation, the characterization step. The task of this step is to take as input the extension of the proposed concept, and produce an intensional definition for it. Recall from chapter 3 that when we speak of a concept in an $\Re$-theory Γ, we refer to a quadruple (p, Γ, I, E) that consists of the concept's *name*, the *theory* of which it is a part, its *intension*, and its *extension*, where the intension is defined as the set of all rules of Γ in which p occurs, either as a premise or as a conclusion, and the extension is the set of all true facts that have p as a functor and are inferrable from Γ.

Since the goal of the characterization process is to find a description that is as general as possible, the learning task for characterization can be described as follows:

Given: the extension of a proposed new concept named p, represented as a set of positive and negated $\Re$ facts in the current knowledge base Γ;

Find: the set of maximally general $\Re$ rules that can be confirmed in Γ (according to a suitably defined criterion, see below), and contain p as premise or conclusion.

In principle, this learning task can be solved by any algorithm that learns concepts from examples and can work with the representation $\Re$. The search for necessary conditions, i.e., rules that use the new concept as their premise, is a little inefficient however with a data-driven learning program such as FOIL [Quinlan, 1990b]. Such programs are constructed to search for clauses with a specified conclusion, and cannot guarantee that their results will contain the newly formed concept as a premise. If such a program is used for characterization (as was done e.g. in the empirical experiments reported in section 5.4.2), we first need to search rules for all predicates in the knowledge base in order to then filter out the ones that mention the new concept.

In this section, we will present how the additional filtering step can be avoided when the learning algorithm RDT [Kietz and Wrobel, 1992] that is part of the MOBAL system is used for characterization. RDT uses a *model-driven* instead of a data-driven approach, and can be used to efficiently find an intensional characterization for a new concept. Based on [Kietz and Wrobel, 1992], we briefly summarize the inner workings of RDT as they are important for our purposes here.

RDT

RDT is a model-driven learner, i.e., its hypothesis space is defined by an explicit model of the kinds of rules for which it is to search. This model, in fact, is a set of rule schemata, i.e., rules with predicate variables as we have already introduced them as parts of metapredicates. For convenience, we repeat their definition from ch. 3, section 3.3.1:

> If R is a rule (of type t), and RS is obtained by replacing in at least one literal of R the functor predicate with a variable (of type t), then RS is a *rule schema* (of type t). The variables introduced into R to produce RS are called the *predicate variables* of RS.

In our context here, we are looking for domain level rules as the intensional definition of the new concept, so $t = 1^1$.

In chapter 3 (section 3.3), we have already defined the notion of a *substitution* that can instantiate variables of all types. In the context of RDT, we often use a specialized type of substitution called an *instantiation*, and usually denoted by capital greek letters. An instantiation Σ is a finite set of pairs P/p, where P is a predicate variable, and p is a predicate symbol, both of the same arity. The set of all p is called the *range* of Σ. The result of applying an instantiation Σ to a rule schema R (denoted $R\Sigma$) is the expression that is obtained when replacing in RS each predicate variable mentioned in Σ by the corresponding predicate symbol. R is called *predicate ground* if all its predicate variables are instantiated, i.e., R is a rule.

Based on the set of rule models $\mathcal{R}$ provided to RDT, and the set of domain predicates $\mathcal{P}$ in the knowledge base, the hypothesis subspace that is searched by RDT is defined as the set

$$\mathcal{H} = \{R\Sigma | R \in \mathcal{R} \wedge range(\Sigma) \subseteq \mathcal{P} \wedge R\Sigma \; predicate \; ground\}$$

i.e., as the set of all possible predicate ground instantiations of rule models with domain predicates[2].

To make the search of this space efficient, RDT uses *schema subsumption*, a form of θ-subsumption [Buntine, 1988] suitably extended for clauses with pred-

---

[1] In fact, within MOBAL, the use of RDT on higher levels is currently not supported.

[2] Further restrictions of the hypothesis space are defined by the predicate topology, see [Kietz and Wrobel, 1992]

with predicate variables. More precisely, a rule schema R (in clausal form) *rule-schema subsumes* another rule schema R' ($R \geq_{RS} R'$) iff there is an instantiation Σ that does not unify different predicate variables, and a substitution σ (which does not replace any predicate variables), such that

$$R\sigma\Sigma \subseteq R'.$$

Using the $\geq_{RS}$ relation, RDT precomputes a *generalization lattice* among the rule schemata that are given to it. Since $\geq_{RS}$ can compare only rule schemata with matching conclusions, i.e., having the same conclusion arity, there are usually lattices for unary, binary, etc. conclusion predicates. Based on the so-defined generalization lattice, RDT performs a general-to-specific breadth-first search by taking the maximally general rule schema whose conclusion matches the target predicate, instantiating its predicate variables in all possible ways, and testing the resulting hypotheses. If a hypothesis H derived from a rule schema R with instantiation Σ ($H = R\Sigma$) is too general, it is specialized by retrieving the most general specialization R' of R from the (precomputed) lattice, and then further instantiating $H' = R'\Sigma$ in all possible ways. If a hypothesis is accepted or already too special, search in this branch of the lattice is pruned. A user-settable *confirmation criterion* is used to decide which rules are considered accepted resp. too general or too special; this allows RDT to be used also in noisy domains. The details of the search process are described in [Kietz and Wrobel, 1992].

RDT is called by providing to it the desired conclusion predicate of the rules to be learned, and guarantees to find all maximally general rules that are instances of rule schemata and meet the user-specified acceptance criterion.

Using RDT for characterization

Just as with a data-driven learner, the search for sufficient conditions, i.e., rules that contain the new concept as their conclusion, is immediately possible with RDT. Given the new concept as the target predicate, RDT can match into the generalization lattice of rule schemata with the appropriate conclusion arity, and then descend into this lattice with its breadth-first search. For necessary conditions and other uses of the concept, this is not directly possible. Since the generalization lattices are organized by their conclusions, first of all we need to call RDT several times, using each predicate in the knowledge base as the target (conclusion) predicate. This alone however, would not guarantee that the rules that are found indeed use the concept to be characterized.

We therefore need to perform an additional step that is made possible by RDT's use of explicit rule models: we can instantiate the existing rule models with the name of the concept to be characterized, thus ensuring that no matter what the conclusion predicate is, the learned rules will indeed be defining conditions for the concept. Performing this instantiation process can be done as follows. Let again $\mathcal{R}$ be the set of all rule schemata available to RDT, and c the concept to be characterized (of arity a). For a rule schema $R \in \mathcal{R}$, where

$$R = L_1 \& \cdots \& L_n \rightarrow L_{n+1},$$

define the set

$$R^{c,a} := \begin{cases} \{R\} & iff\ R\ contains\ c \\ \{R\Sigma | i \in \{1, \ldots, n\}, L_i = P(A_1, \ldots, A_a), \\ \quad \Sigma = \{P/c\}, \not\exists \Sigma_1, j < i : L_j \Sigma_1 = L_i\} & otherwise \end{cases}$$

In other words, each rule schema in $\mathcal{R}$ induces zero or more rule schemata in which at least one premise predicate is c. For example, if a unary concept c is to be characterized, the rule schema

P(X) & Q(X) & R(Y) → S(X,Y)

gives rise to

c(X) & Q(X) & R(Y) → S(X,Y) and P(X) & Q(X) & c(Y) → S(X,Y).

The condition at the end is necessary to avoid redundancy. If it were removed, in the above example, we would also generate the rule schema

P(X) & c(X) & R(Y) → S(X,Y),

which is equivalent to the first one given above[3]. We can then define the rule schema set to be used for necessary condition search as follows:

$$\mathcal{R}^{c,a} := \bigcup_{R \in \mathcal{R}} R^{c,a}.$$

This model indeed will guarantee that all the required rules about the new concept are found.

Lemma 5.1 *If $\mathcal{R}$ is a set of rule schemata, and H the set of hypotheses returned by RDT when using $\mathcal{R}$ as the model on a target predicate c of arity a, then RDT will return exactly the subset of H that corresponds to necessary conditions or uses (see Def. 3.3, p. 50) of c when used with $\mathcal{R}^{c,a}$.*

---

[3] Actually, this equivalence would be detected when the generalization lattice is computed based on $\geq_{RS}$ (see below), but this would be less efficient.

Without proof.

An interesting question is of course whether the generalization lattice for $\mathcal{R}_c$ can be computed from the one for $\mathcal{R}$. After all, we know that

$$R \geq_{RS} R' \; for all \, R' \in R^{c,a}.$$

Unfortunately, we find that the generalization relationship between two rule schemata is not preserved:

$$R_1 \geq_{RS} R_2 \not\rightarrow R'_1 \geq_{RS} R'_2 \; for all \, R'_1 \in R_1^{c,a}, R'_2 \in R_2^{c,a},$$

as the following example shows:

$R_1 = P(X) \rightarrow Q(X), R'_1 = c(X) \rightarrow Q(X) \in R_1^{c,1}$
$R_2 = P(X) \& \, Q(X,Y) \& \, R(Y) \rightarrow S(X)$
$R'_2 = P(X) \& \, Q(X,Y) \& \, c(Y) \rightarrow S(X) \in R_2^{c,1}.$

Clearly, $R_1 \geq_{RS} R_2$, but $R'_1 \not\geq_{RS} R'_2$. The converse is not correct, either:

$$R'_1 \geq_{RS} R'_2 \not\rightarrow R_1 \geq_{RS} R_2 \; for all \, R'_1 \in R_1^{c,a}, R'_2 \in R_2^{c,a},$$

as the following example shows:

$R_1 = c(X) \rightarrow Q(X), R'_1 = c(X) \rightarrow Q(X) \in R_1^{c,1}$
$R_2 = P(X) \& \, Q(X,Y) \& \, R(Y) \rightarrow S(X)$
$R'_2 = c(X) \& \, Q(X,Y) \& \, R(Y) \rightarrow S(X) \in R_2^{c,1}.$

Here, clearly $R'_1 \geq_{RS} R'_2$, but $R_1 \not\geq_{RS} R_2$. This means that the generalization lattice needs to be recomputed. Fortunately, by using Prolog variable sharing in storing the generalization lattice for characterization, the lattice does not need to be recomputed for different new concept names; the characterization process thus simply needs to use the pre-stored lattice just like any regular call to RDT[4]. Table 5.3 summarizes the steps of the characterization process that were described above[5].

5.3.2 Evaluating new concepts

Clearly, not every aggregate proposed by KRT as the basis of a new concept will turn out to be actually useful. Thus, if we indiscriminately introduce

---

[4] Care must be taken, however, to avoid overinstantiating rule schemata that literally contain the target concept.

[5] This way of using RDT for CLT characterization was designed by J.U. Kietz, K. Morik, and the author, and implemented by J.U. Kietz, see the acknowledgments.

---

characterize(Instances,Exceptions,c,Intension)
    invent a new concept name c
    $\forall i \in$ Instances
        add $c(i)$ to Γ
    $\forall e \in$ Exceptions
        add $not(c(e))$ to Γ
    call rdt(c) using $\mathcal{R}$ as the model
    compute $\mathcal{R}^{c,a}$ if necessary
    $\forall p \in \mathcal{P}, p \neq c$
        call rdt(p) using $\mathcal{R}^{c,a}$ as the model
    return the rules found in all calls of RDT as Intension

Table 5.3   Characterization steps in CLT

new concepts, we will increase the size of the representation, and thus the complexity of reasoning and learning, without obtaining a comparable benefit from the new concept. We therefore need some way of evaluating new concepts to decide whether we actually want to keep them. A simple solution to this question is of course to rely on an *oracle*, i.e., to query the user for approval of a proposed new concept. Since KRT and CLT are designed for interactive use in MOBAL, this is a natural choice. The user can decide whether to entirely remove the new concept, keep only its extensional definition (the membership facts), or keep facts and learned rules. Keeping the facts only can be useful if the concept itself is meaningful in the domain, but the found characterization is incorrect, e.g. because the knowledge base is still incomplete. In any case, the user can replace the system-chosen "gensym" name with a more appropriate domain-specific term. To help the user make these choices, the system presents the current list of members and non-members of the concept.

Nonetheless, KRT and CLT are also intended to be used as stand-alone learning modules, so they do need their own internal evaluation criteria. In interactive use, these criteria can be used to provide an initial recommendation that the user can override; in non-interactive use, they are relied upon completely. What, then, are desirable properties of new concepts? How should they affect the existing theory or representation? By definition of the *add_ni* and *add_ne* operators of KRT, new concepts produced by CLT will always be useful for rule reformulation, so this cannot be a distinguishing property. Furthermore, if CLT is used in a different context, e.g., to characterize a user-supplied aggregate, we need a criterion that is independent of KRT.

We have theoretically and empirically examined three different, and progressively weaker, evaluation criteria defined as follows[6]:

Strict criterion Accept c iff $|SC(c)| \geq 2$, and $(|NC(c)| \geq 2$ or $|U(c)| \geq 1)$.

Default criterion Accept c iff $|SC(c)| \geq 1$, and $(|SC(c)| + |NC(c)| + |U(c)| \geq 2)$.

Null Accept c in any case.

Here, SC, NC, and U denote sufficient, necessary, and use conditions of a concept as defined in section 3.2. The first two criteria are motivated by general desirable properties of useful concepts, namely that they be *recognizable*, i.e., have sufficient conditions, and that they be *predictive*, i.e., have necessary conditions or uses. Since our concept representation does not rely on probabilistic correlations, these requirements are implemented as lower bounds on the number of sufficient conditions and uses of the concept. The strict criterion, as we will see in section 5.4, is very strong and results in the introduction of very few concepts, but has interesting theoretical properties with respect to knowledge base structure. The default criterion is less strict, but still requires sufficient and necessary conditions. In our experiment, it turned out to be still strong enough to guarantee that new concepts improve the accuracy of the learning system. The third approach, i.e., introducing a new concept for every specialization (used in the early versions of closed-world specialization [Bain and Muggleton, 1992]) constituted the "control condition" in the empirical experiment of section 5.4.

Note that whereas the aggregation constraint used by CLT is derived from the knowledge revision context, the above evaluation criteria are structural constraints in the classification given at the beginning of the paper. Indeed, the use of contextual constraints to trigger concept formation is orthogonal to the use of other constraints which can be used to judge the concepts so proposed. Also, since an additional inductive step is involved to find the rules upon which the criteria are based, these criteria indeed are an additional strong constraint.

In section 5.4, we will have an opportunity to discuss in more depth the properties of our three criteria, and to present empirical results about their effects on classification accuracy. We will also discuss some other possible practical and theoretical evaluation criteria that could be used to judge proposed concepts. First, however, we will discuss how concept quality is maintained over time, and how accepted concepts are used for restructuring.

---

[6] Before these criteria are applied, CLT also checks whether the new concept has turned out to be a synonym of an existing concept.

Concept garbage collection Since the knowledge base may change after the introduction of a concept, it is not guaranteed that the above evaluation criteria will continue to hold if e.g. a rule in which a concept was used is deleted. To ensure that concepts that have turned out useless are removed from the knowledge base, CLT verifies after each rule modification or deletion whether the evaluation criteria for a CLT-introduced concept are negatively affected, and removes the concept if this is the case. This process is also referred to as *concept garbage collection*. As a final point, the user is of course free to select different evaluation criteria, and can decide whether or not to have the system monitor these criteria over time with the concept garbage collector.

5.3.3   Using new concepts for restructuring

Introducing a new concept may allow further simplifications in a knowledge base in all those cases where parts of the new concept occur in existing rules. First of all, there may be rules which simply become redundant after the introduction of the new concept, because they can be derived from the rules that define the concept. For example, if we had just introduced a concept c defined by

$$p(X) \& q(X) \rightarrow c(X), c(X) \rightarrow r(X)$$

and the knowledge base contained the rule

$$p(X) \& q(X) \rightarrow r(X),$$

we could simply remove this rule without any loss[7]. For more complex new concepts, the savings obtained with this simple operation can be significant (see the example in section 5.3.4). Given the definition of a new concept, the check for redundant rules is easy to perform by deriving via resolution all rules implied by the concept rules found during characterization, and then removing all existing rules that are θ-subsumed by any of those resolvents. The collection of procedures for doing this is also referred to as the *rule set restructuring tool*, or RRT.

More precisely, let $SC(c, \Gamma)$ be the set of all rules in Γ where c occurs in the head, and $NC(c, \Gamma)$ be the set of all rules in Γ where c occurs in the body (both were defined in section 3.2). If

$$R(c, \Gamma) := \{R | \exists R_1 \in SC(c, \Gamma), R_2 \in NC(c, \Gamma) : R = resolvent_{\{c\}}(R_1, R_2)\}$$

---

[7]Without any loss in inferential power, that is. There might be a loss of efficiency because the "compiled" one-step rule may execute faster than the two rules that replace it. Due to the cost of indexing, however, the overall effect of removing a compiled rule could also be a speedup. This is known as the utility-problem of explanation-based learning [Minton, 1990].

then the restructuring operation can be defined as follows.

Definition 5.1 (Redundancy removal) *Given a concept c in a knowledge base* Γ, *rule set restructuring produces the knowledge base*

$$redr(c, \Gamma) := \Gamma \setminus \{R | \exists \theta, R' \in R(c, \Gamma) \wedge R'\theta \subseteq R\}.$$

Beyond the above deductive restructuring operation, which is guaranteed not to change the closure of the theory[8], further changes are possible by also looking for occurrences of parts of the new concept's definition in other rules, and replacing these with a reference to the new concept. For example, if the original knowledge base had contained the rules

p(X) & q(X) & m(X) → s(X),p(X) & q(X) & n(X) → s(X),

these could be simplified to

c(X) & m(X) → s(X),c(X) & n(X) → s(X).

Such a construction may be familiar to the reader from work on inverting resolution, where it is referred to as *absorption* [Muggleton, 1987]. Absorption is a safe operation as long as the new concept is not disjunctive. If another clause

k(X) → c(X)

were added to the definition of c, the above absorption transformation would actually be a generalization, unless of course

k(X) & m(X) → s(X),k(X) & n(X) → s(X)

had been in the knowledge base as well. In RRT, we therefore use the results of the absorption operator as hypotheses which are then either checked against the knowledge base by RDT, or need to be confirmed by the user. The precise definition of the absorption operator is the following.

Definition 5.2 (Absorption) *Let* $SC(c, \Gamma)$ *denote the set of all rules in* Γ *where c occurs in the head and let* $R = P \rightarrow C$ *be a rule in* $SC(c, \Gamma)$, *and* $R' = P' \rightarrow C'$ *be a rule in* $\Gamma \setminus SC(c, \Gamma)$, *where P and P' denote the resp. sets of premises. If there exists a substitution* θ *so that*

$$P\theta \subseteq P',$$

---

[8]This is true only if inference depth limits are not used or set high enough.

then let $P'' := P' \setminus P\theta$, and define the result of the absorption operation as:

$$absrp(R, R') := \left\{ \begin{array}{ll} C\theta \ \& \ P'' \rightarrow C' & if \ C\theta \notin P'' \\ P'' \rightarrow C' & if \ C\theta \in P'' \end{array} \right.$$

Table 5.4 summarizes the rule set restructuring steps.   Interestingly, the

---

rrt(Γ,c,Γ')
   Let $\Lambda := redm(c, \Gamma)$
   For all $R \in SC(c, \Lambda)$ and $R' \in \Lambda \setminus SC(c, \Lambda)$
       if $T := absrp(R, R')$ is defined
          and T can be verified in Λ by RDT
            or T is confirmed by the user
      then
         remove R' from Λ
         add T to Λ unless $\exists T' \in \Lambda : T' \geq_\theta T$.
   return the resulting knowledge base Γ'.

Table 5.4   RRT restructuring steps

overall effect of introducing a new concept and then restructuring the rule set can be similar to the *intra-construction* and *inter-construction* operators of inverse resolution [Muggleton, 1987]. The example given above is an instance of an inter-construction effect. Similarly, if in the above knowledge base, we introduced a new concept d defined by

    m(X) → d(X), n(X) → d(X),

RRT could further simplify the knowledge base, resulting in

    c(X) & d(X) → s(X),

which corresponds to *intra-construction*. The difference between the cited inverse resolution operators, and the restructuring operation used here, is therefore the direction of the operation. Whereas the inverse resolution operators introduce new concepts to capture structural/syntactical commonalities in clauses of the knowledge base, our concept formation approach introduces new concepts based on their problem-solving context, and then *uses* them to perform restructurings that are similar in effect to the inverse resolution operators.

This completes the description of the operations of CLT; table 5.5 summarizes all steps that are performed.

---

clt(Instances,Exceptions,c)
    characterize(Instances,Exceptions,c,Intension)
    evaluate(Intension) (using built-in criterion or user query)
        if positive
            keep c
            restructure Γ with c
        if negative
            remove c from Γ
            fail.

Table 5.5   CLT operation steps

5.3.4   An example

To illustrate the above description of CLT's operation, we now give an example of a concept that was introduced in a knowledge base about traffic violations and their legal implications ("traffic law"). The domain represents the kind of knowledge you might need to take your driver's license test, i.e., knowledge about where to park and where not to park, knowledge about speed limits, traffic safety, traffic violations, fines, etc. In this example, we added descriptions of various traffic violation cases committed by members of the KIT group. After a while, the system had learned the following set of rules Γ_0 in addition to its background knowledge rules:

involved_vehicle(X,Y) & eco_expired(Y) → not(tvr_points_p(X))
involved_vehicle(X,Y) & lights_necessary(X) & not(headlights_on(X,Y))
                                → not(tvr_points_p(X))
parking_violation(X) → not(tvr_points_p(X))

parking_violation(X) & appeals(Y,X) → court_citation(Y)
unsafe_vehicle_violation(X) & appeals(Y,X) → court_citation(Y)

involved_vehicle(X,Y) & owner(Z,Y) → responsible(Z,X)

The above rules (figure 5.1 shows a graphical representation) are correct in our example domain, but overly special, except for the last one which is too general: the owner of a car is responsible regardless of who drove the

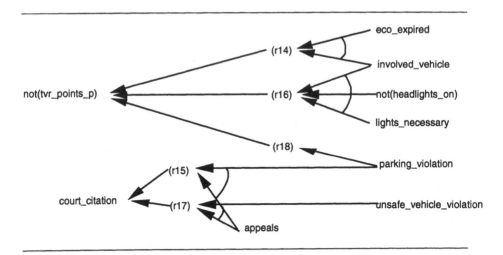

Figure 5.1   Rule set before introduction of minor_violation

car only for minor violations (like false parking); otherwise, the driver is responsible. During knowledge acquisition, we had first focused on parking violations, which are minor violations. Upon entering cases where the driver was responsible, KRT first reduces the support set of the above rule, which becomes:

$$(X, Y, Z) \in \text{all} \times \text{all} \times \text{all} \setminus \{(\text{cab\_event,cab1,ace\_cab\_co}),$$
$$(\text{loan\_event,b\_xs\_400,sw}),(\text{stolen\_event, b\_dx\_986, john})\}$$

After unsuccessfully searching for applications of reformulation operators (1), (2) and (3), KRT then tries to form a new concept (a unary one at first) to add to the rule. In the example,

$Inst = \{$ (event1,b_au_6773,sw),   (event2,b_dx_1385,dj),
           (event3,hh_mo_195,mo),   (event4,b_md_4321,md),
           (event5,b_st_888,st),   (event6,b_ab_89,ab),
           (event7,b_bc_90,bc),   (event8,b_cd_01,cd),
           (event9,b_de_12,de),   (event10,b_ef_23,ef),
           (event11,b_fg_34,fg),   (event12,b_gh_45,ef) $\}$

$Exc = \{$ (cab_event,cab1,ace_cab_co),   (loan_event,b_xs_400,sw),
           (stolen_event,b_dx_986,dx) $\}$.

and therefore, $\pi_3(Inst) \cap \pi_3(Exc) \neq \emptyset$. Concept formation is thus attempted only on variables X and Y. For variable X, *CLT* invents a new name $c1$ and enters the facts corresponding to $\pi_1(Inst)$ and $\pi_1(Exc)$:

```
c1(event1)
c1(event2)
c1(event3) ...
not(c1(tv_event))
not(c1(loan_event)). . .
```

RDT then found the following characterization for $c1$:

$$
\left.
\begin{aligned}
&\text{parking\_violation(X)} \rightarrow \text{c1(X)} \\
&\text{involved\_vehicle(X,Y) \& eco\_expired(Y)} \rightarrow \text{c1(X)} \\
&\text{involved\_vehicle(X,Y) \& lights\_necessary(X)} \\
&\qquad\qquad \text{\& not(headlights\_on(X,Y))} \rightarrow \text{c1(X)} \\
&\text{unsafe\_vehicle\_violation(X)} \rightarrow \text{c1(X)}
\end{aligned}
\right\} SC(c1, \Gamma)
$$

$$
\left.
\begin{aligned}
&\text{c1(X)} \rightarrow \text{not(tvr\_points\_p(X))} \\
&\text{c1(X) \& appeals(Y,X)} \rightarrow \text{court\_citation(Y)}
\end{aligned}
\right\} NC(c1, \Gamma)
$$

Since $|SC(c1, \Gamma)| \geq 2$ and $|NC(c1, \Gamma)| \geq 2$, the evaluation criterion is met, and the concept is renamed by the user to minor_violation, and used to simplify the rule set. As it turns out, all rules in Γ_0 are now θ-subsumed by rules derivable from $SC(c1, \Gamma)$ and $NC(c1, \Gamma)$, so they are removed. Figure 5.2 shows the resulting improvement in rule set structure obtained by introducing the concept minor_violation.

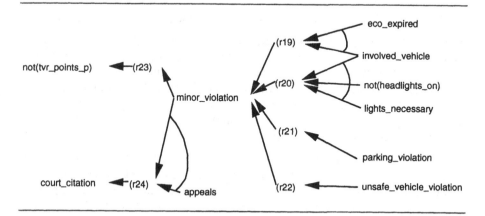

Figure 5.2   Rule set after introduction of minor_violation

5.4 EVALUATION

The demand-driven concept formation process implemented by KRT and CLT can be regarded from a number of different perspectives: as a computational model of concept formation inspired by psychological results about human concept formation, as an algorithm that presents a solution to the representation adjustment problem of machine learning, and as a set of interactive tools to aid the process of knowledge base construction. Consequently, an evaluation of the approach can also be performed along these three dimensions. In section 2.5 of chapter 2 and section 5.2 above, we have already identified where our model takes up the points suggested by psychological research. In this section, we will therefore concentrate on the other two aspects of our model, namely as an interactive tool for knowledge base construction, and as an algorithm that addresses the representation adjustment problem[9].

We begin with an evaluation of the computational properties of the method. As for any algorithmic method, there are two questions we must ask. How expensive is the method, i.e., what is its computational complexity, and how effective is the method, i.e., how good a solution is it to the stated problem? In our context, the latter question subdivides into two issues, namely, what is the quality of concepts that are introduced by this method, both in terms of knowledge base structure and classification accuracy, and how many of the concepts that are needed in a representation does it introduce?

5.4.1   The effect of new concepts on knowledge base structure

A newly introduced concept influences the learning result along several dimensions: the learnability of the desired target concept(s), the classification accuracy of the rules that are learned, the speed of inference of the problem solver, and the structure and understandability of the resulting knowledge base. In the next section, we will discuss the effects of new concepts on learnability and accuracy; here, we first concentrate on the effects of new concepts on the structure and size of a knowledge base.

As Fu and Buchanan [Fu and Buchanan, 1985] have pointed out, a knowledge base consisting of single-step, compiled rules is not optimal in terms of understandability and robustness. The use of intermediate concepts captures knowledge in smaller chunks, summarizes intermediate states of the problem solving process, and provides a partial interpretation of the data even if the final target concept cannot be derived due to incomplete data. The indiscriminate introduction of intermediate concepts, on the other hand, can

---

[9]The relation of this method to human concept formation certainly warrants a deeper examination, e.g. with respect to its power of predicting empirically observable psychological effects. Such studies, however, are outside the scope of this work.

increase the size of the knowledge base, thus reducing understandability. Based on arguments from the philosophy of science, Emde [Emde, 1991, p. 69] (following [Kutschera, 1972]) argues similarly that the introduction of new terms is preferable only if they allow a reduction in size of the other axioms of the theory. We therefore need a measure that balances knowledge base size against the advantages of small chunk size.

Previous work (e.g. [Muggleton, 1987; Muggleton and Buntine, 1988]) has used compactness, i.e., the total size of the knowledge base as approximated by the number of premise and conclusion literals, as a quality measure (call it TS); this measure, however, has counterintuitive effects, as the following simple example with knowledge bases Γ_1 and Γ_2 shows:

$$\Gamma_1 := \left\{ \begin{array}{c} p(X)\,\&\, c(X) \to r(X) \\ a(X) \to c(X) \\ b(X) \to c(X) \end{array} \right\} \qquad \Gamma_2 := \left\{ \begin{array}{c} p(X)\,\&\, a(X) \to r(X) \\ p(X)\,\&\, b(X) \to r(X) \end{array} \right\}$$

According to TS, Γ_2 is the preferred knowledge base, since $TS(\Gamma_2) = 6$, whereas $TS(\Gamma_1) = 7$. We therefore use a compactness measure S that counts only premise literals, thus removing the penalty for extra clauses that TS imposes, while still incorporating a global measure of knowledge base size. According to S, the two theories are equally good, since $S(\Gamma_1) = S(\Gamma_2) = 4$. We then define a quality ordering $>_q$ on knowledge bases such that

$$\Gamma_1 >_q \Gamma_2 \; iff \; S(\Gamma_1) < S(\Gamma_2) \; or \; (S(\Gamma_1) = S(\Gamma_2) \; and \; C(\Gamma_1) > C(\Gamma_2)),$$

where $C(\Gamma)$ denotes the number of predicates in Γ. In our example, we thus find $\Gamma_1 >_q \Gamma_2$.

Equipped with the quality measure $>_q$, we can now show that CLT's strong evaluation criterion, which was motivated on general grounds of recognizability and predictive power above, actually guarantees that a newly introduced concept will improve the quality of the knowledge base.

Let Γ_1 be a knowledge base into which CLT has introduced (perhaps at an earlier time) a new concept c, let $\Gamma_1^H = SC(c, \Gamma_1)$ the set of all rules with head c, similarly $\Gamma_1^B = NC(c, \Gamma_1)$ the set of all rules with c in the body, and $\Gamma_1' := \Gamma_1^B \cup \Gamma_1^H$. Then define

$$\Gamma_2' := R(c, \Gamma_1) = \{R | \exists R_1 \in \Gamma_1^H, R_2 \in \Gamma_1^B : R = resolvent(R_1, R_2)\},$$

and $\Gamma_2 := \Gamma_1 \backslash \Gamma_1' \cup \Gamma_2'$, i.e. Γ_2 is the knowledge base that would result if C were removed. The following holds:

Theorem 5.1 *For any Γ_1 and Γ_2 as defined above, if C meets the strong evaluation criterion of section 5.3.2 at the time of its introduction, and the concept garbage collector is used, then*

$$\Gamma_1 >_q \Gamma_2.$$

Proof: The above can easily be verified by computing S for the new knowledge base with and without the new concept. If the new concept is defined by recursive rules, then there is no equivalent knowledge base without the new concept. If the new concept is defined by non-recursive rules, we see that in producing Γ_2 from Γ_1, all rules in Γ_1^H are simply removed, and in each rule in Γ_1^B, C is replaced by its definitions, resulting in $|\Gamma_1^H|$ new rules each. We thus find that:

$$S(\Gamma_2') = |\Gamma_1^H| \cdot (S(\Gamma_1^B) - |\Gamma_1^B|) + |\Gamma_1^B| \cdot S(\Gamma_1^H)$$

and consequently the S-difference between the two knowledge bases is:

$$
\begin{aligned}
& S(\Gamma_2) - S(\Gamma_1) \\
&= S(\Gamma_2') - S(\Gamma_1') \\
&= |\Gamma_1^H| \cdot (S(\Gamma_1^B) - |\Gamma_1^B|) + |\Gamma_1^B| \cdot S(\Gamma_1^H) - S(\Gamma_1^B) - S(\Gamma_1^H) \\
&= |\Gamma_1^H| \cdot (S(\Gamma_1^B) - |\Gamma_1^B|) + |\Gamma_1^B| \cdot S(\Gamma_1^H) \\
& \qquad -(S(\Gamma_1^B) - |\Gamma_1^B|) - |\Gamma_1^B| - S(\Gamma_1^H) \\
&= (|\Gamma_1^H| - 1) \cdot (S(\Gamma_1^B) - |\Gamma_1^B|) + (|\Gamma_1^B| - 1) \cdot S(\Gamma_1^H) - (|\Gamma_1^B| - 1) - 1 \\
&= (|\Gamma_1^H| - 1) \cdot (S(\Gamma_1^B) - |\Gamma_1^B|) + (|\Gamma_1^B| - 1) \cdot (S(\Gamma_1^H) - 1) - 1
\end{aligned}
$$

From the evaluation conditions imposed by the strong criterion of CLT, we know that C has at least two sufficient conditions, and thus $|\Gamma_1^H| \geq 2$ and $S(\Gamma_1^H) \geq 2$. Also, since it is required that either the concept have at least two necessary conditions, or is used in another rule (with other premises, e.g. in the rule that triggered the knowledge revision in the first place), we know that either (case a) $|\Gamma_1^B| \geq 2$ and $S(\Gamma_1^B) \geq |\Gamma_1^B|$ (if there are at least 2 necessary conditions for C), or (case b) $|\Gamma_1^B| \geq 1$ and $S(\Gamma_1^B) - |\Gamma_1^B| \geq 1$ (if C is used in another, longer rule). In case (a), we find that the difference in size between Γ_1 (incl. C) and Γ_2 (excl. C) is larger than or equal to:

$$\geq (2 - 1) \cdot 0 + (2 - 1) \cdot (2 - 1) - 1 = 0;$$

similarly, in case (b), we find that the difference is larger or equal to:

$$\geq (2 - 1) \cdot 1 + (1 - 1) \cdot (2 - 1) - 1 = 0.$$

The knowledge base including the new concept is thus guaranteed to be smaller or of the same size as the equivalent knowledge base without the concept, and since in any case, $C(\Gamma_1) > C(\Gamma_2)$, it is guaranteed that $\Gamma_1 >_q \Gamma_2$. Since the concept garbage collector maintains the evaluation criteria over time, any intermediate concept found in a knowledge base is guaranteed to be an improvement □.

5.4.2 Empirical evaluation of effects on accuracy

To test the effect of the different evaluation criteria given above on the classification accuracy of the underlying learning system, we have performed a number of empirical tests. To test the generality of our technique for concept formation during theory revision, these tests were performed using Quinlan's FOIL system (version 4)[10] [Quinlan, 1990b] as the underlying learning system, i.e., FOIL was used both to derive an initial set of rules, and also inside CLT to characterize proposed new concepts. This way, unintended effects that could have been caused by different choices of RDT's model knowledge were avoided. Through MOBAL's external tool concept (see appendix), FOIL and other learning algorithms can be used with the same ease as RDT.

The experiments were performed in the kinship domain originally developed by Hinton [1986], and already used by Quinlan [1990b]. This domain consists of the kinship relationships of three generations for two different families as depicted in figure 5.3. These relationships are expressed using twelve different predicates: father, mother, son, daughter, brother, sister, husband, wife, nephew, niece, uncle, aunt. In the factual representation appropriate for MOBAL and FOIL, this domain consists of 112 positive and 6800 negative facts representing the examples. For each experiment, we randomly selected a different subset of these examples for training which included 90 % of the positive examples, and 5 % of the negative examples. FOIL was then run on the training set with the task of finding rules for defining aunt from the other predicates. The accuracy of learned rules was tested on the full set of examples for aunt. Whenever the FOIL-induced rules produced contradictions, i.e., false positives, we applied KRT/CLT in non-interactive mode, searching for unary and binary concepts if necessary according to the search strategy described in section 4.6.3. Whenever a new concept was proposed, FOIL was called again to characterize the proposed concepts as described in section 5.3.1. The characterization produced by FOIL was then evaluated according to one of the three criteria defined above, and if successful, the concept was introduced into the knowledge base. We then removed the rules produced in the revision process, keeping only the rules defining the new CLT concepts. FOIL was

---

[10] We are thankful to R. Quinlan for making FOIL available to other researchers.

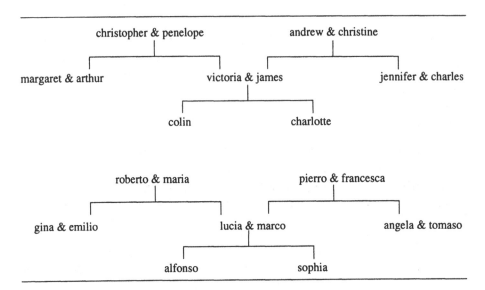

Figure 5.3   The kinship domain of Hinton

then run one more time on the original data, augmented only by the rules defining the new CLT concepts, and accuracy was measured on the examples for aunt again.

Table 5.6 summarizes the results of repeating this experiment 30 times for each of the criteria. The comparison was always made between FOIL on the original knowledge base vs. FOIL on the original knowledge base plus concept definition rules. Surprisingly, these results show that the strict evaluation criterion is much too strict in this domain, and introduced only one concept. For the default criterion, CLT introduced one or more new concepts in 16 out of 30 runs. Among these, almost one half (44 % or 7 runs) led to an improvement in accuracy; in another 3 runs (19 %), the rules learned with CLT concepts had a better fit (less false positives), but reduced coverage, resulting in identical accuracy. In also 3 runs, there was no difference, and in only 3 out of 16 runs, CLT concepts led to a decrease in accuracy when the default criterion was used. Following our expectations, the results with the control criterion were not as good, as the proliferation of new concepts leads FOIL to select many irrelevant rules: without the additional structural check on new concepts, accuracy decreased as often as it increased. Figure 5.4 graphically depicts the results for the default criterion.

Evaluation criterion:	Strict	Default	Null
Total number of runs:	30	30	30
Concepts formed in:	1	16	24
among these:			
Better accuracy using CLT concepts:	0	7 (44 %)	7 (29 %)
Better fit, less coverage using CLT concepts:	0	3 (19 %)	1 (4 %)
Same accuracy using CLT concepts:	0	3 (19 %)	9 (38 %)
Worse accuracy using CLT concepts:	1	3 (19 %)	7 (29 %)

Table 5.6 Summary of experimental results

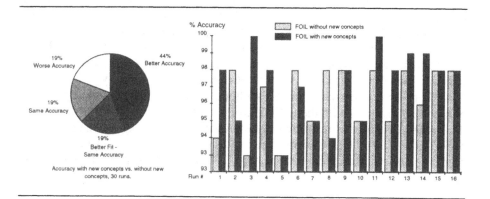

Figure 5.4 Detailed results obtained using the default criterion

5.4.3 Necessity and utility of new concepts

We have thus seen that the new concepts that are introduced by CLT have
a positive effect on the size, structure, and classification accuracy of the
knowledge base. But does CLT introduce all the new concepts that would be
necessary to arrive at a representation that is optimal in terms of structure,
size, learnability, or accuracy? Clearly, by the nature of the technique, there is
one dimension where all necessary concepts are found — namely all concepts
that are necessary for rule reformulation in KRT. By the same token, since the
problem solving context in knowledge revision is the only criterion used for
triggering the introduction of a new concept, we clearly cannot expect CLT to
find all concepts if a different, orthogonal criterion is used.

But what could be the nature of such a criterion anyway? To answer the above question in a more general sense first requires a definition of what it means for a new concept to be "necessary" in a representation, i.e., a definition of what we would consider an optimally structured knowledge base with respect to the set of predicates that is employed. An important distinction in this context is the one between *necessary* and *useful* new terms introduced by Ling [1991c]. According to Ling, a new term is necessary if without it, the learner cannot produce a finite axiomatization of the data being presented to it. Generalizing, we could say that necessary new terms are those without which the learning goal cannot be reached at all, and useful new terms are those without which it can only be reached to a lesser degree.

Stahl ([1993b], a shortened version is [Stahl, 1994]) provides a detailed examination of the situations in which new terms can be necessary to reach a learning goal[11]. In the general case of first-order and first-order Horn logic, is it is undecidable whether there is a finite program that correctly separates positive from negative examples (theorems 2 and 3 of [Stahl, 1993b]). When a fixed language is assumed, it can be shown that in function-free Horn logic, the introduction of new predicates does not change the learnability of a problem — if there was no correct program without the new predicates, there will not be a correct program with them. On the other hand, surprisingly at first sight, if the hypothesis space is restricted even further, as is done e.g. by the schemata of RDT, the introduction of new predicates can affect learnability, as can be seen in a simple example. Assume that RDT is given only one rule schema, namely:

$P(X) \, \& \, Q(X) \rightarrow R(X).$

Using this rule schema, the target rule

$a(X) \, \& \, b(X) \, \& \, c(X) \rightarrow d(X).$

is not learnable as such; if however, we introduce a new term t which corresponds to the conjunction of a and b, the system can learn the equivalent set of rules:

$a(X) \, \& \, b(X) \rightarrow t(X)$
$t(X) \, \& \, c(X) \rightarrow d(X).$

Interestingly, if the language under consideration grows (new constants are introduced after learning), the introduction of new predicates may affect

---

[11] In [Stahl, 1993b], necessary terms according to our definition are referred to as "useful", and useful terms according to our definition are not examined.

learnability and correctness in function-free representations even for learners that do not use schemata or similar restrictions, but whether new predicates are necessary is then again undecidable. Practically, the introduction of strictly necessary new terms seems to be limited to cases where the need for a new term can be precisely identified, as it is the case in KRT/CLT.

So, turning away from the class of necessary new terms, let us examine the class of *useful* new terms, i.e., terms that allow the system to reach its learning goal faster or in a better way. Clearly, CLT's new terms are useful for knowledge revision, and as we already discussed above, they are also useful for improving the structure of the knowledge base. As other criteria for the quality of the learning result, many authors have used the classification accuracy of the resulting knowledge base, or the speed of executing it. At first sight, it seems that the introduction of a new concept by CLT may have both a positive or a negative influence along both of these dimensions. As for classification accuracy, it is clear that any newly introduced concepts increase the hypothesis space for RDT as defined in section 5.3.1. This implies that RDT can now fit its training examples more closely, resulting in increased accuracy on the test data. Depending on the distribution of training examples and the amount of noise, however, precisely fitting the training examples may or may not be advantageous, because the system is in danger of *overfitting* the data (not generalizing enough). It is thus not guaranteed that the good empirical results obtained in the kinship domain will repeat in all other domains.

Similarly, for inference speed, a new concept typically increases the depth of the inference tree by adding more intermediate steps, but reduces the total number of rules. Thus, it depends on the nature of the indexing used for executing rules, and the exact balance between these two effects, whether the resulting knowledge base will execute slower or faster. This is exactly the converse of the *utility problem* of explanation-based learning [Minton, 1990], where newly learned compiled rules may or may not improve the speed of problem solving.

5.4.4 Complexity

Looking at the computational complexity of concept formation with CLT, we see one of the primary advantages of any demand-driven method of representation change. Since no search is involved in finding aggregates, there is no overhead involved in having a demand-driven method in a system as long as it is not triggered. Whenever a demand-driven method of concept formation is triggered, its runtime complexity is mainly determined by the complexity of the characterization step.

Since in CLT, the model-driven learning algorithm RDT is used for character-ization, the complexity of this step depends both on the size of the knowledge base, and the number and kind of rule schemata that are provided. An exact analysis of the runtime of RDT is beyond the scope of this work; we do want to point out however, that the worst-case complexity of any learning algorithm in a true first-order representation is high, since one of the key steps, the decision whether one hypothesis is more general than another, is very complex. In full first-order logic, this question is undecidable if background knowledge is used. Without background knowledge, generality can be tested by using (rule schema) subsumption. First order subsumption, however, is known to be an NP-complete problem ([Garey and Johnson, 1979, p. 264], [Buntine, 1988]) even in a function-free representation like $\Re$. Since θ-subsumption is also used in the restructuring step of CLT, the same applies there as well.

In practice, the length of clauses, and the length of rule schemata is generally small, so that it is usually feasible to compute the subsumption test despite the exponential time complexity of the underlying algorithm. Nonetheless, a careful choice of model knowledge and the confirmation criterion parameter is necessary (see [Kietz and Wrobel, 1992]). For a thorough treatment of the complexity classes entailed by various restrictions on a first-order hypothesis space, the reader is referred to the work of Jörg-Uwe Kietz [Kietz, 1993a; Kietz, 1993b].

5.4.5 Interactive Use

We conclude the evaluation of CLT with a few observations about interactive use. As an interactive tool for knowledge base construction and maintenance, KRT and CLT have to be evaluated in the context of Morik's [1993] *balanced cooperative modeling* paradigm according to which MOBAL is constructed. As pointed out in chapter 1, this paradigm regards knowledge acquisition and knowledge base construction as a cyclic process of interaction between the user and the system. The role of the learning modules in such a system is not primarily that of stand-alone tools that solve the entire problem without human intervention, but that of assistants that suggest improvements, or pinpoint problems in the evolving model.

Consequently, in the above presentation of KRT and CLT, we have assumed that each of the system's proposals, be it a rule to be modified or a concept to be formed, is presented to the user who acts as an oracle that either accepts, modifies, or rejects the system's proposal. In interactive use, we are thus assured that each new concept is valid and useful for the user. More importantly, however, the use of KRT's context to generate new concepts guarantees that the system's proposals are likely to be relevant to the user, i.e., ensuring that the number of nonsensical questions to the oracle is kept low. In practice, users find it relatively easy to evaluate new concepts since the system shows both the instances and exceptions, and the characterization found by RDT whenever a query is asked. Muggleton [Muggleton, 1987] has reported similarly about the query process in the DUCE system.

Besides the traffic law domain that we have been using for illustration in this book, KRT and CLT have also been tested in a highly interactive application developed together with Alcatel Alsthom Recherche, Paris [Fargier, 1991; Sommer *et al.*, 1993] (see section 4.8). In this application, the goal is to construct a system that will aid security managers of telecommunications networks to express, validate, and use security policies expressed as Horn-clause rules; these rules are then used for inferring who may or who may not perform certain operations on a piece of equipment. In this application, KRT and CLT seem to be effective as aids in maintaining a set of security policy rules, since the security manager can simply inspect an individual user's access rights, and have KRT perform the necessary modifications to the general rules if incorrect permissions are found. In the prototype model, CLT was able to find the concept of a "senior operator" which had been missing.

In sum, from our experience so far, we conjecture that in the interactive process of revising an incorrect knowledge base, KRT and CLT are effective tools. An empirical proof of this conjecture would of course require comparative and large scale studies of the structure, speed, and results of the knowledge acquisition process with and without these tools.

5.5 RELATED WORK

CLT is based on the original proposal of exploiting exceptions in METAXA [Emde *et al.*, 1983], and our previous work on concept formation in BLIP resp. the MODELER [Wrobel, 1988; Wrobel, 1989]. In contrast to the previous version in BLIP, CLT as described here uses a much improved concept characterization step based on RDT, is capable of forming relational (n-ary) concepts, employs a theoretically more sound restructuring step based on resolution and θ-subsumption, and includes a concept garbage collector.

The idea of introducing new concepts or predicates in a demand-driven fashion has also been used in a number of other learning systems. We begin with a selection of systems from the field of Inductive Logic Programming (ILP), where this problem is referred to as *predicate invention* (see [Stahl, 1993a] for a complete overview).

5.5.1   Demand-driven concept formation in first-order ILP systems

Closed-World Specialization

As mentioned above, in the early versions of closed-world specialization (CWS), Muggleton and Bain [1992] had also proposed the introduction of new concepts for expressing rule instance and exception sets as they arise during specialization. In contrast to our method, the basic CWS algorithm (see table 4.8) extensionally defines a new predicate containing a rule's exceptions whenever a rule needs to be specialized, i.e., without an additional structural evaluation. To avoid overspecialization, the new predicate is added to the rule as a non-monotonically interpreted negated premise, i.e., the rule only may be applied whenever the bindings of its variables are not yet known to be members of the exception concept. This representation thus is a syntactical variant of the exception set notation used in KRT.

The CWS method thus shares with ours the use of rule instances and exceptions for focusing aggregation, but in its original formulation, does not try to characterize the newly introduced concepts, and thus does not perform any additional quality checking on the proposed concepts. As we have seen in our empirical experiment, this can lead to a proliferation of new concepts without a corresponding increase in classification accuracy. To deal with this, in more recent work, [Srinivasan *et al.*, 1994] have used a compression measure to evaluate the clauses produced by the closed-world specialization algorithm, taking into account the clauses produced when trying to generalize over the exception predicate. In this form, their approach thus is very similar to the way new concepts are evaluated in CLT, the primary difference being that CLT uses structural criteria on the individual concept whereas Srivivasan et.al. evaluate the compression produced by the new concept with respect to the entire theory (see section 4.9.2 for a more detailed description of compression measures). The compression measure (which emphasizes accuracy) thus could be a candidate for replacing the structural criterion of CLT (which emphasizes understandability).

Using modes, dependency graphs or schemata as constraints

The SIERES system [Wirth and O'Rorke, 1992] is a top-down learning system that starts out by building the least general generalization (in the sense of [Plotkin, 1970]) of a given set of examples or abductive hypotheses, and then specializes the resulting clause to prevent overgeneralization. While in KRT, specialization is triggered only by incorrect inferences (covered negative examples), SIERES also triggers specializations when certain structural criteria are not met by the clause. To this end, the system is given mode declarations of all predicates, and specializes whenever an output variable does not appear as an input variable or vice versa ("critical variables"). SIERES also uses additional knowledge in the specialization step: the clause is extented based on a series of *argument dependency graphs*, allowing the introduction of several new literals that must share variables according to the dependency graph. New predicates are introduced whenever a dependency graph cannot be completely instantiated with existing predicates. The argument variables of the new predicates are taken from the graph, respecting the mode declarations, and as in CLT, the instances of the new predicate are taken from the substitutions in proofs of the examples and are used for inducing a definition of the new predicate. SIERES thus shows how additional knowledge could be exploited to replace the general search for new concepts and their arguments in KRT/CLT with a very focused approach. Whereas argument dependency graphs may not always available, mode declarations would certainly be a worthwile addition to KRT.

Instead of argument dependency graphs, some systems have also employed second-order schemata (as used in RDT) for constraining predicate invention. In contrast to SIERES, where the dependency graph is used to constrain *where* to introduce a new predicate, the schemata are used to constrain the *definition* of the new predicate. The first system to use schemata for this purpose was CIA/CLINT [de Raedt and Bruynooghe, 1989]. In CIA/CLINT, concept are induced bottom-up starting from the generalization of a given example and successively generalizing. A set of second-order schemata is compared against the emerging concept definition, and when it matches (θ-subsumes the definition clause), its instantiation is proposed as the target definition. If only the body matches, constructive induction is performed: the user is then asked to name the instantiated head of the schema. FOCL [Silverstein and Pazzani, 1991] have used a variant of schemata called *cliches* in a top-down FOIL [Quinlan, 1990b] like learning system. Whenever adding a single new predicate does not produce sufficient information gain, the system takes a cliche, instantiates it and adds all its body literals to the emerging clause at once. If this proves useful, the set of literals is saved for future use by inventing a new predicate name and adding the corresponding definition.

Other criteria for triggering predicate invention

The "discrimination-based constructive induction" (DBC) approach of the CHAMP system [Kijsirikul *et al.*, 1992] also operates in a demand-driven fashion. Within a top-down learning approach similar to FOIL, new predicates are constructed whenever it is impossible to find a correct clause that meets an encoding-length criterion (cf. section 4.9.2). In comparison, KRT tries to find a new concept whenever no clause can be constructed that correctly separates examples and counterexamples. The approach of CHAMP also presents an interesting replacement for the search strategy that is used in KRTCLT. Instead of beginning with unary concepts and adding arguments if that proves insufficient, DBC first uses all clause variables as arguments for the new predicate and then greedily looks at projections on subsets of these arguments (similar to KRT's *localize* operator, see section 4.6.2). If the projection still correctly separates instances and non-instances, only the projected variables are kept. The starting point for the search of DBC (containing all variables is thus identical syntactically to the CWS approach, and identical semantically to KRT's exception set notation. CHAMP also induces definitions for the newly introduced predicates, and like CWS uses an encoding length restriction to decide whether to keep them, in contrast to the structural criterion used in KRT.

In [Muggleton, 1993], a formal underpinning is provided for the strategy of first using all variables as arguments and then dropping them. Based on the observation that that predicates with fewer arguments can be defined from predicates with more arguments, the former are said to have lower utility. Based on this notion of utility, a clause refinement lattice can be defined within which a unique relative least refinement exists. In an implementation within GOLEM [Muggleton and Feng, 1992], this kind of refinement with predicate invention was triggered heuristically, using the refinement lattice with predicate invention whenever the conventional *lgg* (of a sample pair) was incorrect with respect to negative examples.

Finally, in section 5.4.3, we already briefly mentioned the MENDEL system [Ling, 1991c]. In MENDEL, the demand for a new predicate is defined by the size of the learned theory: new predicates are introduced (with an intraconstruction operator, see below) whenever the learned theory exceeds certain bounds on the size of individual clauses or the entire theory. KRT employs a somewhat similar strategy in using a plausibility criterion to trigger reformulation which is basically a limit on the number of exceptions, and thus on the length of the clause. In KRT, however, this is a local property that immediately points out where to introduce a new concept, whereas MENDEL essentially must perform an unfocused search.

Demand-driven concept formation in description logics

Another way of looking at the aggregation constraint used in MOBAL is that it responds to the need to *refer* to a certain set of objects for which no name is available yet in order to complete a particular task (in our case, the theory revision task). This is why we have often referred to this type of strategy as *demand-driven* concept formation [Wrobel, 1988;

Wrobel, 1989]. Such an aggregation constraint has also been used in the concept formation system KLUSTER [Kietz and Morik, 1994], which forms concepts in a term subsumption representation language similar to KL-ONE. In KLUSTER, objects are first aggregated based on their common occurrence in the same argument place of a predicate; a similar but simpler aggregation rule had also been used in GLAUBER [Langley *et al.*, 1986]. The system then tries to differentiate and characterize these extensional aggregates, and if it needs to refer to a particular set of role fillers for which no existing concept is adequate, a new concept is introduced. KLUSTER thus does not use a task such as theory revision that is external to concept formation, but introduces new concepts as an integral part of its own concept formation activities.

5.5.2   Propositional demand-driven approaches

Using operator applications in LEX/STABB

In a propositional representation, the usefulness of exploiting contextual constraints for introducing new terms has also been demonstrated in Utgoff's STABB system [Utgoff, 1986], an extension of LEX [Mitchell, 1982] capable of introducing new descriptors into LEX's context-free grammar representation language. Where in our method, the context consists of instances and exceptions arising during the specialization of general inference rules, STABB uses the positive and negative instances of LEX's operator applications (as determined by LEX's critic module) as the basis for the introduction of new propositional terms. These are constructed as least disjuncts of existing descriptors, or by collecting all necessary conditions for the successful solution path (regression). The new term is added to the system's grammar vocabulary, but there is no separate characterization step that would search for a concept definition independent of the current operator context. Accordingly, an additional quality check on proposed new terms is not performed. There are also no means for removing a new term once it is no longer needed in the operator condition for which it was constructed.

Local condition formation in EITHER

In a propositional theory revision context, the idea of introducing new concepts system has also been pursued in the revision system EITHER by Ourston and Mooney [1990], albeit in a different fashion than in MOBAL. In EITHER, the system first performs specialization on a theory by using essentially the operators that were defined in table 4.5, augmented by an inductive operator that uses the instances and exceptions of the rule that is to be specialized as an extensional target set for concept learning. Here, however, EITHER only goes halfway, and does not introduce a new, independently named concept — the learned condition is only incorporated into the rule locally. Thus, the theory revision constraint is not exploited for concept formation. Instead, after revision activity has been completed, EITHER uses inverse resolution as described in the preceding paragraph to simplify its theory, which may then lead to predicate introductions. There is also a first-order successor of EITHER called FORTE [Richards and Mooney, to appear]; this system, however, does not introduce new concepts.

5.5.3 Constructive induction

The concept formation method presented here can also be contrasted with work on constructive induction [Michalski, 1983]. In constructive induction (see [Rendell and Seshu, 1990] or [Wnek and Michalski, 1994] overviews), the learning system uses general or domain-dependent operators that examine the existing set of descriptors or predicates, and combine some of them into new descriptors. In contrast, a concept formation approach such as ours starts out by looking at the objects of the domain, decides which ones of them to aggregate, and then inductively characterizes them. In this separate inductive step, a definition for the new concept's predicate is found, i.e., only those combinations of descriptors are acceptable that can inductively be verified in the knowledge base.

In the classical form of constructive induction, the predefined set of operators is applied to the examples once before learning is performed, either exhaustively applying all operators, or controlling them based on example properties (*data-driven constructive induction* [Wnek and Michalski, 1994]). This was done e.g. in the scientific discovery system BACON [Langley *et al.*, 1986], where new numerical descriptors were added whenever interdependencies between original descriptors were detected, or in STAGGER [Schlimmer, 1987] where Boolean combinations of existing attributes were introduced. In more recent constructive induction systems, the application of operators is often based on an analysis of learning results with the original descriptor set. The learning system first performs rule or decision tree induction using the original descriptors, and then analyzes the learning result to find propose new descriptors. These are used and tested in a new learning run, perhaps iterating until a satisfying result is obtained (*hypothesis-driven constructive induction*, [Wnek and Michalski, 1994]). This was done e.g. in FRINGE [Pagallo and Haussler, 1990], where learned decision trees were analyzed to replace replicated feature combinations at the fringes of the tree with new descriptors, or in AQ17-HCI [Wnek and Michalski, 1994] where learned rule sets are analyzed to propose new compound descriptors.

As an example of a constructive operator that also works in a first-order representation, we can look at the intra-construction operator from inverse resolution work (see for instance [Muggleton and Buntine, 1988])[12]. This operator introduces new predicates to group together varying parts of different clauses in a theory which otherwise share the same structure. A new predicate is formed, and extensionally defined to cover the varying parts, while in the original clauses, the varying parts are replaced with the new predicate. As in all constructive induction approaches, there is no separate inductive step, however, to try and relate the new predicate to other knowledge in the system's theory. Thus, other measures, such as proposed in [Muggleton, 1988] or [Muggleton, 1993], are necessary to prevent the introduction of uninteresting new predicates.

5.5.4 Learning in a problem solving context

In the more general context of learning in a problem solving context, there is a large amount of work on approaches that try to improve the performance of the problem solver by analyzing solved problems, and creating generalized compiled rules from them that replace a number of problem solving steps by one single step. Examples of such approaches are the various *explanation-based learning* methods [Mitchell *et al.*, 1986; DeJong and Mooney, 1986], macro-operator learning (e.g. the early STRIPS approach [Fikes *et al.*, 1972]), or chunking in SOAR [Laird *et al.*, 1986]. While all of these approaches exploit the problem-solving context to decide where to learn and what to learn, they do not address the representation or concept formation problem, as the discovered sets of preconditions are local to an individual compiled rule.

More relevant to the work described here are approaches generally referred to as *problem reformulation*, that are exemplified by the work of Amarel [1968], Korf [1980], Subramanian [1990], and others ([Benjamin, 1990] contains a number of relevant papers). While also motivated by the goal of improving problem solver efficiency, these methods generally attempt to reach this goal not by the introduction of compiled rules, but by a change in problem representation that fundamentally changes the search space of the problem solver. This can involve the removal of irrelevant predicates from a theory, as in [Subramanian, 1990], or the creation of abstract states that aggregate states that can be treated identically in planning [Knoblock, 1990]. They are thus much closer in spirit to the work discussed here than compilation methods.

Our work on demand-driven concept formation is also strongly related to a growing body of recent work on *goal-driven learning* [Ram and Leake, to

---

[12]See [Stahl, 1993a] for an excellent overview of other first-order constructive induction operators.

appeara]. Whereas we have used evidence from psychology to argue that the learner's goals play an important role specifically in concept formation (section 2.3.3), work on goal-driven learning now examines the influence of goals on learning in general and from very different perspectives (see [Ram and Leake, to appearb] for a selection of papers). The work presented here can therefore also be seen as part of this new and rapidly developing topic.

5.6 SUMMARY

In this chapter, we have closed the circle back to the goals we had set forth for ourselves at the end of chapter 2, where we had identified a number of points from psychological research that we wanted to take up in a computational model of concept formation. We have now shown that indeed these points can form the basis of such a model, and have described how the problem-solving context defined by the knowledge revision tool KRT in the preceding chapter can be exploited to trigger and focus concept formation.

We also saw how RDT, the first-order rule discovery algorithm incorporated into MOBAL is used to perform the characterization step of concept formation, and how new concepts are evaluated and used for knowledge base restructuring. As we discussed in an evaluation of CLT, the demand-driven method of concept formation described here has proven successful, both theoretically in that it improves the size and structure of the resulting base, as well as empirically, where it has been used successfully in applications, and was shown to improve classification accuracy on a test problem.

Thus having completed the description and discussion of our computational approach, we will now take the opportunity to step back a little from the technical capabilities and limitations of the approach, and answer to some fundamental criticisms that have recently been put forth about the "ungroundedness" of symbolic approaches such as ours.

6

EMBEDDEDNESS

"If an angel is a device with infinite memory and omnipresent attention — a device for which the performance/competence distinction is vacuous — then, on my view, there's no point in angels learning Latin; the conceptual system available to them by virtue of having done so can be no more powerful than the one they started out with."
[Fodor, 1975, p. 86]

6.1 INTRODUCTION

In the preceding chapters, we have discussed the psychological foundations and technical realization of a model of demand-driven concept formation that exploits the problem-solving context of the reasoner to help it decide which new concepts to introduce into the representation. The method constructs new concepts out of concepts (or predicates) already existing in the representation by combining them into rules that express sufficient or necessary conditions on concept membership. This means that the approach must assume the elementary building blocks of concepts as given, and seems unable to account for the origin of truly new features or concepts that are not combinations of existing ones.

A research direction that has recently become popular under the heading of "symbol grounding" [Harnad, 1990] attributes the above problems to one fundamental flaw of symbolic methods, namely the "ungrounded" nature of the symbolic representations that are used. Even though there may be an extrinsic semantics of elementary symbols (i.e. an interpretation), to the system the elementary symbols or features are just uninterpreted, meaningless strings not accessible for further inspection, manipulation, or refinement. This seems to imply that in principle it is impossible to explain the formation of new elementary features in an ungrounded approach, and that consequently any ungrounded model can explain only the smallest part of the concept formation phenomenon — recombining existing features — while leaving the creative part aside.

It is the purpose of this chapter to examine the implications of the above positions for the validity and usefulness of the demand-driven model of concept formation that we have presented. We will proceed by first making more precise in which sense the kind of model we have presented cannot learn any truly new concepts, and what exactly is meant when criticizing symbolic representations as "ungrounded" (section 6.2). After briefly discussing psychological results about the development of human perceptual features (section 6.3), we will then look at two classes of solutions that the critics of symbolic approaches have proposed, and show that they indeed fall prey to the very same fundamental limitation that they set out to remove: they also reduce to abbreviation-building (section 6.4). We conclude that the primary question to be addressed really is the one we have addressed in the preceding chapters, namely which features to form based on which constraints, and propose the requirement of *embeddedness* as a replacement for the one of groundedness (section 6.5). Much of what we have to say in this chapter is not specific to our own model, and so the chapter can also be understood as an argument for the proper treatment of symbolic approaches in general.

6.2 FUNDAMENTAL LIMITATIONS

6.2.1 Concept formation as abbreviation building

What does it mean to form a new feature? As we pointed out in chapter 5, forming a new feature means not only introducing a new name (predicate) into the representation, it also involves somehow acquiring the *meaning* of this new term.

In his 1975 book "The language of thought" [Fodor, 1975], Jerry Fodor uses this observation as a point of departure to show that as long as acquiring the meaning of a new term means formulating and confirming hypotheses about its semantic properties, "one can learn what the semantic properties of a term are only if one already knows a language which contains a term having the same semantic properties." (p.80) The argumentation used to support this conclusion is simple and convincing. If a system is to learn the meaning of a new term p, it must be able to somehow express a hypothesis of the form

"$p(x)$" is true *iff* $G(x)$

where G must of course be an expression constructed from the internal vocabulary already available to the system. This means that p is coextensive with an existing expression, and thus does not increase the expressive power of the representation: two situations that were indistinguishable before will still be indistinguishable with the new concept. In this sense, "there can be no such thing as learning a new concept." (p. 95) Clearly, the above argument applies directly to the kind of concept formation we have described in the preceding chapters — the characterization of a newly introduced concept was performed precisely by formulating and confirming hypotheses about its extension (necessary and sufficient conditions). Thus, it is in this sense that such a model cannot form any truly new concept.

Nonetheless, Fodor is quick to acknowledge that concepts formed by recombining existing terms are useful in *performance* terms, because in a resource-limited system, it may make a crucial difference how complex the expression of a given concept is: even though the new concept can in principle be replaced by its definition wherever it occurs, the resulting expressions may be too complex to be managed within the time and memory limits of the learner. Thus, concepts formed based on existing terms can be understood as *abbreviations* that make a reasoner more effective, and the problem of concept formation, just as we argued in the preceding chapter, remains to decide which of such abbreviations to introduce.

We might add that the usefulness of a newly introduced predicate of course depends on what this new predicate is used for. If the new predicate is only *added* to the representation, the size of expressions that need to be manipulated will actually *increase*, as nothing is deleted. As an example consider the learning technique of *saturation* [Rouveirol and Puget, 1990] that is based on adding to the description of an example all additional statements that can be inferred about it. While this enlarges the set of statements to chose from for learning, it adds to the complexity of the process. Thus, if new concepts are simply added to, instead of replacing, the existing representation, there is a *utility* problem for new predicates that corresponds to the well-known utility problem in explanation-based learning (EBL) [Minton, 1990].

Fodor concludes that learning "essentially involves the use of an *un*learned representational system" (p. 79), and that thus the methodological assumptions of computational psychology (and hence AI) are sound in assuming a set of predetermined elementary symbols as given. At the same time, he is uncomfortable with such a nativist position, and admits that "non-computational processes" (like maturation) may be involved that allow the formation of truly new terms, i.e., terms that increase the expressive power of a representation.

Furthermore, he briefly mentions that the environment could make an essential contribution:

> "The present point is that the process by which one becomes acquainted with the exemplar is not itself a process of hypothesis formation and testing; it is, rather, the process of opening ones eyes and looking." (p. 97)

This possibility, not further considered by Fodor in the "Language of Thought", has been taken up recently, and indeed supplies the ground for a very fundamental criticism of symbolic models, namely that their inability to explain the formation of truly new features is precisely due to the fact that they are not *grounded* in the environment.

6.2.2   The symbol grounding problem

The problem of ungrounded symbolic representations appears in many places in the recent and not-so recent literature. Cottrell *et al.* [Cottrell *et al.*, 1990, p. 307], for example, agree with Woods [Woods, 1975]:

> "While the types of semantic theories that have been formulated by logicians and philosophers do a reasonable job of specifying the semantics of complex constructions involving quantification and combination of predicates with operators of conjunction and negation, they fall down on the specification of the semantics of the basic "atomic" propositions consisting of a predicate and a specification of its arguments — for example, the specification of the meanings of elementary statements such as 'snow is white' or 'Socrates is mortal'."

Brooks [Brooks, 1991, p. 578] even claims that the entire field of knowledge representation

> "is totally ungrounded. It concentrates much of its energy on anomalies within formal systems which are never used for any practical tasks."

The strongest and most relevant critique, however, is the one from Stevan Harnad, because it addresses explicitly the problem of category induction [Harnad, 1987]:

> "*The problem of atomic symbols:* How do the individual words we use in our definitions get *their* meaning? How do they break out of

the circle of dependence on prior definitions and descriptions (and prior words, etc.)?''

This is what Harnad refers to as the "symbol grounding problem", and he illustrates it with an example that turns Fodor's [Fodor, 1975] arguments around: the "Chinese/Chinese dictionary-go-round". Fodor had argued that if a person had a monolingual dictionary of a (partially) unknown language around, then this dictionary would be of no use for learning new words unless the words in the definition (or in some more basic definitions) were already known to the learner. Where Fodor uses this to support the assumption of nativism, Harnad sees this as a prime example of the problems of ungrounded representations: "The trip through the dictionary would amount to a merry-go-round, passing endlessly from one meaningless symbol or symbol-string (the definientes) to another (the definienda), never coming to a halt on what anything meant.''

In Harnad's view, any attempt to address the problem of concept (category) formation on a symbolic level — as we have done in the preceding chapters — cannot be a major contribution, since it leaves unanswered a problem that is of the same magnitude as the entire problem of cognition [Harnad, 1990, p. 7]:

> "The standard reply of the symbolist (e.g., [Fodor, 1980; Fodor, 1985]) is that the meaning of symbols comes from connecting the symbol system to the world in 'the right way.' But it seems apparent that the problem of connecting up with the world in the right way is virtually coextensive with the problem of cognition itself. "

This is indeed a pretty horrible judgment of the work we have described above, and of similar work in "symbolic" machine learning. Unfortunately, as we will see in section 6.4 below, the alternative approaches that have been proposed to solve the symbol grounding problem exhibit the same fundamental limitations, because they focus too much on the symbol-to-world relation and too little on the concept-to-task relation. First, however, let us look at some empirical evidence from psychology with respect to the question of whether elementary perceptual features are innate or acquired.

6.3 PERCEPTUAL FEATURES IN HUMANS

As we saw in the preceding section, there are two fundamentally different conclusions one can draw from an analysis of the problem of elementary features:

one can assume them as innate or at least created by non-computational, non-learning processes, as Fodor did, or postulate that computational mechanisms for their creation should be studied in the context of the grounding problem, as Harnad did. There is a large body of research within developmental psychology relevant to this question[1], and we can only discuss enough of it to show that indeed it seems to support both analyses.

Even though there is no unanimously accepted position on some of the issues, and some of the data are contradictory, it is probably safe to say that in the domain of perception, humans are innately endowed with an important array of capabilities. Most notable, for our purposes here, is the ability to perceive the world in terms of objects and events from very early on: "Some mechanisms for detecting invariants are present at birth [...]." [Gibson and Spelke, 1983, p. 3].

Under suitable conditions, even a newborn infant will reach for a visible object. At 2 to 4 weeks, infants showed avoidant behavior (retracting their heads and interposing their hands) when confronted with an approaching ("looming") object. At one month of age, infants reliably turn their heads towards a target if that target is introduced not too far away from their line of sight. This behavior can be shown both for visual and auditory targets. At the age of 3 months, infants generally swipe at objects, and at 4 1/2 months, they begin to systematically reach for them. At 3 1/2 months, infants attend to the rigidity, and at 6 months, to the weight of objects as indicated by their anticipatory muscle tension. These findings demonstrate that even newborns are capable of perceiving objects and events in their environment and reacting to them, and that attributes such as weight and rigidity are being used relatively early.

Thus, from the outset, there seems to be a precoordinated system of perception and action in humans. This is also reflected in various proposals of representational systems developed e.g. by Piaget [Piaget, 1977], Werner [Werner, 1948; Sigel, 1983], and Bruner [Bruner, 1973; Oerter and Montada, 1982]: they all include a *sensorimotor* level as the basis of the representation system (Bruner uses the term *enactive* representation). Above the sensorimotor level, we find a perceptual level, where experience is represented by a selective organization of percepts and images (Bruner's *iconic* level), and a symbolic level.

We might hypothesize that given a precoordinated sensorimotor level, the finest resolution of our perception of the environment is also fixed at that level, and that upper levels can only performs abstractions of this maximal resolution. This hypothesis was expressed in psychophysics by the assumption

---

[1] We have used, among others, the reviews by Gibson and Spelke [Gibson and Spelke, 1983] about perception, Mandler [Mandler, 1983] about representation, Sigel [Sigel, 1983] about concepts, and by Oerter and Montada [Oerter and Montada, 1982].

of *just noticeable differences* (jnds), which refer to the minimal physical distances that must be between two stimuli so that humans can distinguish between them. *Jnds* have been measured empirically, and were found to follow "Weber's law", which says that the *jnd* is proportional to the magnitude of the signal on the dimension being measured (see [Baird and Noma, 1978] for an overview).

Nonetheless, it is also clear that the perceptual level is not cast in stone. For certain perceptual categories, within-category differences look much smaller than between-category differences even when they are of the same size physically. That is, the size of *jnds* does not vary proportionally as required by Weber's law any more [Pastore, 1987]. Instances of this *perceptual categorization* effect have been observed empirically in color and phoneme perception [Harnad, 1987]. Those effects are dependent on the categories available in the native language of a person, and can therefore not be present at birth. Furthermore, they can be modified by acquiring new categories.

It is these latter data that Harnad draws upon to motivate his model of symbol grounding (see next section), but even the former are no clear indication of how much of human elementary perception is innate, since even within the first weeks, learning processes could be responsible for the rapid development of the perceptual system that we have described.

6.4   TWO INSUFFICIENT SOLUTIONS

Let us now return to the technical side of the problem of grounding symbols and forming new features. We will examine two classes of proposed computational solutions to these problems — connectionist networks and so-called "grounded" approaches — to see whether they are just technically different, or indeed break out of the limitations of the symbolic paradigm in a fundamental way.

6.4.1   Connectionism

An apparently obvious way to get rid of the symbol grounding problem is to get rid of symbols altogether, and this brings into focus a class of approaches that have optimistically been termed *non-symbolic* or *sub-symbolic* [Smolensky, 1988]: *connectionist networks* (also referred to as *(artificial) neural networks*).

The design of connectionist networks is generally thought of as modeled after the structure of the human brain. In this context, the brain is seen as a highly parallel network of neurons, heavily interconnected by synapses that carry experimentally measurable electrical potentials and thus "implement" the brain's functionality. Learning is seen as consisting of a change in synaptic connection strength. By capturing these properties of the brain, it is hoped that connectionist networks will also share some of the advantageous properties that characterize the brain, like natural parallelism, and failure tolerance.

Technical realization

In their technical realization, connectionist networks consist of a number of simple processing units or nodes (the "neurons") connected by directed weighted links (the "synapses"). The architecture of connectionist networks varies, but many are organized into a number of layers, such that the first layer is thought of as an input layer, subsequent layers are seen as hidden layers, and the final layer as an output. In such a configuration, each unit of layer i normally receives input from each unit of layer $i - 1$ (totally connected feedforward networks). However, configurations where higher layers feed back into lower layers are receiving increasing attention (recurrent networks). Since two-layer feedforward networks (*Perceptrons*) have shown to be severely limited in the types of functions they can learn [Minsky and Papert, 1969], most networks consist of at least one input, one hidden, and one output layer.

In connectionist networks with *local* representation, each unit is interpreted as indicating the presence of a certain concept in the domain (the "grandmother" neuron); whereas in networks with *distributed* representation, only the pattern of activation of units can be interpreted as encoding a certain concept. It is especially the distributed representations that give rise to the view of connectionist networks as non-symbolic.

Computation in a connectionist network proceeds by the weighted propagation of activation values from node to node along the directed links. This computation proceeds as follows. Each node i has an activation value $a(i)$ (a real number). The state of the network can thus be described by the vector of activation values $a(i)$ for all units i. The activation value of a unit is computed from the activation values of its neighbors according to the following rule:

$$a(i) := f(\sum_{j \neq i} w_{j,i} a(j) + b_i)$$

where $w_{j,i}$ is the weight on the link from j to i, and b_i is a unit-specific bias (pre-activation, often zero). f is usually a totally differentiable "sigmoid" function like:

$$f(x) := \frac{1}{1 + e^{-x}}$$

In feedforward networks, these values can be computed simply by setting $a(i)$ to the corresponding values of the input vector for all units of the input layer, then computing the values for each hidden layer in turn until the output layer is reached.

Learning proceeds by comparing the output vector generated by the network with the intended output vector, and then adjusting the weights in the network such that the difference between the two is reduced or eliminated. Various methods for doing this have been proposed [Hinton, 1989]; one of the most popular is the "back propagation" method, also known as the generalized delta rule [Rumelhart *et al.*, 1986]. It adjusts the weight of each connection as follows (ignoring the momentum term):

$$\Delta w_{i,j} := \alpha \delta_j a(i)$$

where

$$\delta_j := a(j)(1 - a(j))(o(j) - a(j))$$

if j is an output unit, and $o(j)$ is the intended output value for j, and

$$\delta_j := a(j)(1 - a(j)) \sum_k \delta_k w_{j,k}$$

if j is a hidden unit, and k are the successor units in the next higher layer. α is a user-set scaling factor called the learning rate.

Connectionist networks as gradient descent methods

Even though derived from the brain metaphor, it is not clear at all whether connectionist networks are sufficiently brain-like, or even whether they are brain-like in the right way: the model of electrical signal transmissions completely ignores that the neuronal cells are immersed in a biochemical environment containing hormones and other chemical substances that may play a crucial role of which the electrical processes are only the most visible indication.

Furthermore, if stripped of the brain metaphor, connectionist networks can of course be analyzed as a technological approach or a mathematical method which makes them lose their privileged status.

The important point is that the back-propagation rule is only an instance of a general class of function approximation methods that work by a gradient descent search, as pointed out e.g. in [Sutton, 1988]. Such methods all use variants of the following prototypical weight update procedure:

$$\Delta w := \alpha(o - a)\nabla_w a$$

where w, o, and a are interpreted as vectors spanning the entire network (i.e. all weights, all target outputs, all activations), and where $\nabla_w a$ is the vector of partial derivatives of a with respect to each component of w. This gradient thus reflects how the total error depends on each individual weight, and back-propagation is a method to compute this gradient for the kind of network we have described above.

Gradient-descent methods in general, and back-propagation in particular, have many desirable, but also many undesirable properties. They generally require repeated presentations of the training instance set on the order of several hundred or more, and in the general case cannot be guaranteed to converge to the global minimum. The parameter α, the learning rate, needs to be fine-tuned by hand: if α is too small, the network is more likely to be trapped in local minima; if α is too large, the network can jump out of false minima, but may also jump out of the intended global minimum. To improve the learning speed, a special-purpose design of network architecture (number of layers, hidden units, connectivity) and perhaps even a specialized learning rule are often used. Worst-case results for these methods are as discouraging as worst-case results for symbolic methods: The learning problem is infeasible (NP-complete) in the general case without any domain-specific knowledge, even for concepts representable by very simple 2-node networks with only one hidden unit [Lin and Vitter, 1991].

Given that the architecture (nodes and links) of a network, its learning rate α, and perhaps even the learning rule are the result of the system designer's efforts, it should have become clear that even without symbols, connectionist networks must suffer from the same grounding problem as symbolic systems, because in a modification of Harnad's original question about symbol systems, we can ask: Where does α, where do the nodes or activation patterns of a network get their meaning? What is the meaning of the input and the output nodes? And the answer is, just as for symbolic systems, that their meaning is extrinsic, and available only in the interpretation of the user of such a network. In the network itself, we find real numbers and threshold functions — but no intrinsic meaning.

Feature formation in the hidden layer

A similarly sobering conclusion applies to the often noted capacity of neural networks to automatically develop an emergent, customized representation of the input patterns in the hidden units (see [Hanson and Burr, 1990] for a discussion of learning and representation in connectionist networks). This statement refers to the fact that after training is complete, each hidden unit (in a local representation) or pattern of hidden units (in a distributed representation) picks out (represents) a certain relevant feature of the input set. By analyzing such hidden units (often with special tools such as cluster analysis [Hanson and Burr, 1990], researchers have indeed been able to find that many units had discovered semantically meaningful (and sometimes previously unknown) properties of the input vector. An example is Hinton's [Hinton, 1989] family relations network the internal units of which indeed coded for features such as age or nationality even though those features were not present in the input.

While this certainly demonstrates the technical potential of connectionist networks, it is no more of an answer to the problem of new features than symbolic abbreviation-building methods. Recall that the activation of a (hidden) unit is determined by a function similar to the following:

$$a(i) := f(\sum_{j \neq i} w_{j,i} a(j) + b_i)$$

The building blocks of this function, the $a(j)$, are (recursively) taken from the given (and unchangeable) set of input activations determined by the network designer, i.e. the hidden units functionally recombine existing values into a new value, their own activation. This of course shows a marked similarity to symbolic concept definition rules that recombine existing predicates into a new predicate, their concept membership predicate.

Thus, the features formed in connectionist networks are abbreviations just as the concepts defined by symbolic rules are. Consequently, the features discovered by the hidden units are not "truly new" either: They do not change the representational power of the network, because two input vectors that were identical without the hidden-unit features will be still identical with them. Of course, if the network were embedded into a larger context, encountering two identical input vectors with different associated output vectors could lead the system to request more information — but this applies to symbolic systems as well as to artificial neural systems.

Discreteness of network implementations

We should finally point out that the apparent distinction between the continuous processing of connectionist networks and the discrete processing of symbolic models disappears as soon as one assumes a digital implementation of such networks. Then, each real-numbered input activation will really have a fixed precision of p bits, so if N input nodes are used, this input can be regarded as a bit vector of length pN. Such a bit vector can be trivially encoded as the propositional-logic expression

$$\theta_1 b_1 \wedge \theta_2 b_2 \wedge \cdots \wedge \theta_{pN} b_{pN}$$

where

$$\theta_j := \neg \leftrightarrow a(j) = 1.$$

Consequently, the processing going on in the network can also be described on this propositional logic level. We should emphasize that this "reduction" is not intended as a technical point; indeed, such an implementation of connectionist networks would certainly be useless. It is intended only to show that differences between connectionist networks and symbolic models are of a technical nature (how to cope with the complexity implied by this input representation space), not of a fundamental one as far as the (symbol) grounding or new feature problems are concerned[2].

All of this might change only if truly analog processes were employed, because then presumably the dynamics of the environment could be passed directly to the inner workings of the agent; indeed, the distinction between inside and outside would not be so clear anymore. As long as digitization is used, we are back to the maximal resolution argument.

In sum, the use of connectionist networks *per se* does not change the problem, and the mere absence of symbols still does not allow for a representation change that would increase expressive power, i.e., produce "truly new" features. So let us turn our attention to a second class of approaches that address the grounding problem directly.

6.4.2   Grounded Approaches

The approaches we want to discuss here take up Fodor's point of "opening ones eyes and looking", and consequently place an emphasis on grounding

---

[2] Indeed connectionist networks and symbolic algorithms can be applied and compared on the same tasks [Shavlik *et al.*, 1991].

meaning in perception, i.e. sensory data. Incidentally, for such approaches, connectionist networks are often used, but not because of their "internal" properties, but simply because they can solve certain learning problems.

In the recent literature, there have been several approaches explicitly designed to address the symbol grounding problem, e.g. by Lee *et. al.* [Lee *et al.*, 1990], Cottrell *et. al.* [Cottrell *et al.*, 1990], or Harnad [Harnad, 1987; Harnad, 1990; Harnad *et al.*, 1991; Harnad, 1992]. We will concentrate on Harnad's proposal, because it is well developed, and well embedded in a theory about how symbol grounding should function in the context of concept formation. The arguments, however, apply to the other models also.

Background

In his 1987 paper [Harnad, 1987], Harnad motivates his model of symbol grounding with reference to data about categorical perception which show that in humans, low-level perception (e.g. of colors) is strongly linked to the high-level categories that are available (section 6.3). Consequently, Harnad tries to capture in his model the entire range of phenomena on the "path" from real-world objects to symbolic categories, in order to demonstrate both how symbols could be grounded in the world, and more specifically, how categorical perception effects could be explained.

His view of the concept formation process is largely congruent with our discussion in chapter 2, and centers upon the classificatory goal of concept formation: Category formation is seen as an approximative process of continuous refinement, and sorting of objects into categories is based on extracting and encoding those invariant features that will "reliably subserve the categorizations one must make" in the "context of confusable alternatives", where this context is supplied by a higher-order (parent) category[3]. An example would be having to differentiate poisonous from non-poisonous mushrooms in the context of plants found in a forest.

Representation

Harnad proposes a three-level representation system as the basis for his approach that is quite similar to what developmental psychologists have proposed (see section 6.3). It consists of the following levels:

---

[3]Incidentally, in the actual model described in [Harnad, 1990; Harnad, 1992], the idea of context is not modeled, whereas it is captured by many "symbolic" learning algorithms, like the TDIDT family [Quinlan, 1983] or recent clustering algorithms (e.g. [Lebowitz, 1987; Fisher, 1987a; Kietz and Morik, 1994]).

Iconic The iconic level is an analog of the sensory input, i.e., of the "proximal projection of the distal stimulus on the device's transducer surfaces". (p. 14) The iconic representation is unbounded, i.e. not governed by category boundaries.

Categorical Categorical representations are still analog/sensory, but have category boundaries, i.e., group each stimulus into a class based upon distinctive features. The categorical representation selectively reduces iconic representations to those invariant features that will "reliably distinguish a member of a category from any non-members with which it could be confused." [Harnad, 1990, p. 10].

Symbolic Symbolic representations are the kind we are familiar with; their elementary symbols are labels for categorical representations, and thus grounded in perception.

Implementation

The crucial transformation in this model is, according to Harnad, between the iconic and categorical levels, where invariants must be found. In its first incarnations [Harnad, 1987; Harnad, 1990], the model was not very precise about how this could be done, or even exactly how the various representational levels were to be understood; more recently, however, Harnad, Hanson, and Lubin [Harnad *et al.*, 1991; Harnad, 1992] have presented an implementation based on connectionist networks that allows a more detailed evaluation.

The task selected for this implementation was to categorize 8 lines, with lengths from 1 to 8, into two categories the boundary of which was between length 4 and 5. The lines were represented in an 8-unit input layer of a backpropagation network either by a place code, i.e. a line of length 4 would be 00010000, or by a thermometer code, i.e. the same line would be 11110000. The nets, which had 8 output units and one hidden layer with varying numbers of units (2 to 12), were first trained to do autoassociation, i.e. reproduce the input in their output units. Once auto-association was learned, the "stimulus distance" between each pair of lines was measured as the Euclidean distance of the hidden layer activations of each line.

In the second part of the experiment, an additional output bit was added that indicated the category of the input, weights were reloaded, but not fixed, and training was repeated with the additional bit to learn. When comparing stimulus distances after successful learning in this case with the distances found before, they were found to be decreased for pairs within a category, and increased for pairs between categories, i.e., a categorical perception effect could be demonstrated.

Criticism

Even though Harnad points out that these results may not generalize to the full scale of the symbol grounding problem, his presentation in [Harnad, 1992] justifies an evaluation of the model against the published goals. The representational levels that are proposed have some psychological validity in a very general sense when compared to other models from developmental psychology. Nonetheless, as Harnad points out himself, in assuming that all stimuli are already normalized, i.e., appear in the sensory projection in the same orientation, size, and temporally separated, an important part of the path from object to symbol is already left out, rendering incomplete the intended model of symbol grounding in the world.

The more important criticism in our context, however, is the nature of the categorical representation level which is supposed to pick out invariants that successfully allow the separation of stimuli into different categories. In both the general description of the model, and the particular implementation for line categorization, however, these categories were supplied by the experimenter, or assumed to be supplied from some other source. What is left of the category formation phenomenon if we already know which categories to form? What is left is the problem of learning from examples, so this model of grounded category formation reduces to a model of concept-learning-from examples, and consequently has no more explanatory power for concept formation, or the formation of "truly new" features from perceptual data than any other learning-from-examples algorithm[4].

The only difference is in the interpretation given to results by the experimenter (interpreting the inputs 11110000 as pictures or sensorial stimuli, and the hidden layer as categorial invariants). This, however, is *extrinsic* meaning, and that is precisely what Harnad has criticized about symbolic models. When stripped of this extrinsic interpretation of its input bits, one can also see that the argument made above (section 6.4.1) about the hidden layer of connectionist networks applies to "grounded" models as well: Independent of how the transformation from an iconic to a categorical representation is realized, and independent of whether we even assume such levels, as long as our sensors are digital, any model will be limited to abbreviation-building in the Fodorian sense, i.e., in a fixed and predetermined representation space defined by the resolution of our inputs.

So again, we are back to abbreviation building, and again the crucial point is the one made in the previous chapters: How to decide which abbreviations to build (which concepts to form) in order to cope with the complexity of the

---

[4]The same is true for the model of Cottrell *et. al.* [Cottrell *et al.*, 1990].

available representation space, and *not* which form of input or representation to use. And as we saw in Harnad's model, the relation of symbols to sensory data alone cannot help us at all in making this choice (so Harnad leaves it to the experimenter).

6.5   EMBEDDEDNESS

We can finally return now to the question posed at the beginning of the chapter, namely the implications of the "grounding problem" for the validity and contribution of purely symbolic research on concept formation. As we have seen in the preceding sections, the concept of groundedness is incapable of answering the questions that motivated its introduction in the first place. As long as we assume the use of digital sensors, Fodor's argument applies, and concept formation always reduces to the building of abbreviations in the space determined by the elementary inputs, independent of whether those inputs are propositions or bit vectors interpreted as perceptual, leaving us with the problem of deciding which "abbreviations" to form.

As we will see, in identifying the importance of a problem solving context for constraining concept formation, the model of demand-driven concept formation that we have developed in this book has thus addressed not a peripheral, but the very central problem of concept formation.

6.5.1   Embeddedness vs. groundedness

Furthermore, in its emphasis on a problem-solving context, our model of demand-driven concept formation points the way towards replacing groundedness with an improved notion of what it means for an agent to be connected to the world: it is not the purely perceptual relation of concepts to objects in the world as it is emphasized by groundedness, it is rather the relation between concept and task in a world, between concept and problem solving or acting in a world.

While it is true that the existence of goals or problem solving activity presupposes the existence of a world (in which goals can be acted out), this is still a different point from the one implied by groundedness, as what is important is not that the agent be perceptually connected to the real world in order to widen its vocabulary by "looking" into the world. What matters is that the agent can use constructs made of its existing vocabulary to interact with the world in order to achieve its goals. An example[5] may illustrate this

---

[5] Suggested by K. Morik.

point. Consider a color-blind person trying to play the once-popular game of MasterMind. This game involves guessing the color of 4 pins placed by the opponent in a hidden row of the gameboard. The guessing player proposes a solution, and the opponent indicates how many correct colors and positions it contains. It is not possible to play this game successfully if one cannot distinguish all the colors properly, and the answers of the opponent will vary on apparently identical proposals. Nonetheless, if one can interact with the world, it is possible to attach paper labels to different pins, or otherwise mark them so that they become distinguishable.

What are the crucial components of the environmental interaction taking place in this example? In our view, the minimal requirements that enable goal-oriented activity are captured by the following abstraction:

- the agent receives input from the world in some form, directly or indirectly

- the agent, based on current goals, generates action recommendations that are executed, directly or indirectly, and influence the state of the world

- the agent can judge the quality of the recommendation, and the resulting new state of the world, as positive or negative, and change its policy accordingly.

Note that this framework allows the agent to notice when it needs to gather additional information from the world. Since we have assumed that the outcome of actions can be evaluated, additional information is necessary whenever identical actions in apparently identical situations lead to varying results. Borrowing from research on reinforcement learning [Kaelbling, 1990], and to properly separate these requirements from the ones implied by a "grounded" approach, we will refer to such an agent as *embedded*.

6.5.2 Assistants vs. Robots

At this point, it is useful to go back and look at the possible environments in which agents can be "embedded". The real world, sensorially experienced and motorically acted upon e.g. by a robot, certainly exhibits these properties, but other "worlds" that are equally interesting and important do so as well, namely all worlds where the learning agent is embedded in some problem-solving context. This context could for example be a plant or a process to be controlled, in which case the descriptions received by the agent, and the actions generated by the agent, need not have the perceptual character implied by the notion of groundedness any more.

Furthermore, there is a completely different, often overlooked paradigm that also exhibits the required properties for embeddedness of an agent: the assistant paradigm [Hoschka, 1991]. Where a lot of research in AI, and especially robotics, is aimed at reconstructing intelligent beings (perhaps humans), and thus replacing humans completely in a given context, the line of research governed by the assistant paradigm aims at constructing systems that aid a human in whatever it is that the human wants to achieve in the world.

This configuration offers a type of indirect grounding in the world that nonetheless shows all the elements of embeddedness: the systems receives input about the world from a user, perhaps in the form of symbolic descriptions. The system can then generate advice about the world, and pass it on to the user. If the user then follows this advice, the system — if it allows this — can be given feedback about the quality of these actions. Thus, even though the system itself does not perceive directly, and does not itself act directly, it is still embedded, and can exploit the constraints offered by goal-oriented activity to focus its concept formation activities.

So it is an admittedly simple form of embeddedness that allowed our model of demand-driven concept formation to exploit goal-derived constraints for concept formation: the system has indeed received input about the world in the form of symbolically described cases, has then generated from these descriptions a very simple form of action recommendation (a categorization inference based on the implicit goal of classifying a case), and has finally received feedback about the correctness of this inference which it exploits to form new concepts that are relevant for its (categorization) task.

6.5.3 Embeddedness vs. Situatedness

We conclude by briefly pointing out the relationship between the notion of embeddedness, and the concept of "situatedness", as it has been discussed in robotics [Brooks, 1991], or as a general AI model [Sandberg, 1991; Clancey, 1991]. Situatedness makes the same requirements as embeddedness, i.e., the relation to a world, but it augments them with other, methodological assumptions that make the term unsuitable for methodologically neutral use.

Clancey [Clancey, 1991], for example, proposed an entire program of research under this label, and adds very strong postulates to its meaning, namely that representations have no internal reality in humans, i.e., that they are objects that are available only externally, never stored, and always constructed on the spot. Brooks [Brooks, 1991], gives a slightly different meaning to situatedness in stating that "the key idea from situatedness is: The world is its own best model.", i.e., making a methodological commitment to *reactive* systems. A reactive system is defined as a system that generates behavior directly from a descriptions of its inputs, e.g. by a situation-action table, and does not construct an internal model of its environment.

In our view, this link between the notion of goal-oriented acting in some context, and assumptions about the internal structure of an agent that is embedded in such a context, are premature, since, as both Clancey [Clancey, 1991, p. 111] and Brooks [Brooks, 1991, p. 582] agree, the existing AI methodology that uses explicit representations and models is still legitimate. Sandberg and Wielinga [Sandberg and Wielinga, 1991] have argued in a similar fashion. Indeed the choice of whether we want to construct explicit models, as in the symbolic approaches, or rely on situation-action maps, as in reactive systems, is a methodological choice, and its appropriateness depends on the research goals that are being pursued (see section 1.1). The notion of embeddedness is thus intended to capture the idea of placing an agent in a context *without* making any methodological commitments about the use or non-use of explicit models. In other words, embeddedness is neutral on whether the agent should be realized by symbolic inference procedures based on representations, or reactive procedures not involving explicit representation.

6.6 SUMMARY

In this chapter, we have discussed the apparent incapability of the demand-driven concept formation approach, and other "ungrounded" approaches, to explain the creation of "truly new" features. Following an argument by Fodor, we saw that indeed this type of concept formation must amount to mere abbreviation building in a fixed maximal space of representations. We then saw that two approaches often said not to suffer from this problem — connectionist networks and grounded approaches — unfortunately have the very same limitation as long as digital input devices are assumed. From this we could see that grounded or not, the real issue to be addressed is the one we have addressed, namely which constraints to use in order to decide which abbreviations (concepts) to form. We concluded by proposing embeddedness as an alternative notion to groundedness, focusing less on the relation between concept and sensorially perceived object, and more on the relation between concept and task context.

7

CONCLUSIONS

At the end of this book, we want to conclude with an assessment of areas where we hope this book will make a contribution, a description of problems that are still open, and a discussion of possible future work.

7.1   CONTRIBUTIONS OF THIS BOOK

Following our main perspective, one area where we hope that this book will make a contribution is in the domain of representation adjustment and concept formation. While most previous work on the representation adjustment problem has concentrated on finding operators that map a set of existing terms into a new combined term, we have emphasized the dual view that regards the introduction of a new term as a concept formation problem. While this does not totally eliminate the search control problem, it makes the constraints found in psychological and AI work on concept formation applicable to the new term problem. We showed that contextual constraints, which had not received much attention in previous research, can be used profitably to focus concept formation in the context of knowledge revision. For the future, we hope this book can contribute to a continued strong focus on interdisplinary issues in Machine Learning, and to further developments in the emerging topic of goal-driven learning [Ram and Leake, to appearb].

With respect to first-order knowledge revision and the field of Inductive Logic Programming (ILP) [Muggleton and De Raedt, 1994], in this book we have identified a set of base revision postulates that any theory revision operation should satisfy, and showed that it should replace the notion of minimal specializations previously used in ILP. We defined a base revision operation that is minimal with respect to the postulates, and showed how this operator can be computed efficiently and controlled by a two-tiered confidence model.

199

Hopefully, this work will help to further strengthen the awareness that besides algorithms for inducing theories from examples, work on revising theories when they are incorrect is just as important.

With respect to knowledge representation in ILP, we have defined a knowledge representation formalism $\Re$ with selected higher-order statements that allows contradictions to be handled gracefully. We analyzed the semantics of this representation and its computational properties and showed that both have satisfactory answers. Hopefully, this will lead to a greater acceptance of such multi-valued logics also as a basis for ILP work.

Finally, we hope this book contributes to the on-going discussion of paradigms of AI, taking issue with the claim that only systems that are grounded in the real world, i.e., sensorially connected to it, can form truly new concepts, and demonstring that it is the connection to a problem-solving context that makes all the difference. Here we hope to have given additional arguments for replacing the concept of groundedness with the concept of embeddedness.

7.2   OPEN PROBLEMS AND FUTURE RESEARCH

In the preceding chapters, in particular in their related work sections, we have already identified a number of questions and areas for future work. Here, we want to focus again on some of the questions that we consider important for the future.

The most important open problem for our topic is certainly the characterization of the set of concepts that are *necessary* in a representation. We were able to show that the concepts we do introduce are useful, but were unable to define a criterion against which to show that we find *all* useful concepts. As pointed out in section 5.4.3, this is a general unsolved problem in work on representation adjustment, as so far all approaches can only nshow that with a newly introduced term, the performance of the learning system or problem solver increases, or the structure of the knowledge base improves. Existing first steps towards a definition of the necessity and utility of new concepts have been made towards evaluating the effect of new concepts on accuracy (e.g. based on compression measures, see section 5.4.3), but more work is needed to identify structural criteria that could identify concepts useful to improve the *understandability* of a domain theory for users.

Furthermore, an important question with respect to our approach to concept formation is whether we have actually captured the use of goal-derived constraints in a psychologically valid fashion. As pointed out in the introduction (section 1.1), for this book we constrained ourselves to taking up the hints from psychology, and then demonstrating that they make sense technically. Given the operational implementation of the model, the open question is which psychological predictions it makes, and how these could be tested empirically. As a related issue, a promising topic for further research would be to see where else in problem-solving and learning systems goal-derived constraints could be used to trigger concept formation; our work has identified only one such possibility. In section 5.5, some related work exploring this issue was identified.

As for the issue of "truly new" terms, our discussion in chapter 6 has shown that the criticism of symbolic approaches as ungrounded, and thus incapable of introducing truly new terms, is unfounded, as the competing grounded approaches fall prey to the same fundamental limitation, i.e., they too can only introduce new terms that are abbreviations of their input features. We showed that it is the embeddedness into an environment that matters, and argued that for symbolic approaches such as ours, the feedback from the environment consists of the classification of the system's inferences as correct or incorrect, which indeed is what triggers concept formation in our approach.

While this defends the legitimacy of symbolic approaches, it still leaves the interesting question of how goal-driven methods could be used if a more intensive feedback from the environment were provided, i.e., a feedback that would identify not only incorrect inferences, but evaluate each action of the system in its environment. Since this is a question of great interest in work on *reinforcement learning*, we want to briefly indicate how goal-driven representation change could be examined in future research in such a setting.

7.3 GOAL-DRIVEN REPRESENTATION CHANGE IN REINFORCEMENT LEARNING

The reinforcement learning paradigm [Kaelbling, 1990] assumes an agent that inspects its environment with a number of sensors, processes the inputs it receives, and then selects an action to perform from a limited set of available actions. This operation cycle is assumed to be discrete, i.e., there is a fixed cycle of sensing, interpretation, and then acting on the world. After each executed action, we assume that the system receives a feedback or *reinforcement* value which indicates the pay-off of the chosen action, i.e., how much it contributes to the problem solving goals of the agent. This feedback can be computed by the agent from its sensor values according to a fixed function that reflects its problem solving goals ("reward center", see [Whitehead and Ballard, 1990]), or is externally provided.

A concrete instantiation of this situation can be found in *process control*, a domain where AI techniques are already being applied (e.g. [Rowan, 1989]). There, a control system takes multiple-process sensor inputs, analyzes the data, makes decisions about the operating conditions of the process, and adjusts certain control parameters. Thus, in this concrete setting, the agent's sensors are the process measurement devices, its actions consist of setting one of the process' parameters, and its problem solving goal is to keep the process operating optimally, which can be measured by certain key parameters.

For the simple model sketch that we develop here, we use the assumptions that all sensor values are real numbers, and that there are minimum and maximum values, and that all actions consist of assigning a value of 0 or 1 to a parameter. We will further assume that feedback consists of a classification of each action as positive or negative, thus simplifying the reinforcement learning model where generally a pay-off boundary (above which actions are "good") is not provided. Figure 7.1 graphically shows the outline of a model that could be used as the basis for future research on representation change in this scenario.

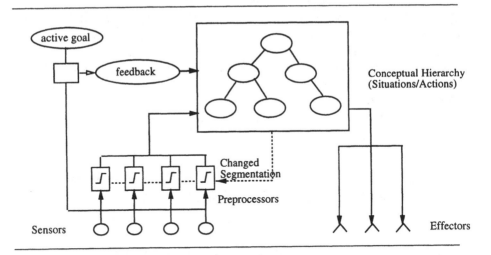

Figure 7.1   Basic model for future research

Since according to our methodological assumptions, we are still committed to symbolic models because of their explicit nature, we assume that the agent uses a symbolic mechanism to compute its action choices based on a given set of inputs[1]. In order to use this (unspecified) symbolic action selection

---

[1] As pointed out in [Wrobel, 1991], a possible choice for action selection would be a hierarchy of situation-action descriptions into which a new situation is classified.

mechanism, the system needs to compute a discrete symbolic representation from the numerical data supplied by its sensors. To this end, a preprocessing element segments the real-numbered value range of each sensor into a number of disjoint intervals that are each represented by a symbolic value; those values then constitute the system's set of features — its elementary symbolic vocabulary[2].

In this general context, a goal-directed strategy of representation adjustment is indeed possible. Whenever the system has classified a situation into its conceptual hierarchy, it executes the action that is associated with the chosen concept, and expects a positive feedback in the next sampling interval. If a negative feedback is observed instead, the system must modify its concept hierarchy by splitting the chosen concept in such a way that the erroneous action is no longer predicted. This corresponds to splitting an overly general rule into several more specific rules.

Splitting a concept node, however, is possible only if the existing concept is not maximally special yet, i.e., if the chosen concept is not a completely specified leaf of the hierarchy. Otherwise, a refinement of the existing features is necessary: the segmentation rules in the preprocessors are changed so that the segments corresponding to the attribute values of the current situation are split in half. The reverse process, i.e., a coarsening of the available vocabulary, can be performed by analyzing the use of attribute values in the action selection module, and combining the segments of those neighboring values that represent noninformative distinctions[3].

In contrast to learning systems that directly use numerical attributes in their concept hierarchies, such as UNIMEM [Lebowitz, 1987], CLASSIT [Gennari et al., 1989], and many of the decision tree systems of the ID3/CART family [Quinlan, 1983; Breiman et al., 1984], the model sketched above, if properly instantiated, could thus be used to acquire a global symbolic vocabulary precisely adapted to a given task; the above-mentioned systems only acquire an implicit vocabulary that is different for each of their decision nodes.

The above model is clearly only a sketch of how goal-driven feature formation could work in a reinforcement learning setting; whether it can be properly instantiated must be left as a topic for future research.

---

[2]The initial vocabulary could either be a maximally coarse, i.e., binary segmentation, or a specific pre-determined segmentation that the agent could have inherited through evolution-like processes. This opens up the interesting possibility of using genetic algorithms [DeJong, 1988] to study the development of elementary feature sets.

[3]A distinction is *non-informative* if the conditional probability of a (predicted) effector value given an attribute value is identical or nearly identical for both values. If a probabilistic concept hierarchy is used, this can be computed from the attribute probabilities stored with the concepts.

7.4 CONCLUDING REMARKS

This chapter has concluded our treatment of the topic of concept formation and knowledge revision in this book. Our hope is that we have been able to supply a small building block of an encompassing computational theory of concept formation and knowledge revision. Many questions had to be left open, and a lot of areas of future work have been identified in this chapter and the preceding ones. If concept formation and knowledge revision remain as active a research topic as they are today, answers to the remaining questions may not be too far away.

MOBAL
SOFTWARE INFO PAGE

MOBAL [Morik *et al.*, 1993] (see also section 1.6) is a sophisticated system for developing, validating, and maintaining operational models of application domains. It integrates a manual knowledge acquisition and inspection environment, a powerful inference engine, machine learning methods for automated knowledge acquisition, and a knowledge revision tool.

By using MOBAL's *knowledge acquisition environment*, a user can incrementally develop a model of an application domain in terms of logical facts and rules, i.e., in a representation that is much more powerful than attribute-based formalisms. The entered knowledge can be viewed and inspected in text or graphics windows, augmented, or changed at any time. The built-in *inference engine* can immediately execute the rules that have been entered to show the consequences of existing inputs, or answer queries about the current knowledge. MOBAL also builds a dynamic *sort taxonomy* that provides information about the objects that have been used in a domain. The system can automatically construct a *predicate topology* reflecting the inference structure of a knowledge base. Machine learning methods can be used to automatically *discover rules* based on the facts that have been entered, or to *form new concepts*. If there are contradictions in the knowledge base due to incorrect rules or facts, there is a *knowledge revision* tool to help locate the problem and fix it by recording exceptions or modifying rules.

User Interaction

MOBAL is a system constructed according to the *balanced cooperative modeling* paradigm that regards knowledge acquisition as a continuing interactive process of model construction. Consequently, in MOBAL, the distribution of work between system and user is flexible: the user can input all the knowledge needed for problem solving in a particular domain by hand, or can start by simply entering facts and using the various structuring and learning tools of MOBAL to extend this initial knowledge. Learning results are immediately incorporated into the knowledge base where they can be modified further. This contrasts with one-shot learning systems that run like a compiler and do not support the cyclic acquisition process. Consequently, use of MOBAL is highly interactive, and does not need to follow a fixed script.

Application domains

MOBAL is applicable to all types of classification or advice-given problems, such as medical or technical diagnosis, assignment of objects or cases to a certain class, type or group, advice based on constraint violations, ... It is especially suitable if the domain requires the representation of time-dependent or other relational data, and in domains where frequent interactive changes are necessary. In the the MLT project, MOBAL has been applied to the problem of diagnosing and treating Maldecensus testis diseases (with ICS Forth), and to the problem of deciding whether a given user has certain access rights in a telecommunication network (with Alcatel Alsthom Recherche).

News in Release 3.0

As the most visible change, the new release 3.0 no longer requires OpenWindows, but features an X11 graphical user interface built using Tcl/Tk. This should make installation trouble-free for most users, and through its networked client-server structure, allows easy integration with other programs.

As a second change resulting from work in the ILP ESPRIT basic research project, MOBAL 3.0 now offers an "external tool" facility that allows other (ILP) learning algorithms to be interfaced to the system and used from within the same knowledge acquisition environment. The current release of MOBAL includes interfaces e.g. to GOLEM by S. Muggleton and C. Feng (Oxford University), GRDT by V. Klingspor (Univ. Dortmund) and FOIL 6.1 by R. Quinlan and M. Cameron-Jones (Sydney Univ.).

Availability

The Mobal system (release 3.0) is currently available in a runtime version for SUN systems running SunOS UNIX 4.1.* and X-Windows. Mobal is a copyrighted program and *not* in the public domain. GMD grants a cost-free license to use Mobal for non-commercial academic purposes. The system is available via anonymous FTP from ftp.gmd.de, directory /ml-archive/GMD/software/Mobal.

B

GLOSSARY OF SYMBOLS

This glossary lists the important symbols and abbreviations that are used in the text, in the order of first occurrence. The first column of the table contains the symbol or abbreviation, the second provides a short reminder of its meaning, and the third lists the page or pages where the symbol is defined or first mentioned.

Chapter 3

Symbol	Meaning	Page
$\Re$	the knowledge representation used in this book	46, 55
Γ	a logical theory (usually of $\Re$)	
$Int(c, \Gamma)$	intension of a concept (name) c in a theory Γ	49
$Ext(c, \Gamma)$	extension of a concept (name) c in a theory Γ	49
$SC(c, \Gamma)$	sufficient condition rules for a concept (name) c in a theory Γ	50
$NC(c, \Gamma)$	necessary condition rules for a concept (name) c in a theory Γ	50
$U(c, \Gamma)$	other rules that use a concept (name) c in a theory Γ	50
Ω	alphabet of $\Re$	55
$\mathcal{M}, \mathcal{C}, \mathcal{V}, \mathcal{P}$	punctuation, constant, variable, predicate symbols of Ω	55
$arity(p)$	arity of predicate p	55
$\mathcal{T}$	the terms of $\Re$	55
τ	type (level) function on terms and statements	55
L	usually denotes a literal (of $\Re$)	56
$vars(L)$	variables occurring in L	56
D^*	domain of interpretation for $\Re$	57
I	an interpretation for $\Re$	57
δ	a domain substitution (replace vars. by constants)	58
$\models$	logical (semantical) entailment	58

Chapter 3, contd.

Symbol	Meaning	Page
σ, θ	substitutions	59
$\vdash_1$	(syntactical) derivation in one step	59
Γ^*	closure of Γ under $\vdash/\vdash_1$	59
$\vdash$	(syntactical) derivation operator for $\Re$	59
$\Re^+$	positive literal subset of $\Re$	60
t_{max}	number of highest level used in a theory	65
F_{max}	maximal number of facts expressible with a given Ω	66
$\mathcal{T}_{\sqsubseteq}$	set of truth values for multi-valued semantics	71
$\geq_{\mathcal{T}_{\sqsubseteq}}$	truth value ordering in multi-valued semantics	72

Chapter 4

Symbol	Meaning	Page
$\hat{-}$	The minimal base revision (MBR) operator of KRT	81, 101
$\hat{+}$	Consistent addition of a fact to a theory	82
$\hat{\pm}$	Resolution of an inconsistency	82
ϕ	Function that chooses "side" of contradiction	82, 108
Cn	Logical consequence operation	84
Γ	a logical theory (usually in $\Re$)	
B	base of a theory	84
$\dot{-}$	denotes closed theory contraction operations	85
$\Gamma \downarrow f$	Set of maximally correct subsets of Γ	86
γ	Function that chooses among elements of $\Gamma \downarrow f$ (or $\Gamma \downarrow_\Pi f$)	87, 101, 107
$\geq_g$	"more general than" relation	87
$\dot{\sim}$	denotes base contraction operations	91
$\diamond$	Denotes addition of a premise to a clause.	93, 99
$\in_\sigma$	Extended membership predicate allowing substitutions	94
$S(R)$	support set of a rule	95
GE	global exception set of a support set	95
LE	local exception set of a support set's variable	95
$\Delta(f, \Gamma)$	derivation of f in Γ	96

Chapter 4, contd.

Symbol	Meaning	Page
$\Pi(f,\Gamma)$	clause applications occurring in $\Delta(f,\Gamma)$	97
$\Sigma(C,P)$	substitutions used for C in application set P	98
$I(C,P)$	instances of C in application set P	98
$C(P)$	clauses occurring in application set P	99
$\Gamma_\Pi(P)$	theory corresponding to application set P	99
$\Gamma\times_\Pi f$	factorization of Γ wrt. f	99
$\Gamma\downarrow_\Pi f$	set of maximally correct subsets of $\Pi(f,\Gamma)$	100
$\Gamma\downarrow_\Pi f$	minimal removal sets (complements of members of $\Gamma\downarrow_\Pi f$)	100
$add(C,f,P)$	set of statements to replace a statement C removed by application set P wrt. f	100
χ	continuous confidence function	106, 108
κ	discrete confidence class function	106
$Exc(R,P,\Gamma)$	exception set of a rule wrt. application set P	117
$Inst(R,P,\Gamma)$	instance set of a rule wrt. application set P	117
Exc	abbreviates $Exc(R,P,\Gamma)$	118
$Inst$	abbreviates $Inst(R,P,\Gamma)$	118
$\geq_\gamma$	dual of $\geq_\gamma$	119
$\pi_{i_1,\ldots,i_m}(S)$	projection of a tuple set	124
$\geq_{ref}$	comparison predicate for selecting reformulations	129

Chapter 5

Symbol	Meaning	Page
Σ	instantiation (a substitution restricted to predicate variables)	150
$\mathcal{R}$	set of rules models used by RDT	150
$\mathcal{H}$	hypothesis space of RDT	150
$\mathcal{R}^{c,a}$	rule models for characterization	152
$>_q$	quality measure on knowledge bases	163

REFERENCES

[Aben and van Someren, 1990] M. Aben and M. van Someren. Heuristic refinement of logic programs. In *Proc. of the 9 th ECAI*, pages 7 – 12. Stockholm, 1990.

[Ade *et al.*, 1993] H. Ade, L. De Raedt, and M. Bruynooghe. Theory revision. In S. Muggleton, editor, *Proceedings of the 3rd International Workshop on Inductive Logic Programming*, pages 179–192, 1993.

[Aha, 1989] D. Aha. Incremental, instance-based learning of independent and graded concept descriptions. In *Proc. Sixth Intern. Workshop on Machine Learning*. Morgan Kaufman, San Mateo, CA, 1989.

[Aha *et al.*, 1991] D. Aha, D. Kibler, and M. Albert. Instance-based learning algorithms. *Machine Learning*, 6:37 – 66, 1991.

[Alchourron and Makinson, 1982] C. E. Alchourron and D. Makinson. On the logic of theory change: contraction functions and their associated revision functions. *Theoria*, 48:14 – 37, 1982.

[Alchourron *et al.*, 1985] C. E. Alchourron, P. Gärdenfors, and D. Makinson. On the logic of theory change: Partial meet contraction and revision functions. *The Journal of Symbolic Logic*, 50:510 – 530, 1985.

[Amarel, 1968] S. Amarel. On representations of problems of reasoning about actions. In D. Michie, editor, *Machine Intelligence 3*, pages 131 – 171. Edinburgh University Press, 1968. Reprinted in Readings in Artificial Intelligence, ed. B. L. Webber and N. J. Nilsson, Morgan Kaufmann, 1981.

[Armstrong *et al.*, 1983] S. Armstrong, L. Gleitman, and H. Gleitman. What some concepts might not be. *Cognition*, 13:263 – 308, 1983.

[Bain and Muggleton, 1992] M. Bain and S. Muggleton. Non-monotonic learning. In S. Muggleton, editor, *Inductive Logic Programming*. Academic Press, London, New York, 1992.

[Baird and Noma, 1978] J. C. Baird and E. Noma. *Fundamentals of Scaling and Psychophysics*. Wiley and Sons, New York, 1978.

[Bareiss and Porter, 1987] E. Bareiss and B. Porter. Protos: An exemplar-based learning apprentice. In P. Langley, editor, *Proc. 4th Int. Workshop on Machine Learning*, pages 12–23. Morgan Kaufman, 1987.

[Barsalou, 1982] L. Barsalou. Context-independent and context-dependent information in concepts. *Memory & Cognition*, 10:82 – 93, 1982.

[Barsalou, 1983] L. W. Barsalou. Ad hoc categories. *Memory & Cognition*, 11(3):211 – 227, 1983.

[Benjamin, 1990] D. P. Benjamin, editor. *Change of Representation and Inductive Bias*. Kluwer, Dordrecht, Netherlands, 1990.

[Bergadano *et al.*, 1992] F. Bergadano, S. Matwin, R. Michalski, and J. Zhang. Learning two-tiered descriptions of flexible concepts: The POSEIDON system. *Machine Learning*, 8(1):5 – 43, 1992.

[Blair and Subrahmanian, 1989] H. A. Blair and V. S. Subrahmanian. Para-consistent logic programming. *Theoretical Computer Science*, 68:135 – 154, 1989.

[Bostrom and Idestam-Almquist, 1994] H. Bostrom and P. Idestam-Almquist. Specialization of logic programs by pruning SLD-trees. In S. Wrobel, editor, *Proc. MLNet Familiarization Workshop on Theory Revision and Restructuring (at ECML-94, Catania, Italy)*, pages 8–9. Arbeitspapiere der GMD, Pf. 1316, D-53754 Sankt Augustin, 1994. Available via FTP from ftp.gmd.de as /ml-archive/MLnet/Catania94/theory-revision.ps.

[Brachman and Schmolze, 1985] R. J. Brachman and J. G. Schmolze. An overview of the KL-ONE knowledge representation system. *Cognitive Science*, 9:171 – 216, 1985.

[Breiman *et al.*, 1984] L. Breiman, J. Friedman, R. Olshen, and C. Stone. *Classifikation and regression trees*. Belmont, Wadsworth, 1984.

[Brooks, 1991] R. A. Brooks. Intelligence without reason. In *Proc. 12th International Joint Conference on Artificial Intelligence*, pages 569 – 595. Morgan Kaufman, San Mateo, CA, 1991.

[Bruner, 1973] J. Bruner. The course of cognitive growth. In J. M. Anglin, editor, *Beyond the information given: studies in the psychology of knowing*. Norton, New York, 1973.

[Buntine, 1988] W. Buntine. Generalized subsumption and its applications to induction and redundancy. *Artificial Intelligence*, 36:149 – 176, 1988.

[Carey, 1985] S. Carey. *Conceptual change in childhood*. MIT Press, Boston, 1985.

[Ceri *et al.*, 1990] S. Ceri, G. Gottlob, and L. Tanca. *Logic Programming and Databases*. Springer Verlag, Berlin, New York, 1990.

[Chang and Lee, 1973] C. L. Chang and R. C. Lee. *Symbolic Logic and Mechanical Theorem Proving*. Academic Press, London, New York, 1973.

[Chapman and Chapman, 1969] L. J. Chapman and J. P. Chapman. Illusory correlation as an obstacle to the use of valid psycho-diagnostic signs. *Journal of Abnormal Psychology*, 74:272 – 280, 1969.

[Charniak and McDermott, 1985] E. Charniak and D. McDermott. *Introduction to Artificial Intelligence*. Addison-Wesley, Reading, Massachusetts, 1985.

[Chi *et al.*, 1982] M. Chi, R. Glaser, and E. Rees. Expertise in problem solving. In R. Sternberg, editor, *Advances in the Psychology of Human Intelligence*, chapter 1, pages 7 – 75. Lawrence Earlbaum Associates, Hillsdale, NJ, 1982.

[Clancey, 1991] W. J. Clancey. Situated cognition: Stepping out of representational flatland. *AI Communications*, 4(2/3):109 – 112, 1991.

[Cohen and Younger, 1983] L. B. Cohen and B. A. Younger. Perceptual categorization in the infant. In E. K. Scholnick, editor, *New trends in conceptual representation: Challenges to Piaget's theory?*, pages 197 – 220. Erlbaum, Hillsdale, NJ, 1983.

[Collins and Loftus, 1975] A. Collins and E. F. Loftus. A spreading activation theory of semantic processing. *Psychological Review*, 82:407 – 428, 1975.

[Cottrell *et al.*, 1990] G. W. Cottrell, B. Bartell, and C. Haupt. Grounding meaning in perception. In H. Marburger, editor, *Proc. GWAI-90, 14th German Workshop on Artif. Intelligence*, pages 307 – 321. Springer Verlag, Berlin, New York, 1990.

[Crocker, 1981] J. Crocker. Judgment of covariation by social perceivers. *Psychological Bulletin*, 90:272 – 292, 1981.

[de Raedt and Bruynooghe, 1989] L. de Raedt and M. Bruynooghe. Constructive induction by analogy: a method to learn how to learn? In *Proc. Fourth European Working Session on Learning (EWSL)*, pages 189 – 199. Pitman/Morgan Kaufman, London/Los Altos, CA, 1989.

[DeJong, 1988] K. DeJong. Learning with genetic algorithms: An overview. *Machine Learning*, 3(2/3):121 – 138, 1988.

[DeJong and Mooney, 1986] G. DeJong and R. Mooney. Explanation-based learning: An alternative view. *Machine Learning*, 1:145 – 176, 1986.

[DeRaedt, 1991] L. DeRaedt. *Interactive Concept-Learning*. PhD thesis, Kath. Univ. Leuven, Leuven, Belgium, February 1991.

[DeRaedt and Bruynooghe, 1989] L. DeRaedt and M. Bruynooghe. Towards friendly concept-learners. In *Proc. of the 11th Int. Joint Conf. on Artif. Intelligence*, pages 849 – 854. Morgan Kaufman, San Mateo, CA, 1989.

[DeRaedt and Bruynooghe, 1992] L. DeRaedt and M. Bruynooghe. Interactive concept-learning and constructive induction by analogy. *Machine Learning*, 8(2):107–150, 1992.

[Donini *et al.*, 1991] F. Donini, M. Lenzerini, D. Nardi, and W. Nutt. Tractable concept languages. In *Proc. 12th International Joint Conference on Artificial Intelligence*, pages 458 – 463. Morgan Kaufman, San Mateo, CA, 1991.

[Easterlin and Langley, 1985] J. D. Easterlin and P. Langley. A framework for concept formation. In *Seventh Annual Conference of the Cognitive Science Society*, pages 267 – 271. Irvine, CA, 1985.

[Emde, 1989] W. Emde. An inference engine for representing multiple theories. In K. Morik, editor, *Knowledge Representation and Organization in Machine Learning*, pages 148–176. Springer Verlag, Berlin, New York, 1989.

[Emde, 1991] W. Emde. *Modellbildung, Wissensrevision und Wissensreprasentation im Maschinellen Lernen*. Informatik-Fachberichte 281. Springer Verlag, Berlin, New York, 1991. Dissertation.

[Emde, August 1987] W. Emde. Non-cumulative learning in METAXA.3. In *IJCAI-87*. Morgan Kaufman, San Mateo, CA, August 1987.

[Emde *et al.*, 1983] W. Emde, C. U. Habel, and C.-R. Rollinger. The discovery of the equator or concept driven learning. In *IJCAI-83*, pages 455 – 458. Morgan Kaufman, San Mateo, CA, 1983.

[Emde *et al.*, 1989] W. Emde, I. Keller, J.-U. Kietz, K. Morik, S. Thieme, and S. Wrobel. Abschlussbericht des BMFT-Projektes 3 b LERNER. KIT-Report 71, Technische Universität Berlin, D-1000 Berlin, West Germany, April 1989.

[Entwistle, 1966] D. R. Entwistle. *The word associations of young children.* Johns Hopkins Univ. Press, Baltimore, Md., 1966.

[Ervin, 1961] S. M. Ervin. Changes with age in the verbal determinants of word associations. *American Journal of Psychology*, 74:361 – 372, 1961.

[Everitt, 1980] B. Everitt. *Cluster analysis.* Halsted Press, New York, 1980.

[Fargier, 1991] H. Fargier. Using Mobal : overview and remarks. Technical note AAR/P2154/40/1, Alcatel Alsthom Recherche, August 1991.

[Feng and Muggleton, 1992] C. Feng and S. Muggleton. Towards inductive generalisation in higher order logic. In D. Sleeman, editor, *Procs. Of IML-92*. Morgan Kaufmann, San Mateo, CA, 1992.

[Fikes *et al.*, 1972] R. E. Fikes, P. E. Hart, and N. J. Nilsson. Learning and executing generalized robot plans. *Artificial Intelligence*, 3:251 – 288, 1972.

[Fisher, 1987a] D. H. Fisher. Knowledge acquisition via incremental conceptual clustering. *Machine Learning*, 2:139 – 172, 1987.

[Fisher, 1987b] D. H. Fisher. Knowledge acquisition via incremental conceptual clustering. Technical Report 87-22, Department of Information and Computer Science, Univ. of California Irvine, Irvine, CA, 1987. Doctoral Dissertation.

[Fodor, 1975] J. A. Fodor. *The language of thought.* Thomas Y. Crowell, New York, 1975.

[Fodor, 1980] J. A. Fodor. Methodological solipsism considered as a research strategy in cognitive psychology. *Behavioral and Brain Sciences*, 3:63 – 109, 1980.

[Fodor, 1985] J. A. Fodor. Precis of the modularity of mind. *Behavioral and Brain Sciences*, 8:1 – 42, 1985.

[Fu and Buchanan, 1985] L.-M. Fu and B. Buchanan. Learning intermediate concepts in constructing a hierarchical knowledge base. In *Proc. 9th International Joint Conference on Artificial Intelligence*, pages 659 – 666. Morgan Kaufman, San Mateo, CA, 1985.

[Gärdenfors, 1988] P. Gärdenfors. *Knowledge in Flux — Modeling the Dynamics of Epistemic States.* MIT Press, Cambridge, MA, 1988.

[Garey and Johnson, 1979] M. R. Garey and D. S. Johnson. *Computers and Intractability - A Guide to the Theory of NP-Completeness.* Freeman, San Francisco, Cal., 1979.

[Gennari *et al.*, 1989] J. H. Gennari, P. Langley, and D. Fisher. Models of incremental concept formation. *Artificial Intelligence*, 40:11 – 61, 1989.

[Gibson and Spelke, 1983] E. J. Gibson and E. S. Spelke. The development of perception. In P. H. Mussen, editor, *Handbook of Child Psychology*, volume III, chapter 1, pages 1 – 76. John Wiley & Sons, New York, fourth edition, 1983.

[Gluck and Corter, 1985] M. Gluck and J. Corter. Information, uncertainty, and the utility of categories. In *Proc. of the 7th Annual Conf. of the Cognitive Science Society*, pages 283 – 287. Academic Press, 1985.

[Goodman, 1955] N. Goodman. *Fact, Fiction and Forecast.* Bobbs-Merrill, Indianapolis, 1955.

[Habel and Rollinger, 1981] C. Habel and C.-R. Rollinger. Aspekte der rechnergestutzten Generierung von Inferenzregeln durch Regelschemata. In J. Siekmann, editor, *Procs. German Workshop on Artificial Intelligence 1981.* Springer, Berlin, 1981.

[Hampton, 1979] J. A. Hampton. Polymorphous concepts in semantic memory. *Journal of Verbal Learning and Verbal Behavior*, 18:441 – 461, 1979.

[Hanson and Bauer, 1989] S. J. Hanson and M. Bauer. Conceptual clustering, categorization, and polymorphy. *Machine Learning*, 3(4):343 – 372, 1989.

[Hanson and Burr, 1990] S. J. Hanson and D. J. Burr. What connectionist models learn: Learning and representation in connectionist networks. *Behavioral and Brain Sciences*, 13:471 – 518, 1990.

[Harnad, 1987] S. Harnad. Category induction and representation. In S. Harnad, editor, *Categorical Perception*, chapter 19, pages 535 – 565. Cambridge University Press, 1987.

[Harnad, 1990] S. Harnad. The symbol grounding problem. *Physica D*, 42(1):335 – 346, 1990.

[Harnad, 1992] S. Harnad. Connecting object to symbol in modeling cognition. In A. Clark and R. Lutz, editors, *Connectionism in Context.* Springer Verlag, Berlin, New York, 1992. To appear.

[Harnad *et al.*, 1991] S. Harnad, S. J. Hanson, and J. Lubin. Categorical perception and the evolution of supervised learning in neural nets. Pres. at the 1991 AAAI Symp. on Symbol Grounding: Problem and Practice; available via anonymous ftp from Princeton University (princeton.edu), 1991.

[Hayes-Roth and Hayes-Roth, 1977] B. Hayes-Roth and F. Hayes-Roth. Concept learning and the recognition and classification of exemplars. *Journal of Verbal Learning and Verbal Behavior*, 16:321 – 338, 1977.

[Hinton, 1986] G. E. Hinton. Learning distributed representations of concepts. In *Proc. Eigth Annual Conf. of the Cognitive Science Society*. Lawrence Earlbaum Associates, Hillsdale, NJ, 1986.

[Hinton, 1989] G. E. Hinton. Connectionist learning procedures. *Artificial Intelligence*, 40:185 – 234, 1989.

[Hinton, 1990] G. H. Hinton. Connectionist learning procedures. In Y. Kodratoff and R. Michalski, editors, *Machine Learning — An Artificial Intelligence Approach, Vol. III*, chapter 20, pages 555 – 610. Morgan Kaufman, San Mateo, CA, 1990.

[Holyoak and Glass, 1975] K. J. Holyoak and A. L. Glass. The role of contradictions and counterexamples in the rejection of false sentences. *Journal of Verbal Learning and Verbal Behavior*, 14:215 – 239, 1975.

[Hoschka, 1991] P. Hoschka. Assisting-computer — a new generation of support systems. In W. Brauer and D. Hernandez, editors, *Verteilte K¨ unstliche Intelligenz und Kooperatives Arbeiten. Proc. 4. Int. GI-Kongre Wissensbasierte Systeme*, pages 219 – 230. Springer Verlag, Berlin, New York, 1991.

[Johnson-Laird, 1980] P. N. Johnson-Laird. Mental models in cognitive science. *Cognitive Science*, 4:71 – 115, 1980.

[Kaelbling, 1990] L. P. Kaelbling. Learning in embedded systems. Technical Report STAN-CS-90-1326, Stanford University, Stanford, CA, 1990. Ph.D. thesis.

[Keil, 1979] F. C. Keil. *Semantic and Conceptual Development: An Ontological Perspective*. Harvard Univ. Press, Cambridge, MA, 1979.

[Kietz, 1988] J.-U. Kietz. Incremental and reversible acquisition of taxonomies. *Proceedings of EKAW-88*, pages 24.1–24.11, 1988. Also as KIT-Report 66, Technical University Berlin.

[Kietz, 1993a] J.-U. Kietz. A comparative study of structural most specific generalisations used in machine learning. In *Proc. Third International Workshop on Inductive Logic Programming*, pages 149 – 164. J. Stefan Institute Technical Report IJS-DP-6707,, Ljubljana, Slovenia, 1993. Also as Arbeitspapiere der GMD 667.

[Kietz, 1993b] J.-U. Kietz. Some lower bounds for the computational complexity of inductive logic programming. In *Proc. Sixth European Conference on Machine Learning (ECML-93)*, pages 115 – 123, 1993. Also as Arbeitspapiere der GMD No. 718.

[Kietz and Morik, 1994] J.-U. Kietz and K. Morik. A polynomial approach to the constructive induction of structural knowledge. *Machine Learning*, 14:193–217, 1994. Revised and extended version of a paper presented at Workshop W8 of the 12th IJCAI-91: Evaluating and changing representations in machine learning. Also as Arbeitspapiere der GMD No. 716.

[Kietz and Wrobel, 1992] J.-U. Kietz and S. Wrobel. Controlling the complexity of learning in logic through syntactic and task-oriented models. In S. Muggleton, editor, *Inductive Logic Programming*, chapter 16. Academic Press, London, New York, 1992.

[Kijsirikul *et al.*, 1992] B. Kijsirikul, M. Numao, and M. Shimura. Discrimination-based constructive induction of logic programs. In *AAAI-92 Proc. Tenth Natl. Conference on Artif. Intelligence*, pages 44 – 49. AAAI Press/The MIT Press, Menlo Park, Cambridge, London, 1992.

[Klingspor, 1991] V. Klingspor. MLT Deliverable 4.3.2/G: MOBAL's predicate structuring tool. GMD (German Natl. Research Center for Computer Science), P.O.Box 1240, W-5205 St. Augustin 1, Germany, September 1991.

[Knoblock, 1990] C. A. Knoblock. Learning abstraction hierarchies for problem solving. In *Proc. 9th National Conference on Artificial Intelligence*, pages 923 – 928, 1990.

[Kolodner, 1992] J. Kolodner. An introduction to case-based reasoning. *Artificial Intelligence Review*, 6:3 – 34, 1992.

[Korf, 1980] R. E. Korf. Toward a model of representation changes. *Artificial Intelligence*, 14(1):41 – 78, 1980.

[Kuhn, 1962] T. S. Kuhn. *The Structure of Scientific Revolutions*. Cambridge University, 1962.

[Kutschera, 1972] F. v. Kutschera. *Wissenschaftstheorie II*. Wilhelm Fink Verlag, Munchen, 1972.

[Laird *et al.*, 1986] J. E. Laird, P. S. Rosenbloom, and A. Newell. Chunking in SOAR: the anatomy of a general learning mechanism. *Machine Learning*, 1(1):11 – 46, 1986.

[Landau, 1982] B. Landau. Will the real grandmother please stand up? the psychological reality of dual meaning representations. *Journal of Psycholinguistic Research*, 11:47 – 62, 1982.

[Langley *et al.*, 1986] P. Langley, J. M. Zytkow, H. A. Simon, and G. L. Bradshaw. The search for regularity: Four aspects of scientific discovery. In R. Michalski, J. Carbonell, and T. Mitchell, editors, *Machine Learning Volume II*, pages 425 – 469. Morgan Kaufman, Los Altos, CA, USA, 1986.

[Le Compte and Gratch, 1972] G. K. Le Compte and G. Gratch. Violation of a rule as a method of diagnosing infants' level of object concept. *Child Development*, 43:385 – 396, 1972.

[Lebowitz, 1987] M. Lebowitz. Experiments with incremental concept formation: UNIMEM. *Machine Learning*, 2:103 – 138, 1987.

[Lee *et al.*, 1990] G. Lee, M. Flowers, and M. G. Dyer. Learning distributed representations of conceptual knowledge and their application to script-based story processing. *Connection Science*, 4(2):313 – 346, 1990.

[Lenat, 1982] D. B. Lenat. Am: Discovery in mathematics as heuristic search. In R. Davis and D. Lenat, editors, *Knowledge-Based Systems in Artificial Intelligence*, pages 1 – 225. McGraw-Hill, New York, NY, 1982.

[Levesque and Brachman, 1985] H. Levesque and R. Brachman. A fundamental tradeoff in knowledge representation and reasoning. In Brachman and Levesque, editors, *Readings in Knowledge Representation*, pages 41–70. Morgan Kaufmann, Los Altos, CA, 1985.

[Levi, 1977] I. Levi. Subjunctives, dispositions, and chances. *Synthese*, 34:423 – 455, 1977.

[Li and Vitanyi, 1993] M. Li and P. Vitanyi. *An introduction to Kolmogorov complexity and its applications*. Springer Verlag, Berlin, New York, 1993.

[Lin and Vitter, 1991] H.-H. Lin and J. S. Vitter. Complexity results on learning by neural nets. *Machine Learning*, 6(3):211 – 230, 1991.

[Ling, 1991a] C. Ling. Non-monotonic specialization. In *Proc. Inductive Logic Programming Workshop, Portugal*, 1991.

[Ling, 1991b] C. Ling. Non-monotonic specialization. In *Proc. Inductive Logic Programming Workshop, Portugal*, 1991.

[Ling, 1991c] C. X. Ling. Inventing necessary theoretical terms in scientific discovery and inductive logic programming. Report 302, Dept. of CS, Univ. of Western Ontario, London, Ontario, Canada N6A 5B7, 1991.

[Lloyd, 1987] J. Lloyd. *Foundations of Logic Programming*. Springer Verlag, Berlin, New York, 2nd edition, 1987.

[Makinson, 1985] D. Makinson. How to give it up: A survey of some formal aspects of theory change. *Synthese*, 62:347 – 363, 1985.

[Mandler, 1983] J. M. Mandler. Representation. In P. H. Mussen, editor, *Handbook of Child Psychology*, volume III, chapter 7, pages 420 – 494. John Wiley & Sons, New York, fourth edition, 1983.

[McCloskey and Glucksberg, 1978] M. McCloskey and S. Glucksberg. Natural categories: Well defined or fuzzy sets? *Memory & Cognition*, 6:462 – 472, 1978.

[Medin and Schaffer, 1978] D. L. Medin and M. M. Schaffer. A context theory of classification learning. *Psychological Review*, 85:207 – 238, 1978.

[Medin and Schwanenflugel, 1981] D. L. Medin and P. L. Schwanenflugel. Linear separability in classification learning. *Journal of Experimental Psychology: Human Learning and Memory*, 7:355 – 368, 1981.

[Medin and Smith, 1984] D. L. Medin and E. E. Smith. Concepts and concept formation. *Annual Review of Psychology*, 35:113 – 138, 1984.

[Medin et al., 1982] D. L. Medin, M. W. Altom, S. M. Edelson, and D. Freko. Correlated symptoms and simulated medical classification. *Journal of Experimental Psychology: Learning, Memory, and Cognition*, 8:37 – 50, 1982.

[Medin et al., 1987] D. L. Medin, W. D. Wattenmaker, and S. E. Hampson. Family resemblance, conceptual cohesiveness, and category construction. *Cognitive Psychology*, 19(2):242 – 279, 1987.

[Mendelson, 1987] E. Mendelson. *Introduction to Mathematical Logic*. Wadsworth & Brooks, Belmont, CA, third edition, 1987.

[Michalski, 1983] R. S. Michalski. A theory and methodology of inductive learning. In R. Michalski, J. Carbonell, and T. Mitchell, editors, *Machine Learning — An Artificial Intelligence Approach, Vol. I*, pages 83 – 134. Morgan Kaufman, San Mateo, CA, 1983.

[Michalski, 1987] R. Michalski. How to learn imprecise concepts: A method for employing a two-tiered knowledge representation in learning. In P. Langley, editor, *Proc. 4th Int. Workshop on Machine Learning*, pages 50–58. Morgan Kaufman, 1987.

[Michalski, 1990] R. Michalski. Learning flexible concepts: Fundamental ideas and a method based on two-tiered representation. In Y. Kodratoff and R. Michalski, editors, *Machine Learning — An Artificial Intelligence Approach, Vol. III*, chapter 3, pages 63 – 112. Morgan Kaufman, San Mateo, CA, 1990.

[Michalski and Stepp, 1983] R. S. Michalski and R. E. Stepp. Learning from observation: Conceptual clustering. In R. Michalski, J. Carbonell, and T. Mitchell, editors, *Machine Learning — An Artificial Intelligence Approach, Vol. I*, volume I, pages 331 – 363. Tioga, Palo Alto, CA, 1983.

[Miller and Johnson-Laird, 1976] G. A. Miller and P. N. Johnson-Laird. *Language and perception*. Harvard University Press, Cambridge, MA, USA, 1976.

[Minsky and Papert, 1969] M. Minsky and S. Papert. *Perceptrons*. MIT Press, Cambridge, MA, 1969.

[Minton, 1990] S. Minton. Quantitative results concerning the utility of explanation-based learning. *Artificial Intelligence*, 42:363 – 392, 1990.

[Mitchell, 1982] T. M. Mitchell. Generalization as search. *Artificial Intelligence*, 18(2):203 – 226, 1982.

[Mitchell et al., 1986] T. Mitchell, R. Keller, and S. Kedar-Cabelli. Explanation-based generalization: A unifying view. *Machine Learning*, 1:47 – 80, 1986.

[Morik, 1987] K. Morik. Acquiring domain models. *Intern. Journal of Man Machine Studies*, 26:93–104, 1987. also appeared in *Knowledge Acquisition Tools for Expert Systems*, volume 2, J. Boose, B. Gaines, eds., Academic Press, 1988.

[Morik, 1989a] K. Morik. Integration issues in knowledge acquisition systems. *ACM Sigart Newsletter*, 108:124 – 131, 1989. Special Issue on Knowledge Acquisition.

[Morik, 1989b] K. Morik. Sloppy modeling. In K. Morik, editor, *Knowledge Representation and Organization in Machine Learning*, pages 107–134. Springer Verlag, Berlin, New York, 1989.

[Morik, 1990] K. Morik. Integrating manual and automatic knowledge aquisition - BLIP. In K. L. McGraw and C. R. Westphal, editors, *Readings in Knowledge Acquisition › Current Practices and Trends*, chapter 14, pages 213 – 232. Ellis Horwood, New York, 1990.

[Morik, 1991] K. Morik. Underlying assumptions of knowledge acquisition and machine learning. *Knowledge Acquisition Journal*, 3, 1991.

[Morik, 1992] K. Morik. Einfuhrung in die Künstliche Intelligenz. Vorlesungsskript, Universität Dortmund, Fachbereich Informatik, Lehrstuhl VIII, 1992.

[Morik, 1993] K. Morik. Balanced cooperative modeling. *Machine Learning*, 10(1):217 – 235, 1993. Revised version of the paper presented at: Proc. First Int. Workshop on Multistrategy Learning (MSL-91), Michalski, Ryszard S. and Tecuci, Gheorghe, George Mason Univ., pages 65 - 80, 1991.

[Morik and Kietz, 1989] K. Morik and J.-U. Kietz. A bootstrapping approach to conceptual clustering. In *Proc. Sixth Intern. Workshop on Machine Learning*, 1989.

[Morik *et al.*, 1991] K. Morik, K. Causse, and R. Boswell. A common knowledge representation integrating learning tools. In R. S. Michalski and G. Tecuci, editors, *Proc. First Int. Workshop on Multistrategy Learning (MSL-91)*, pages 81 – 96. George Mason Univ., 1991.

[Morik *et al.*, 1993] K. Morik, S. Wrobel, J. Kietz, and W. Emde. *Knowledge Acquisition and Machine Learning: Theory, Methods and Applications*. Academic Press, London, New York, 1993. To appear.

[Muggleton, 1987] S. Muggleton. Structuring knowledge by asking questions. In I. Bratko and N. Lavrac, editors, *Progress in Machine Learning — Proc. Second European Working Session on Learning (EWSL)*, pages 218 – 229. Sigma Press, Wilmslow, UK, 1987.

[Muggleton, 1988] S. Muggleton. A strategy for constructing new predicates in first order logic. In D. Sleeman, editor, *Proc. of the 3rd European Working Session on Learning*, pages 123 – 130. Pitman, London, 1988.

[Muggleton, 1993] S. Muggleton. Predicate invention and utility. *Journal of Experimental and Theoretical Artificial Intelligence*, 1993.

[Muggleton and Buntine, 1988] S. Muggleton and W. Buntine. Machine invention of first-order predicates by inverting resolution. In *Proc. Fifth Intern. Conf. on Machine Learning*. Morgan Kaufman, San Mateo, CA, 1988.

[Muggleton and De Raedt, 1994] S. Muggleton and L. De Raedt. Inductive logic programming: Theory and methods. *Journal of Logic Programming*, 1994. To appear.

[Muggleton and Feng, 1992] S. Muggleton and C. Feng. Efficient induction of logic programs. In S. Muggleton, editor, *Inductive Logic Programming*. Academic Press, 1992.

[Murphy and Medin, 1985] G. L. Murphy and D. L. Medin. The role of theories in conceptual coherence. *Psychological Review*, 92(3):289 – 316, 1985.

[Nebel, 1989] B. Nebel. *Reasoning and Revision in Hybrid Representation Systems*. Springer Verlag, Berlin, New York, 1989. Doctoral Dissertation.

[Nebel, 1992] B. Nebel. Syntax based approaches to belief revision. In P. Gärdenfors, editor, *Belief Revision*, Cambridge Tracts in Theoretical Computer Science, pages 52 – 88. Cambridge University Press, Cambridge, UK, 1992.

[Nedellec and Causse, 1992] C. Nedellec and K. Causse. Knowledge refinement using Knowledge Acquisition and Machine Learning Methods. In *Proceedings of EKAW*. Springer Verlag, May 1992.

[Nelson, 1977] K. Nelson. The syntagmatic–paradigmatic shift revisited: A review of research and theory. *Psychological Bulletin*, 84:93 – 116, 1977.

[Nelson, 1979] K. Nelson. Explorations in the development of a functional semantic system. In W. A. Collins, editor, *Children's language and communication*. Lawrence Erlbaum Associates, Hillsdale, NJ, 1979.

[Nelson, 1983] K. Nelson. The derivation of concepts and categories from event representations. In E. K. Scholnick, editor, *New Trends in Conceptual Representation: Challenges to Piaget's Theory?*, chapter 6, pages 129 – 149. Lawrence Earlbaum Associates, Hillsdale, NJ, 1983.

[Nersessian, 1984] N. J. Nersessian. Aether/or: The creation of scientific concepts. *Studies in History and Philosophy of Science*, 15(3):175 – 212, 1984.

[Newell, 1982] A. Newell. The knowledge level. *Artificial Intelligence*, 18:87 – 127, 1982.

[Newell and Simon, 1963] A. Newell and H. A. Simon. GPS, a program that simulates human thought. In E. A. Feigenbaum and J. Feldman, editors, *Computers and Thought*. McGraw-Hill, New York, 1963.

[Oerter and Montada, 1982] R. Oerter and L. Montada, editors. *Entwicklungspsychologie*. U&S Psychologie. Urban & Schwarzenberg, Munchen, Wien, Baltimore, 1982.

[Ourston and Mooney, 1990] D. Ourston and R. Mooney. Changing the rules: A comprehensive approach to theory refinement. In *Proc. 9th National Conference on Artificial Intelligence*, pages 815 – 820. Morgan Kaufman, San Mateo, CA, 1990.

[Pagallo, 1989] G. Pagallo. Learning DNF by decision trees. In *Proc. 11th International Joint Conference on Artificial Intelligence*, pages 639 – 644. Morgan Kaufman, San Mateo, CA, 1989.

[Pagallo and Haussler, 1990] J. Pagallo and D. Haussler. Boolean feature discovery in empirical learning. *Machine Learning*, 5:71 – 99, 1990.

[Pastore, 1987] R. E. Pastore. Categorical perception: Some psychophysical models. In S. Harnad, editor, *Categorical Perception — The Groundwork of Cognition*, chapter 1, pages 29 – 52. Cambridge University Press, Cambridge, 1987.

[Pazzani and Brunk, 1991] M. Pazzani and C. Brunk. Detecting and correcting errors in rule-based expert systems: An integration of empirical and explanation-based learning. *Knowledge Acquisition*, 3(2):157 – 173, 1991.

[Pazzani et al., August 1986] M. Pazzani, M. Dyer, and M. Flowers. The role of prior causal theories in generalization. In *AAAI-86*, pages 545 – 550. Philadelphia, PA, August 1986.

[Piaget, 1977] J. Piaget. *The development of thought*. Viking Penguin, New York, 1977.

[Plotkin, 1970] G. D. Plotkin. A note on inductive generalization. In B. Meltzer and D. Michie, editors, *Machine Intelligence 5*, chapter 8, pages 153 – 163. Edinburgh Univ. Press, Edinburgh, 1970.

[Quine, 1964] W. V. O. Quine. *From a logical point of view*. Harvard University Press, Cambridge, Mass., 1964.

[Quinlan, 1983] J. R. Quinlan. Learning efficient classification procedures and their application to chess end games. In R. Michalski, J. Carbonell, and T. Mitchell, editors, *Machine Learning — An Artificial Intelligence Approach*, pages 463 – 482. Tioga, Palo Alto, CA, 1983.

[Quinlan, 1990a] J. R. Quinlan. Probabilistic decision trees. In Y. Kodratoff and R. Michalski, editors, *Machine Learning — An Artificial Intelligence Approach, Vol. III*, chapter 5, pages 140 – 152. Morgan Kaufman, San Mateo, CA, 1990.

[Quinlan, 1990b] J. Quinlan. Learning logical definitions from relations. *Machine Learning*, 5(3):239 – 266, 1990.

[Ram and Leake, to appeara] A. Ram and D. Leake. A framework for goal-driven learning. In A. Ram and D. Leake, editors, *Goal-Driven Learning*. MIT Press/Bradford Books, Cambridge, MA, to appear.

[Ram and Leake, to appearb] A. Ram and D. Leake, editors. *Goal-Driven Learning*. MIT Press/Bradford Books, Cambridge, MA, to appear.

[Rendell and Seshu, 1990] L. Rendell and R. Seshu. Learning hard concepts through constructive induction: framework and rationale. *Computational Intelligence*, 6:247 – 270, 1990.

[Richards and Mooney, to appear] B. L. Richards and R. J. Mooney. Automated refinement of first-order horn-clause domain theories. *Machine Learning*, to appear.

[Rips *et al.*, 1973] L. Rips, E. Shoben, and E. Smith. Semantic distance and the verification of semantic relations. *Journal of Verbal Learning and Verbal Behavior*, 12(1 – 20):1 – 20, 1973.

[Rosch, 1975] E. Rosch. Cognitive representations of semantic categories. *Journal of Experimental Psychology: General*, 104:192 – 233, 1975.

[Rosch, 1978] E. Rosch. Principles of categorization. In E. Rosch and B. B. Lloyd, editors, *Cognition and Categorization*, pages 27 – 48. Erlbaum, Hillsdale, NJ, 1978.

[Rosch *et al.*, 1976] E. Rosch, C. B. Mervis, W. D. Gray, D. M. Johnson, and P. Boyes-Braem. Basic objects in natural categories. *Cognitive Psychology*, 8:382 – 439, 1976.

[Rouveirol and Puget, 1990] C. Rouveirol and J. F. Puget. Beyond inversion of resolution. In B. Porter and R. Mooney, editors, *Proc. Seventh Intern. Conf. on Machine Learning*, pages 122 – 130. Morgan Kaufmann, Palo Alto, CA, 1990.

[Rowan, 1989] D. R. Rowan. On-line expert systems in process industries. *AI Expert*, pages 30 – 38, August 1989.

[Rumelhart *et al.*, 1986] D. E. Rumelhart, G. e. Hinton, and R. J. Williams. Learning internal representations by error propagation. In D. E. Rumelhart and J. E. McClelland, editors, *Parallel distriguted systems: Explorations in the microstructure of cognition (Vol. I & II)*, pages 318 – 362 (Vol. I). MIT Press, Cambridge, MA, 1986.

[Saitta *et al.*, 1993] L. Saitta, M. Botta, and F. Neri. Multistrategy learning and theory revision. *Machine Learning*, 11(2/3):153 – 172, 1993.

[Salzberg, 1985] S. Salzberg. Heuristics for inductive learning. In *IJCAI-85*, pages 603 – 609. Los Angeles, CA, 1985.

[Sammut and Banerji, 1986] C. Sammut and R. B. Banerji. Learning concepts by asking questions. In R. Michalski, J. Carbonell, and T. Mitchell, editors, *Machine Learning — An Artificial Intelligence Approach*, volume II, chapter 7, pages 167 – 191. Morgan Kaufman, San Mateo, CA, 1986.

[Sandberg, 1991] J. Sandberg. Invited speaker: Bill Clancey (Summary of a talk given at the DELTA conference, Den Haag, Oct. 1990. *AI Communications*, 4(1):4 – 10, 1991.

[Sandberg and Wielinga, 1991] J. Sandberg and B. Wielinga. How situated is cognition? In *Proc. 12th International Joint Conference on Artificial Intelligence*, pages 341 – 346. Morgan Kaufman, San Mateo, CA, 1991.

[Schank and Abelson, 1977] R. Schank and R. A. Abelson. *Scripts, plans, goals, and understanding*. Lawrence Earlbaum Associates, Hillsdale, NJ, 1977.

[Schlimmer, 1987] J. C. Schlimmer. Incremental adjustment of representations for learning. In *Proc. Fourth Intern. Workshop on Machine Learning*, pages 79 – 90. Irvine, CA, 1987.

[Shapiro, 1983] E. Y. Shapiro. *Algorithmic Program Debugging*. ACM Distinguished Doctoral Dissertations. The MIT Press, Cambridge, Mass., 1983.

[Shavlik *et al.*, 1991] J. W. Shavlik, R. J. Mooney, and G. G. Towell. Symbolic and neural learning algorithms: An experimental comparison. *Machine Learning*, 6(2):111 – 143, 1991.

[Shortliffe, 1976] E. H. Shortliffe. *Computer-based Medical Consultations: MYCIN*. Elsevier, New York, 1976.

[Sigel, 1983] I. E. Sigel. Is the concept of the *concept* still elusive or What do we know about concept development? In E. K. Scholnick, editor, *New Trends in Conceptual Representation: Challenges to Piaget's Theory?*, chapter 12, pages 239 – 273. Lawrence Earlbaum Associates, Hillsdale, NJ, 1983.

[Silverstein and Pazzani, 1991] G. Silverstein and M. Pazzani. Relational cliches: Constraining constructive induction during relational learning. In Birnbaum and Collins, editors, *Procs. of the Eighth International Workshop on Machine Learning*, pages 203–207. Morgan Kaufmann, San Mateo, CA, 1991.

[Smith and Medin, 1981] E. E. Smith and D. L. Medin. *Categories and Concepts.* Harvard University Press, London, England, 1981.

[Smolensky, 1988] P. Smolensky. On the proper treatment of connectionism. *Behavioral and Brain Sciences*, 11:1 – 74, 1988.

[Sommer, 1994] E. Sommer. Learning relations without closing the world. In F. Bergadano and L. D. Raedt, editors, *Machine Learning: ECML-94, European Conference on Machine Learning, Catania, Italy, April 1994, Proceedings*, pages 419 – 422. Springer-Verlag, Berlin, 1994.

[Sommer *et al.*, 1993] E. Sommer, K. Morik, J.-M. Andre, and M. Uszynski. What online machine learning can do for knowledge acquisition — a case study. To appear, 1993.

[Sommer *et al.*, 1994] E. Sommer, K. Morik, J.-M. Andre, and M. Uszynski. What online machine learning can do for knowledge acquisition — a case study. *Knowledge Acquisition (to appear)*, 1994. also appeared as GMD Report No. 757.

[Srinivasan *et al.*, 1994] A. Srinivasan, S. Muggleton, and M. Bain. The justification of logical theories based on data compression. In K. Furukawa, D. Michie, and S. Muggleton, editors, *Machine Intelligence 13*, chapter 4, pages 87 – 123. Oxford University Press, Oxford, 1994.

[Stahl, 1993a] I. Stahl. Predicate invention in ILP — an overview. In *Proc. Sixth European Conference on Machine Learning (ECML-93)*, pages 313 – 322. Springer Verlag, Berlin, New York, 1993. A longer version is available as a technical report from Univ. Stuttgart.

[Stahl, 1993b] I. Stahl. Predicate invention in ILP — decidability, utility and decision criteria. Technical report, Univ. Stuttgart, FB Informatik, Breitwiesenstraße, Stuttgart, Germany, 1993. ILP-Project Deliverable STU1.1.

[Stahl, 1994] I. Stahl. On the utility of predicate invention in inductive logic programming. In *Machine Learning: ECML-94 (Proc. Seventh European Conference on Machine Learning)*, pages 272 – 286. Springer Verlag, Berlin, New York, 1994. A longer version is available as a technical report from Univ. Stuttgart.

[Stegmüller, 1970] W. Stegmüller. *Probleme und Resultate der Wissenschaftstheorie und Analytischen Philosophie, Band II: Theorie und Erfahrung*. Springer Verlag, Berlin, New York, 1970. (Studienausgabe, Teil A).

[Stepp and Michalski, 1986] R. E. Stepp and R. S. Michalski. Conceptual clustering of structured objects: A goal-oriented approach. *Artificial Intelligence*, 28:43–69, 1986.

[Subramanian, 1990] D. Subramanian. A theory of justified reformulations. In D. P. Benjamin, editor, *Change of Representation and Inductive Bias*, pages 147 – 167. Kluwer, Boston, 1990.

[Sutton, 1988] R. S. Sutton. Learning to predict by the methods of temporal differences. *Machine Learning*, 3(1):9 – 44, 1988.

[Tversky, 1977] A. Tversky. Features of similarity. *Psychological Review*, 84:327 – 352, 1977.

[Utgoff, 1986] P. E. Utgoff. Shift of bias for inductive concept learning. In R. Michalski, J. Carbonell, and T. Mitchell, editors, *Machine Learning — An Artificial Intelligence Approach*, volume II, pages 107 – 148. Morgan Kaufman, San Mateo, CA, 1986.

[Weber and Bell, 1994] S. Weber and S. Bell. A note on paraconsistent entailment in machine learning. LS-8 Report 10, Universität Dortmund, 44221 Dortmund, Germany, 1994.

[Werner, 1948] H. Werner. *Comparative psychology of mental development*. Follett, Chicago, rev. edition, 1948.

[Whitehead and Ballard, 1990] S. D. Whitehead and D. H. Ballard. Active perception and reinforcement learning. In *Proc. Seventh Intern. Conf. on Machine Learning*, pages 179 – 188. Morgan Kaufman, San Mateo, CA, 1990.

[Winston, 1975] P. H. Winston. Learning structural descriptions from examples. In P. Winston, editor, *The Psychology of Computer Vision*. McGraw-Hill, New York, 1975.

[Winston, 1992] P. H. Winston. *Artificial Intelligence*. Addison-Wesley, Reading, Massachusetts, third edition, 1992.

[Wirth, 1989] R. Wirth. Completing logic programs by inverse resolution. In K. Morik, editor, *Proc. Fourth European Working Session on Learning (EWSL)*, pages 239 – 250. Pitman/Morgan Kaufmann, London/San Mateo, CA, 1989.

[Wirth and O'Rorke, 1992] R. Wirth and P. O'Rorke. Constraints for predicate invention. In S. Muggleton, editor, *Inductive Logic Programming*, chapter 14, pages 299 – 318. Academic Press, London, New York, 1992.

[Wnek and Michalski, 1994] J. Wnek and R. S. Michalski. Hypothesis-driven constructive induction in AQ17-HCI: A method and experiments. *Machine Learning*, 14:139 – 168, 1994.

[Wogulis, 1991] J. Wogulis. Revising relational domain theories. In *Proc. Eighth Intern. Workshop on Machine Learning*, pages 462 – 466. Morgan Kaufman, San Mateo, CA, 1991.

[Woods, 1975] W. A. Woods. What's in a link? In D. Bobrow and A. M. Collins, editors, *Representation and Understanding: Studies in Cognitive Science*. Academic Press, New York, 1975.

[Wright and Murphy, 1984] J. C. Wright and G. L. Murphy. The utility of theories in intuitive statistics: the robustness of theory-based judgments. *Journal of Experimental Psychology: General*, 113:301 – 322, 1984.

[Wrobel, 1987] S. Wrobel. Higher-order concepts in a tractable knowledge representation. In K. Morik, editor, *GWAI-87 11th German Workshop on Artificial Intelligence*, Informatik-Fachberichte Nr. 152, pages 129 – 138. Springer Verlag, Berlin, New York, October 1987.

[Wrobel, 1988] S. Wrobel. Automatic representation adjustment in an observational discovery system. In D. Sleeman, editor, *Proc. of the 3rd Europ. Working Session on Learning*, pages 253 – 262. Pitman, London, 1988.

[Wrobel, 1989] S. Wrobel. Demand-driven concept formation. In K. Morik, editor, *Knowledge Representation and Organization in Machine Learning*, pages 289–319. Springer Verlag, Berlin, New York, 1989.

[Wrobel, 1991] S. Wrobel. Towards a model of grounded concept formation. In *Proc. 12th International Joint Conference on Artificial Intelligence*, pages 712 – 717. Morgan Kaufman, San Mateo, CA, 1991.

[Wygotski, 1964] L. S. Wygotski. *Denken und Sprechen*. Conditio humana. S. Fischer, 1964. (First published in Russian 1934, english translation ''Thought and language'' 1962 by MIT Press).

[Younger and Cohen, 1984] B. A. Younger and L. B. Cohen. Infant perception of correlations among attributes. *Child Development*, 54:858 – 867, 1984.

INDEX